Creating Universes with SAP BusinessObjects

Create and maintain powerful SAP BusinessObjects Universes with the SAP Information Design Tool

Taha M. Mahmoud

[PACKT] enterprise 𝕏
PUBLISHING   professional expertise distilled

BIRMINGHAM - MUMBAI

Creating Universes with SAP BusinessObjects

First published: September 2014

Production reference: 1180914

Published by Packt Publishing Ltd.
Livery Place
35 Livery Street
Birmingham B3 2PB, UK.

ISBN 978-1-78217-090-7

www.packtpub.com

Cover image by Tony Shi (shihe99@hotmail.com)

Credits

Author
Taha M. Mahmoud

Reviewers
Dmitry Anoshin
David Lai
Didier Valat

Commissioning Editor
Edward Gordon

Acquisition Editor
Gregory Wild

Content Development Editor
Madhuja Chaudhari

Technical Editors
Mrunmayee Patil
Siddhi Rane

Copy Editors
Karuna Narayanan
Laxmi Subramanian

Project Coordinator
Akash Poojary

Proofreaders
Simran Bhogal
Stephen Copestake
Maria Gould
Lawrence A. Herman
Paul Hindle

Indexers
Hemangini Bari
Tejal Soni

Production Coordinators
Saiprasad Kadam
Nilesh R. Mohite
Alwin Roy

Cover Work
Nilesh R. Mohite
Alwin Roy

About the Author

Taha M. Mahmoud (PMP, TOGAF, ITIL, and CSM) is a senior BI consultant, BI project manager, and a solution architect. He has more than 7 years of experience working on, consulting for, and deploying successful business objects' projects in the banking and telecom industries.

I would like to thank my mother and father for raising me and helping me to be different. I love you and will always do. I would also like to thank my wife, Rasha, for supporting me during the period of writing this book—there is always a woman behind every great man. Special thanks to my son, Ali, daughter, Ruqayyah, and my family and friends.

About the Reviewers

Dmitry Anoshin is a datacentric technologist and recognized expert in building and implementing Business Intelligence solutions. He has a successful track record of implementing BI/DWH projects in numerous industries, such as retail, finance, and e-commerce industries.

He has an in-depth knowledge of BI technologies and is experienced in various projects as a BI consultant and a hands-on ETL/DWH developer.

He has more than 7 years of experience in BI/DWH. In addition, he is certified in Teradata database, SAP BusinessObjects, SAS BI, and Pentaho DI.

He has also reviewed the book, *SAP BusinessObjects Reporting Cookbook*, *Packt Publishing*.

I would like to thank my wife, Svetlana, and my children, Vasily and Anna, for their patience while I was reviewing this book. I love them very much. Thank you, my beloved family.

Didier Valat is a certified technical leader in Business Intelligence. He graduated from Paul Sabatier, a French University, with a Master's degree in Statistics and Business Intelligence in 2009.

After completing his Master's degree, he joined an IT service company as a BI consultant in Toulouse. He worked for major clients such as EADS Airbus and Toulouse town council, and developed SAP expertise both on BusinessObjects and Business Warehouse. He worked as the Lead of Projects in the finance and supply chain domains, where his hard work and strong team spirit were recognized and appreciated.

In 2012, he joined the Teradata company in Paris to become an expert in data warehouse solution implementation. He was quickly identified as a technical and functional team leader when he worked for the main French lottery company, and he was involved in each part of the project: architecture, modeling, and development.

He is now taking part in data science challenges, mainly on R and Big Data solutions.

I would like to thank all the people behind this project who trusted me and made this book possible. I would also like to thank my family for all their love and support.

www.PacktPub.com

Support files, eBooks, discount offers, and more

You might want to visit www.PacktPub.com for support files and downloads related to your book.

Did you know that Packt offers eBook versions of every book published, with PDF and ePub files available? You can upgrade to the eBook version at www.PacktPub.com and as a print book customer, you are entitled to a discount on the eBook copy. Get in touch with us at service@packtpub.com for more details.

At www.PacktPub.com, you can also read a collection of free technical articles, sign up for a range of free newsletters, and receive exclusive discounts and offers on Packt books and eBooks.

http://PacktLib.PacktPub.com

Do you need instant solutions to your IT questions? PacktLib is Packt's online digital book library. Here, you can access, read, and search across Packt's entire library of books.

Why subscribe?

- Fully searchable across every book published by Packt
- Copy and paste, print, and bookmark content
- On demand and accessible via web browser

Free access for Packt account holders

If you have an account with Packt at www.PacktPub.com, you can use this to access PacktLib today and view nine entirely free books. Simply use your login credentials for immediate access.

Instant updates on new Packt books

Get notified! Find out when new books are published by following @PacktEnterprise on Twitter, or the *Packt Enterprise* Facebook page.

Table of Contents

Preface

This year (2014) was an amazing year for German football fans as their national team won the World Cup 2014 title. A few days later, I received a subscription e-mail from SAP with the title *How SAP helped Germany win the World Cup*. It was very interesting for me to know how. As SAP is one of the leading IT companies in the world, it was not clear to me how IT can help a sports team or even a football team to win a title or a medal. You can have a look at the e-mail body in the following screenshot:

How SAP helped Germany win the World Cup
By using SAP Match Insights and SAP HANA, the German National Team coaches simplified training to improve performance, making the 'beautiful game' even more beautiful to fans worldwide.

Dear Partner,

Did you know that SAP helped the German football team with their tactics and that CIO named Big Data as Germany's 12th Man at the World Cup?

A combination of great talent, great teamwork, great training...and Big Data.

Working in collaboration with the German Football Association (DFB) and SAP, the team used SAP Match Insights (powered by SAP HANA) to analyse matches by processing vast amounts of data. Video data was captured from 8 on-field cameras and crunched into thousands of data points per second. This data was converted into simulations and graphs viewable on a tablet or smartphone, enabling coaches and players to identify and assess key metrics such as player speed, position and possession time in each match. These insights were then used during pre-match preparations to improve player and team performance.

"SAP's involvement has transformed the football experience for coaches, players, fans, and the media," said Oliver Bierhoff, SAP Ambassador and manager of the German national football team.

"Imagine this: In just 10 minutes, 10 players with three balls can produce over 7 million data points. SAP HANA can process these in real time. With SAP, our team can analyse this huge amount of data to customise training and prepare for the next match."

As well as enabling the German team to analyse its own performance, SAP Match Insights can help coaches and players to identify opponents' strengths and weaknesses, and inform defensive tactics. The software can extract data on individual players, and present it in the form of digital personas, so that it is "as simple to use as their favorite video game", according to Chris Burton, general VP of global sponsorships at SAP.

So it is all about Business Intelligence (BI). Now, we can see BI participating in almost every single aspect of our life, even in sports. SAP used the Big Data concept to handle vast amount of data, SAP HANA to assure optimum response time, and SAP BO BI 4.x to make data available to the right users in the right format (reports, dashboards, and analysis), as we can see in the previous example. The results were amazing, Germany won the World Cup title with the aid of BI. This era is not the "hard work one", but rather it is the "intelligent work one".

SAP BO BI 4.x is a complete BI solution with many tools bundled together to satisfy different needs of BI. One important tool is Information Design Tool, which is used to create and build the BO semantic layer (Universe). Universe is an intermediate layer between database and BI tools that will transform database entities and joins into business objects stored in the Business layer. These business objects can be consumed later on by different BO reporting solutions.

In this book, we will learn how to create a Universe from scratch. We will cover all related topics in detail along with step-by-step hands-on and real examples. We will discuss design best practices, the Universe development life cycle, Universe testing, security, and the multiuser development environment.

Congratulations on taking a step toward learning how to create a Universe using SAP BO BI 4.x! Are you ready? Let's go…

What this book covers

Chapter 1, Introduction to BI and the Semantic Layer, introduces Business Intelligence (BI), BI concepts, and Information Design Tool (IDT).

Chapter 2, Aligning BI Solutions with Business Demands, explains how to download the Northwind MS Access database and configure it in order to use it in the remaining chapters of this book. We will also discuss the business case for Northwind and will explain its data model.

Chapter 3, Creating Our First Universe, facilitates a quick walkthrough that will guide you to build your first Universe from start to finish. We will talk about the main building blocks for any Universe and we will start creating a project, connection, as well as the Data Foundation and Business layers; then we will publish this Universe. We will continue building and enriching this Universe in the remaining chapters of this book.

Chapter 4, Creating the Data Foundation Layer, introduces us to our core chapter that will cover in detail all you need to know about data connection and Data Foundation resources.

Chapter 5, Creating the Business Layer, covers in detail all that you need to know about the Business layer. Here, you can also find many best practices on how to deal with business requirements.

Chapter 6, Testing Your Universe, discusses the Universe development life cycle, how to use the Check Integrity wizard to complete the System Integration Test (SIT) for the Universe, and how to use the Queries tab in the Business layer resource to complete the User Acceptance Test (UAT).

Chapter 7, The Data Foundation Layer – Advanced Topics, covers advanced design topics that we need to take care of during the Data Foundation design phase. We will start with design concepts, then we will cover Data Foundation advanced techniques that we will use to enhance our Data Foundation design. Finally, we will talk about SQL design traps and how to fix and avoid them.

Chapter 8, The Business Layer – Advanced Topics, discusses Business layer topics such as list of values (LOV), navigation paths (hierarchies), index awareness, aggregate awareness, and Business layer's BO advanced functions (@functions).

Chapter 9, Data Security and Profiles, covers the important topic of security in detail. We will start with differentiating between the two main types of security profiles (Data Security Profile and Business Security Profile). We will learn how to use the Security Editor to create security rules and how to assign them. Finally, we will talk about security implementation best practices and how to create the security matrix.

Chapter 10, A Multiuser Development Environment, explains how designers can work more efficiently in teams and how to use Information Design Tool in the multiuser development environment using the synchronization wizard to synchronize local and shared projects. It also explains how to migrate and upgrade a Universe among BO environments.

What you need for this book

You need to have the SAP BO BI 4.x client installed on your machine. You also will need to have access to the BO BI 4.x server to be able to complete some parts that require establishing a session with the BO server. It is also important to complete the setup and configuration steps mentioned in *Chapter 2, Aligning BI Solutions with Business Demands*, in order to be able to complete the hands-on and real examples described in this book.

Who this book is for

This book is a step-by-step walkthrough supported with real-life examples and illustrator diagrams that will help you to build robust Universes. This is the perfect book for you if you are a beginner and want to learn how to use SAP BO Information Design Tool to create a Universe from scratch. You will also find all that you need to upgrade from Universe Design Tool (BO 6.x, BO XI2.x, and BO XI3.x) to Information Design Tool (the new SAP BO semantic layer tool introduced since BO BI 4.0). You will find information about how to map your current knowledge and experience in the UDT in a very fast and efficient way and to start using the new IDT. This book is also for professional Universe designers who work with the IDT to build SAP BO Universes. As a professional IDT designer, you will still find many tips, tricks, and best practices. Finally, this book is a complete guide that you can always refer to irrespective of your current level of experience.

Conventions

In this book, you will find a number of styles of text that distinguish between different kinds of information. Here are some examples of these styles, and an explanation of their meaning.

Code words in text, database table names, folder names, filenames, file extensions, pathnames, dummy URLs, user input, and Twitter handles are shown as follows: "To convert a .unv Universe, let's perform the following steps:"

A block of code is set as follows:

```
SELECT A.CUSTOMER_ID, COUNT (C.CREDIT_CARD_NO), COUNT
(B.ACCOUNT_NUMBER)
FROM CUSTOMERS A, CURRENT_ACCOUNTS B, CREDIT_CARDS C
WHERE A.CUSTOMER_ID =B.CUSTOMER_ID
AND A.CUSTOMER_ID = C.CUSTOMER_ID
GROUP BY A.CUSTOMER_ID
```

When we wish to draw your attention to a particular part of a code block, the relevant lines or items are set in bold:

```
EMPLOYEES.AGE BETWEEN "AGE BUCKET".AGE_LOWER_BOUND AND "AGE BUCKET".
AGE_UPPER_BOUND
```

New terms and important words are shown in bold. Words that you see on the screen, in menus or dialog boxes for example, appear in the text like this: "Navigate to **Administrative Tools**, and then double-click on **Data Sources (ODBC)**."

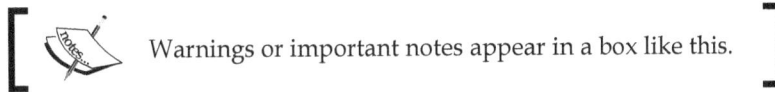

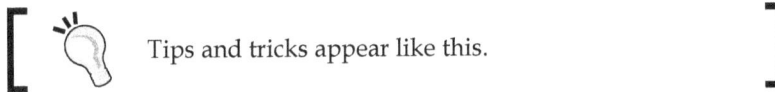

> Warnings or important notes appear in a box like this.

> Tips and tricks appear like this.

Reader feedback

Feedback from our readers is always welcome. Let us know what you think about this book—what you liked or may have disliked. Reader feedback is important for us to develop titles that you really get the most out of.

To send us general feedback, simply send an e-mail to feedback@packtpub.com, and mention the book title via the subject of your message.

If there is a topic that you have expertise in and you are interested in either writing or contributing to a book, see our author guide on www.packtpub.com/authors.

Customer support

Now that you are the proud owner of a Packt book, we have a number of things to help you to get the most from your purchase.

Downloading the example code

You can download the example code files for all Packt books you have purchased from your account at http://www.packtpub.com. If you purchased this book elsewhere, you can visit http://www.packtpub.com/support and register to have the files e-mailed directly to you.

Errata

Although we have taken every care to ensure the accuracy of our content, mistakes do happen. If you find a mistake in one of our books—maybe a mistake in the text or the code—we would be grateful if you would report this to us. By doing so, you can save other readers from frustration and help us improve subsequent versions of this book. If you find any errata, please report them by visiting http://www.packtpub.com/submit-errata, selecting your book, clicking on the **errata submission form** link, and entering the details of your errata. Once your errata are verified, your submission will be accepted and the errata will be uploaded on our website, or added to any list of existing errata, under the Errata section of that title. Any existing errata can be viewed by selecting your title from http://www.packtpub.com/support.

Piracy

Piracy of copyright material on the Internet is an ongoing problem across all media. At Packt, we take the protection of our copyright and licenses very seriously. If you come across any illegal copies of our works, in any form, on the Internet, please provide us with the location address or website name immediately so that we can pursue a remedy.

Please contact us at copyright@packtpub.com with a link to the suspected pirated material.

We appreciate your help in protecting our authors, and our ability to bring you valuable content.

Questions

You can contact us at questions@packtpub.com if you are having a problem with any aspect of the book, and we will do our best to address it.

1
Introduction to BI and the Semantic Layer

Before getting started with SAP Business Object Universe, you need to first understand what **Business Intelligence (BI)** is and how **SAP Business Objects (SAP BO)** Universe fits in. It is very important to know the terms and language used in the BI world, and this is the aim of this chapter.

In this chapter, we will cover the following topics:

- What Business Intelligence is and how it helps organizations and decision makers make the best use of the information they have
- The important terms and concepts that everyone working in the BI field should be aware of
- The BI reporting architecture models, starting with the basic and simple single-tier model until we reach the most matured three-tier model
- Defining the semantic layer, and describing its functionality and main role in the BI reporting model
- Introduction to the SAP BO Universe, which represents the semantic layer in SAP BO's reporting solution, and Information Design Tool, which is mainly used to create and publish Universes

What is Business Intelligence?

Business Intelligence (BI) is a complex term to describe. It is not a tool or a theory but a combination of methodologies, concepts, and technologies that enable you to get business value of raw data by transforming it into a format that can be used to do the required analysis and make decisions based on past trends.

To make it simple, let's start with a small example that illustrates the difference between using BI and not using it. We all know and play card games. Let's imagine that we have two players. Player number one is the smart BI guy, and player number two is the lazy, old-fashioned player. The old-fashioned player just plays cards based on his gut feeling, without trying to think or make use of the cards already played in the previous turns. He's actually not sure what the right card to play now is, or what cards he should play later on and in which sequence to win. He doesn't have the right tools and information to make his decision.

He is compared to the BI player who spends his time tracking all the cards played in the previous rounds. Then, he will try to predict and forecast the remaining cards for each player. He also spends time tracking the behavior of other players, their actions, and their impressions. This will help him predict their succeeding moves. He will start classifying the other players into categories such as a *risky* player who will rush to play his valuable cards in the early rounds, while other players will prefer to keep their valuable cards up to the end. The BI player simply uses historical information (past) to know what card to play now (current), and in the long run, he will build a strategy and vision on what cards he shall play in his upcoming turns to finally win the game.

Let's have a deeper look at our example to be able to define BI. BI means to extract historical information and then analyze it to help us decide what we shall do in the current situation and explore opportunities. In the long run, it will help build a strategy and vision by predicting and forecasting for the future.

Business Intelligence concepts

In this section, we will try to explain some of the most important BI concepts that you need to be familiar with. Before we start creating Universes, we need to make sure that we are talking the same language. The concepts, terms, and language used here are generic BI terminologies, and they are not related to specific BI reporting tools.

We will start with a knowledge pyramid that describes how data evolves from information to knowledge and finally, to wisdom. This is important because BI focuses on achieving knowledge and wisdom.

We will then talk about the difference between hindsight, insight, and foresight. After that, we will go through a fast overview of a **data warehouse** (**DWH**) and how it is related to BI.

The knowledge pyramid

The knowledge pyramid is also known as the data, information, knowledge, and wisdom model. Here is an example that describes each stage of the knowledge pyramid:

- **Data**: This consists of scattered discrete facts that you can't understand alone, because they are not in a context. The following facts are an example of data:

  ```
  [is 200 Temperature C].
  ```

  These facts cannot be understood in the current order and format. This is because they are discrete, scattered, and without a context. This means that data alone is not useful and somehow needs to evolve to the other levels in the knowledge pyramid in order to gain some extra value.

- **Information**: This consists of some discrete facts (data) evolved by putting them in a context. **Context** is a specific order of facts that will help us understand them and gain information. Let's check out the following example:

  ```
  [Temperature is 200 C].
  ```

  Now, we start having a context after reordering the discrete facts presented in the previous data example. We know that 200 is a number representing the temperature of something and that it is measured in Celsius.

- **Knowledge**: This can be achieved by adding more context to the information. Let's check out the following example:

  ```
  [Car engine temperature is 200 C].
  [Car engine normal temperature is between 100 and 150].
  ```

  Now, you have more information grouped together in a context, and you know that your car engine's temperature is above the normal temperature. You might take an action, but you still need some more information to be able to take the right decision at the right time.

- **Wisdom**: We will reach wisdom when we increase the context level by adding more knowledge and information together in the right order that can help us gain information and take actions. Let's check out the following example:

  ```
  [Car engine temperature is 200 C].
  [Car engine normal temperature is between 100 and 150].
  [Car engine temperature red zone starts from 200 C].
  [You need to stop your car if engine temperature reaches the red zone].
  ```

Now, you can take a precise action based on the data, information, knowledge, and wisdom you have, and you will stop your car and go to check your engine. This is because you realized that your car temperature is higher than normal, and it is in the red (dangerous) zone.

The different stages of the knowledge pyramid are shown in the following diagram:

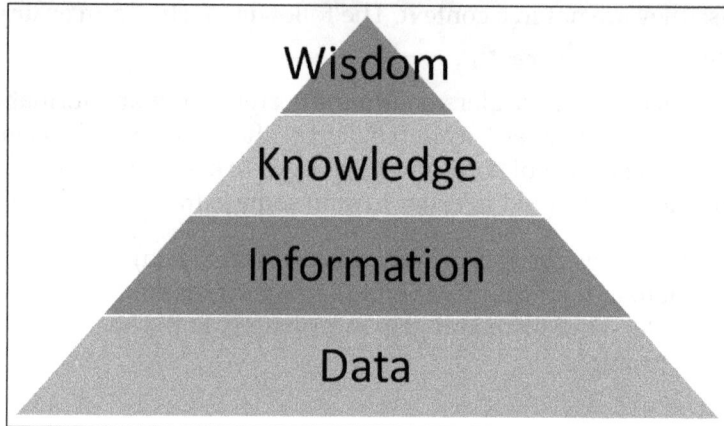

Now, after you have learned the knowledge pyramid, we need to find out what the relation between the pyramid and BI is. BI will evolve as data evolves. BI starts with raw data that will evolve into information after presenting it in a format that is suitable for analysis. Information will evolve to knowledge after doing the proper analysis on the information. Historical information and current knowledge will evolve and lead to future wisdom. It will help us take the right action in the current situation and make the right decisions in the future.

> More information on the knowledge pyramid is available at
> http://en.wikipedia.org/wiki/DIKW_Pyramid.

Hindsight, insight, and foresight

You will hear these three words, hindsight, insight, and foresight, many times if you work in BI field. They are strongly connected with BI because they simply describe what BI is. We've already explored these concepts in the *What is Business Intelligence?* section; now, we're going to discuss them in more detail:

- **Hindsight**: This refers to focusing on the past and history. We learn from our past to avoid making the same mistakes and to explore new opportunities that we didn't catch.

- **Insight**: This refers to the balance and start point for both hindsight and foresight. The action that we will take now will be history in a few moments and will shape our future. We can have a better present by learning from our history, and this will lead to a better future.

- **Foresight**: This refers to what we expect in future, that is, how we will predict what will happen based on what has already happened.

BI is a mix of hindsight, insight, and foresight. As they are somehow related and connected, the main target of BI is to learn from our hindsight to take the right decision in our insight to have a better foresight.

> For more information, you can refer to `http://www.learnthelessons.com/Ponderables/sights.htm`.

BI and DWH

The **data warehouse (DWH)** is a central big repository to hold extracted data from multiple source systems across the organization. This is an important thing to think about before starting any BI initiative in your organization. The DWH will act as a single source for your BI reporting, and you will be able to integrate your isolated source systems and make your information available to top management and decision makers.

In the following diagram, you can see the data flow, which starts from source systems and ends at knowledge and wisdom, delivered to BI users in many formats:

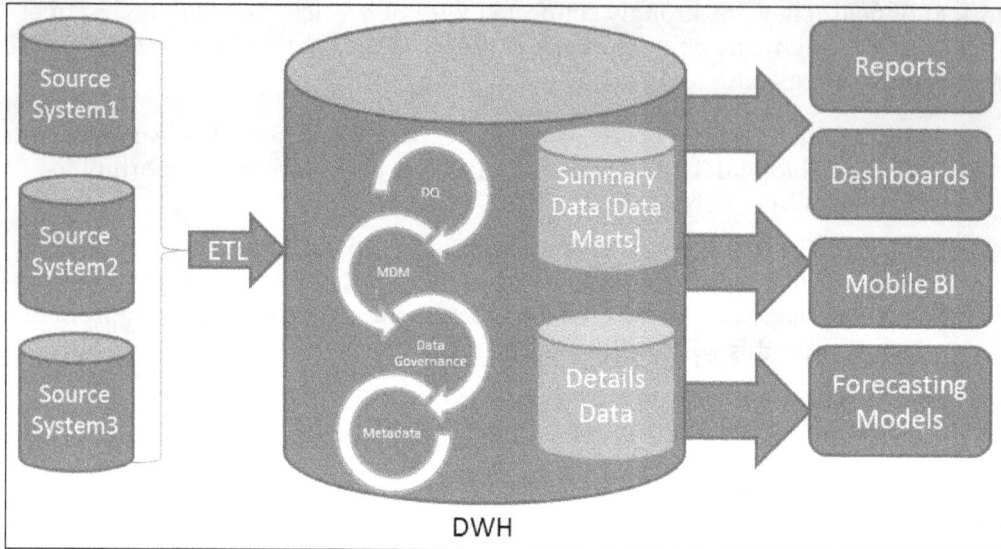

DWH comes with many other concepts, which are given as follows:

- **Data Quality (DQ)**: This focuses on enhancing the quality of the data extracted from source systems to get more accurate information and build more valuable knowledge. Also, it takes care of enhancing source systems' user interfaces by doing the required data validation to make sure that the proper data is being entered and stored.

- **Master Data Management (MDM)**: This will focus on unifying the data to get the most accurate records. For example, let's take a customer's information. You might have a customer's mobile number and address stored in more than one system, but you know that a specific system contains the most accurate phone number of the customer, because it is used to perform transactions through calls. So, you will consider this system to get the most accurate phone number for your clients and other customer information such as address and name. This will help us get the most accurate and unified record for the customer from across our organization's source systems and also get what we call the customer golden record.

- **Metadata**: Imagine that you have many source systems in your organization that you need to consider for data extraction. In some organizations, DWH contains thousands of tables and hundreds of thousands of columns and billions of records. For example, banking and telecommunication industries. For such huge DWH, you need to track what kind of information you have, where this information is stored, and how to access it. Metadata is data about data, and it will help you answer all questions raised earlier.

- **Data Governance**: This is your DWH police. It will govern DWH by controlling the data flow between DWH and source systems. It will help unify business rules and criteria across the organization. Finally, it will control the process as well. Data Governance is the big umbrella that holds everything that we talked about in this section.

Besides data governance, there are many other types of governance that can run in your organization, such as IT governance, enterprise governance, and BI governance. In the following diagram, you can see just an example of multiple levels of governance:

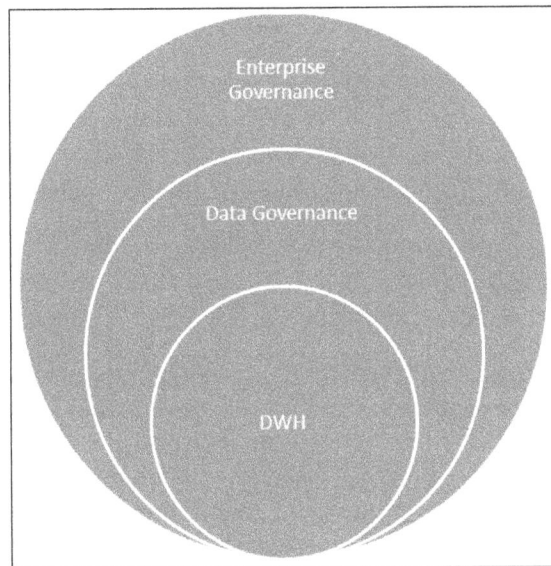

DWH will act like the single point of truth, as everyone is accessing the same information that is stored in the same location with the same business logic and rules applied.

As you can see, there is a strong relation between BI and DWH as both of them complement each other. BI needs DWH to achieve its goals, and DWH needs BI to avail its data and make it utilized.

> For more information on data warehouse and BI, you can visit
> http://en.wikipedia.org/wiki/Data_warehouse and
> http://en.wikipedia.org/wiki/Business_intelligence.

BI reporting tools architecture

To achieve BI, we need tools. Some tools will be used to extract and transform data (ETL tools: extract, transform, and load) which is out of the scope of our book. We also need reporting tools to display the information and help us perform a proper analysis of the information that we have, to achieve the required knowledge and wisdom. Also, we might need some other tools to help us in data mining and forecasting. Here, we will concentrate on BI reporting tools as it is the entrance point to our main title. In this section, we will talk about the generic BI reporting tools architecture, and then, we will give special attention to SAP Business Objects.

The BI reporting architecture model evolved as BI evolved. It started as a one-tier model, **client applications**, that can access the data files directly. It then evolved into a two-tier model, by adding a **database-server tier**. The main purpose of the database-server tier is to enhance the security model for the previous model by isolating data access from the client tools. However, in this model, the client application will perform all the calculation and data processing before displaying the final results to the end user. This is why we call the client application in this model the **thick** client, as it will require high-standard hardware on the client machines.

Later on, the BI reporting architecture model evolved to the three-tier or multitier model, which is the most common architecture used nowadays. In this model, we added one extra business or BI tier to act as an intermediate layer between the client application and database-server tier. This layer will enhance the overall end user experience, because it will perform data calculation and processing after getting the data from the database server and before sending it to the client application. This is why we call the client in this model a **thin** client, because it will be used just to draw and display the results for the end user.

The following diagram displays the one-tier, two-tier, and three-tier models:

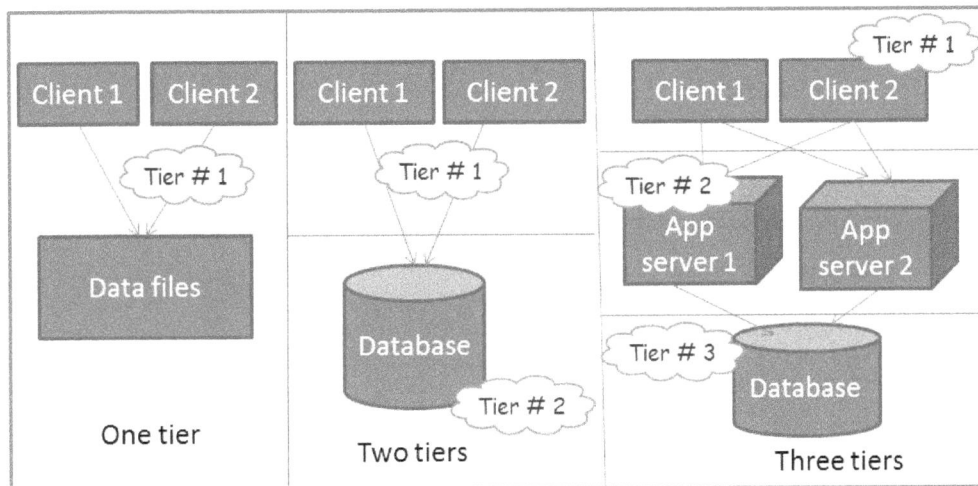

In the following sections, we will discuss the BI reporting architecture models in more detail.

The one-tier architecture model

In the one-tier architecture model, you have only one client application that connects directly to the data files. There is no authentication, and the user can modify, update, or even delete the master data files because he or she has complete access to data. The main characteristics of this model are:

- We don't have a server, and we have only a client application
- All calculations and processing are done by the client
- The data is not secured, as the end user can access it directly using the client tools
- You can't operate an efficient multiple user environment
- It is a cheap and simple solution
- The example tools are MS Excel, MS Access, and so on

The two-tier architecture model

In the two-tier architecture model, we have one extra tier, which is the database tier, besides a client-side application. This is why we call this model a client-server architecture model. To make it simple, let's just list the role of each component.

The database server is responsible for:

- Receiving data queries from client applications
- Communicating directly with the database and retrieving the required data
- Sending it back to the client

The client-side application is responsible for:

- Acting as an interface for the user
- Sending user requests to the database server
- Processing the data sent by the database server

The main characteristics of this model are:

- It supports multiuser environment
- It is more secured than the one-tier model
- The client application is a thick client

A Java application (client) generates and submits SQL queries to the database server (server). Then, this application will process the retrieved data to display the final output as an example of the two-tier model.

The three-tier architecture model

The three-tier architecture model is the same as the previous model, but we will add one extra tier for business logic. This is also known as the application server, and the main purpose of this tier is to process the information before submitting it to the client application.

The main characteristics of this model are:

- Data is more secured as end users don't have direct access to it
- It supports multiuser environment
- The semantic layer will isolate the physical layer from the Business layer
- The application server will generate SQL queries using the semantic layer and then submit them to the database

- Data calculation and processing are done on the application server
- Client applications are thin clients and just used to display information

We will not go deep into this as it is out of the scope of our book and is related to server administration, but all that you should know for now is that SAP Business Objects platform 4.x is a multitier model. We can see a simple representation of the SAP BO 4 solution architecture in the following diagram. First, we have client tools (first tier) at the top of the graph. We have many client and reporting tools in SAP BO 4, such as Crystal Reports, Web Intelligence, and Dashboards. Then, we have the application server (second tier) in the middle. We have many modules in the application server, but our main concern here is the semantic layer, which will be managed and maintained by the Information Design Tool. Finally, we have the third tier represented in data sources and source systems at the bottom of the graph.

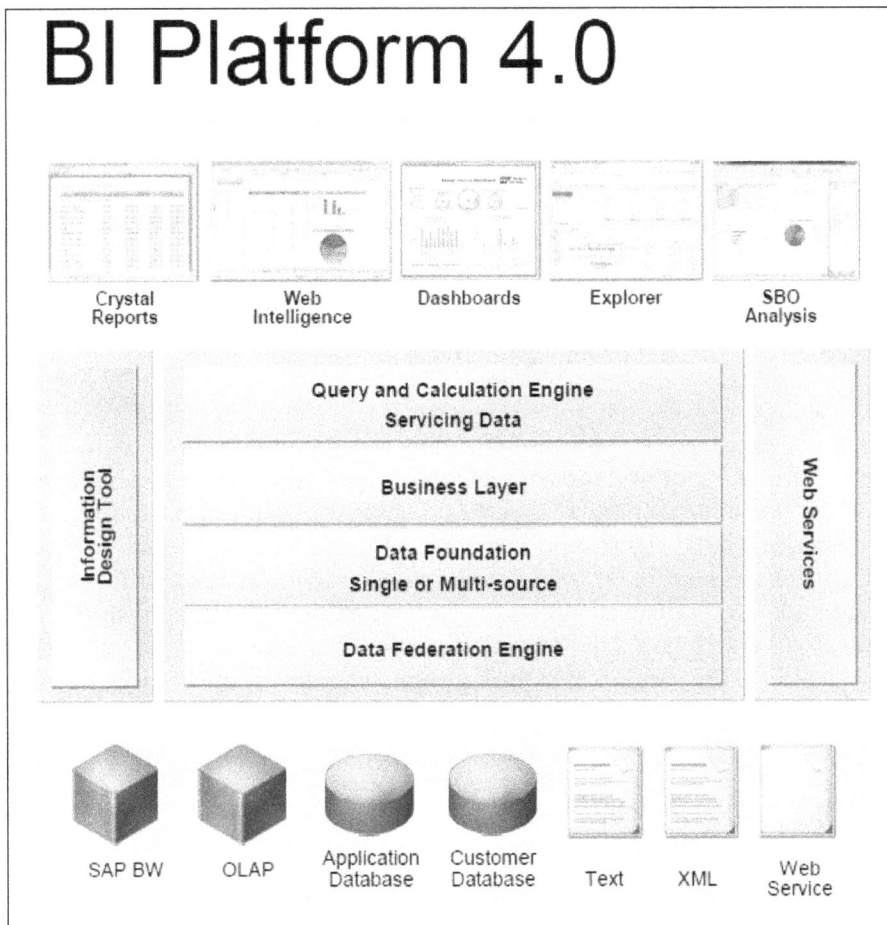

What is a semantic layer?

In this section, we will define the semantic layer and then describe the main role of semantic layers in BI reporting solutions.

The semantic layer acts like a translator. A translator is an expert in two languages at least. During a conversation, he or she will listen to the first person, understand what they said, and then translate the same message into a language that the other person can understand and vice versa.

The semantic layer does exactly the same thing. The end user can understand it and communicate with it, because it talks the same business language. Then, the other part translates the request into a technical language that can be submitted to the database. After that, it does the opposite by receiving the data from the database in a raw format and then translates it in a format that can be interpreted by the end user. So, it is like a man with two faces. One face is the technical face (evil one), which talks to the database, and the other one is the business user face (good one), which talks to the business end users.

The main idea of the semantic layer is to translate and simplify complex technical information in a way that business people can understand and utilize. The information is stored in a database, and it requires many technical skills to access it directly and do the required analysis. The semantic layer will isolate all technical staff from the actual business information needed, and it provides an easy way to understand and use a business model that can be accessed directly by the business to do their own reports and on-the-fly analysis.

The semantic layer will consist of two layers at least. The first one is the physical layer that will contain the technical part. In this layer, you will set up your data model by adding the required tables/views and create the proper joins between them. Usually, technical experts will be responsible for building this part as it requires technical skills. The second layer is the business model, which will be visible to the business users. This layer will contain attributes that business users can understand. Every attribute will have its own mapping to the physical layer either directly or it will be a driven attribute (calculated from other physical database columns). This will hide and isolate the complex technical part behind the frontend business model.

> For more information on the semantic layer, you can visit http://en.wikipedia.org/wiki/Semantic_layer.

Introduction to Universes and the Information Design Tool

All reporting tools use semantic layers for the same purpose. However, they just give it different names such as **Framework** in IBM Cognos, **Project** in Oracle BI, and **Universe** in SAP Business Objects. All semantic layers have exactly the same functionality: isolation of the technical part from the end business user by acting like a translator. They will translate the business requests into technical SQL queries submitted to the database. Also, they interpret the data returned into a format that can be understood by the end user.

SAP BO introduced a new tool to create your Universe (SAP BO semantic layer) in SAP BO 4.1; this is the Information Design Tool. They are still supporting the old Universe designer tool for compatibility purposes, but they clearly mention that they will stop supporting the Universe designer soon, and you will be able to create your Universes using the Information Design Tool only.

Before we conclude this chapter, let's have a look at the main components of Universe:

- **Connection**: Every Universe should have at least one data connection. The data connection will define how Universe will access the data based on the connection type. If you have an Oracle connection, for example, you will need to define your Oracle database and set your connection parameters. We will talk about this in detail later on.
- **The Data Foundation layer**: This is the physical layer in the Universe.
- **The Business layer**: We define our business model in this layer. We might have more than one Business layer that shares the same Data Foundation.

History of SAP Business Objects

Business Objects is one of the leading companies in the BI and reporting field. The company was created in 1990 and finally taken over by SAP in 2007. There were many products offered by Business Objects, but the most famous one is Business Objects XI. The first official SAP release was SAP Business Objects XI3. The last available version of SAP Business Objects is BO 4.x, and the framework was completely changed in this version to comply with the Microsoft Ribbon technology. The integration between Business Objects and other SAP products was dramatically enhanced in this version, as shown in the following table:

Release name	Number of the service pack	Release date
BusinessObjects 3.x	NA	1995
BusinessObjects 5	11	1999
BusinessObjects Enterprise 6.x	9	2003
BusinessObjects Enterprise XIR2	5	2005
SAP BusinessObjects Enterprise XI3	5	2008
SAP BusinessObjects BI4	NA	2011

Summary

This concludes our first chapter. After reading this chapter, you should be able to describe what BI is and how this will help your organization achieve its goals. Then, we went through some of the most important aspects of BI such as the knowledge pyramid and the difference between foresight, insight, and hindsight. We also had an introduction to DWH and how BI can benefit from it. We also had an overview of the BI reporting tiers and how the BI architecture model evolved as BI evolved. Then, we talked about the semantic layer as our entrance to Universe building. Finally, we had a brief introduction to Universes and the Information Design Tool.

Now that we've been introduced to BI and SAP Business Objects Universe, in the next chapter, we will talk about the data model for the Universe that we will build together in the remaining chapters.

2
Aligning BI Solutions with Business Demands

In the previous chapter, we learned what BI is and how it can enhance the decision-making process in our organization. Now, let's discuss a business case. In this chapter, we will find how BI will help an example company, Northwind, to track their sales, orders, and inventories. We will go through a complete simulation on how Northwind will start adopting BI. Then, we will download the Northwind Microsoft Access database from the Microsoft site. After that, we will get to know their data model and business processes. At the end, we will set up the **Open Database Connectivity (ODBC)** connection, which will be used in the next chapter to build our first Universe.

In this chapter, we will cover the following topics:

- A business process and how it applies to the Northwind's example
- The BI Maturity Model
- How to download the Northwind Microsoft Access database, and how to set up and configure the ODBC connection linked to this database
- Some important database terminologies by explaining the differences between dimensions, measures, and attributes
- The differences between facts, dimensions, and mapping tables
- The data model used by Northwind

> Understanding a business process is the key to building a relevant Universe.

Northwind

Northwind is a small company that offers many products to its customers. The company starts growing, and there is no way to maintain customer orders and inventory details manually. The company doesn't have an IT department, and they are using Microsoft Excel to perform their data analysis. The data is stored on many isolated Microsoft Access databases. Currently, reporting is done through Microsoft Excel and some basic Microsoft Access reports. The top management of Northwind is facing difficulties finding the required information at the right time. The available information is also not 100 percent accurate, as it is stored and processed manually. As you can see, they need to build a complete system to store all this information and to act as a source for a complete BI solution.

Management was worried about the cost of implementing such a system, and they are also not sure whether Northwind is ready to take this step yet. Market competition was another key factor to consider at this point of time as well, because wrong decisions might lead to big losses. Finally, Northwind needs to make a good profit this year to maintain their share price on the market and to keep their shareholders satisfied.

Northwind's top management formed a special team from many departments across the Northwind organization to come up with a recommendation on this subject. They needed to come up with a recommendation on how to establish a BI reporting system to act as a foundation for a complete BI solution.

The formed committee comes up with the following recommendations:

- Northwind can implement a DWH system to store all the analytics data needed for reporting and analysis purposes. They can also start implementing robust and reliable source systems instead of using isolated Microsoft Excel and Microsoft Access files to store their information.

- Northwind can start an assessment for the available BI reporting tools and select one to start and implement.

- Northwind can establish a new department to own the DWH system as well as the new BI reporting system.

> The best practice is to load your DWH with either summarized or detailed information, which is required for analysis and reporting purposes, instead of operational, atomic, transactional, and system logs data. This will help us to achieve the main target of DWH system, which is availing analytical data for the right users at the right time in the right format.
>
> The **operational data store** (**ODS**) is the right place to store your operational detailed data. You can refer to `http://en.wikipedia.org/wiki/Operational_data_store` for more information on the ODS.

The formed committee recommends SAP BusinessObjects based on the following assessment:

- SAP BO is one of the leading BI tools in the market.

- The SAP BO interface is user friendly, flexible, and can be used by end business users to build their own reports and do on-the-fly analysis without referring back to the technical IT team.

- SAP BO's **web intelligence** (**Webi**) report interface is similar to Microsoft Excel. This will ensure a fast-learning curve for all BI users.

- SAP BO's semantic layer (Universe) is powerful and can handle complex business logic.

- A SAP BO Universe can establish a connection to various databases as well as external source files such as Microsoft Excel and Microsoft Access database. This means that we can start building our reporting solution now, without the need to wait for a complete DWH solution.

- SAP BO Universes are able to have multiple data connections to different **database management systems** (**DBMS**) as a multisource Universe.

- A SAP BO Universe supports OLAP cubes as well as relational databases.

- A SAP BO Universe supports multiuser development environments.

- A SAP BO Universe's security model can be customized and configured to fulfill any security requirements or needs.

As discussed earlier, Northwind lacks the information that can help their top management make strategic decisions. This will lead them to act based on their gut feeling and experience, instead of facts and numbers. They don't have any idea about what they should plan for in order to achieve their goals and objectives. The solution recommended by the committee will help by giving a data repository that holds all the required information as well as a BI reporting system to build the required reports. These reports will help top management do the required analysis on the historical information that they have, and based on this, they will be able to act on the current situation and take the proper actions that will lead to good results.

> A well-designed Universe will help end business users be independent and facilitate the creation of analytics reports as well as on-the-fly analysis. An IT-oriented Universe will lead business users to be IT dependent, and they will fail to access information. Thus, the entire BI solution might fail.

The BI Maturity Model

As we know, an organization will take time to adopt BI and start getting the desired results. This will not happen within a day. In this section, we will talk about BI Maturity Models, and we will try to identify at which stage Northwind will start and what required actions to reach high-maturity levels are needed. The different levels of the BI Maturity Model are shown in the following diagram:

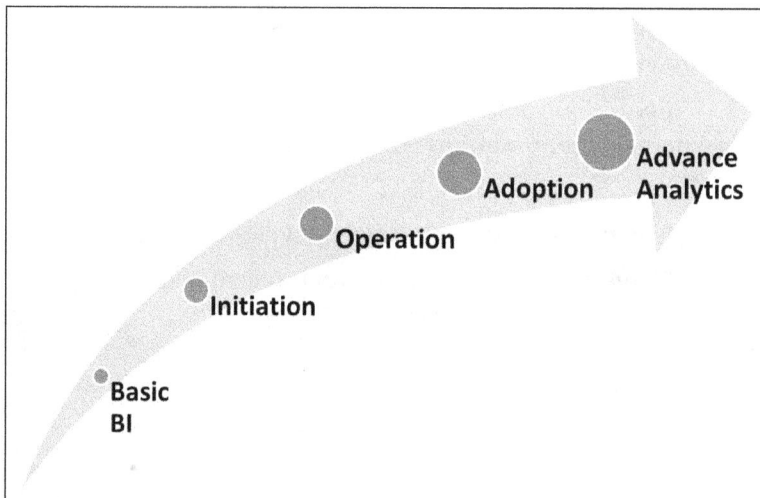

Let's take a look at the levels of the BI Maturity Model:

- **Basic BI**: At this stage, BI is very limited, and the organization will mainly depend on spreadsheets for analysis and data scattered in many disconnected data sources (data silos).

- **Initiation**: At this stage, the organization will try to start and establish a BI system after sensing its value, and after the internal assessment, it will select a BI reporting tool and plan for it. Normally, the cost of establishing a BI solution is high at the beginning, but it will decrease over time, while the value you are getting from your BI system will be small at the beginning, but it will increase over time. The semantic layer (Universe) will be basic at this stage, and end business users need training on how to use the selected BI reporting tool.

- **Operation**: At this stage, the organization will start to have some detailed operational reports, ad hoc queries, and simple reports. The organization will be reactive at this stage, as they will act after the fact (in a reactive way). The management will be able to get the required information, but it's of a poor quality and is late. The business users will start using Universes, and they will be able to develop some basic reports. The Universes are developed, and many subject areas are covered across the organizations, but they are still not matured and need a lot of enhancements.

- **Adoption**: At this stage, the BI maturity level will be very high. Everyone in the organization knows the importance of BI and will start sensing its value. Business users will start using the system and start getting familiar with it. They will start creating their own reports and will interact with the system. The Universe maturity and usability level will be high at this stage. The organization will start gaining the expected value of adopting BI. The organization will be active at this stage, and they will act on the fact.

- **Advanced Analytics**: This is the highest maturity level, and the organization will start using data mining and forecasting models. The organization will be proactive as they will act before the fact. End business users will get the required information in high quality and on time.

As we can see, Northwind is in the initiation phase.

> The subject area is a group of related information. It is not mandatory to be sourced from the same location (source system).

Configuring and setting up Northwind's database

In this section, we will find out how to download the Northwind Microsoft Access sample database. Then, we will create and configure the ODBC connection that we will use in the remaining chapters to build our Universe.

Getting the Northwind sample database

There are two methods to get the Northwind Microsoft database Access file:

- **Downloading it from the Microsoft website**: Northwind is a sample Microsoft Access database that you can download and use. To download it, we need to go to the Microsoft office website, then type Northwind in the **Home** page's search box and navigate to the **Template results** section or simply use the following links:

    ◦ **The Microsoft link**: www.microsoft.com

    ◦ **The direct link**: http://office.microsoft.com/en-001/ templates/Northwind-sales-web-database-TC101114818.aspx

    There are two database versions; one is Microsoft Access 2007, and the other one is Microsoft Access 2010. We will use the 2007 version, as you can open it by both Microsoft Access 2007 as well as Microsoft Access 2010. This is also to make sure that we are using the same database version.

- **Getting it from the SAP BusinessObjects samples directory**: You can also find the same Microsoft Access database file under the installation folder located at [BO4_INSTALLATION_DIRECTORY]\SAP BusinessObjects\SAP BusinessObjects Enterprise XI 4.0\Samples\webi.

    In this folder, you will find three sample databases (Northwind, eFashion, and Club) that we will use in the remaining chapters. There are two ready-to-use Universes: one for Northwind and the other one for eFashion. However, we will build our own NorthWind Universe from scratch.

You can also find the same Microsoft Access database file on the Packt Publishing website.

Creating the ODBC Connection

After getting the Northwind sample database file, we need to create the ODBC connection for this file. We will use this connection later on to connect to the Northwind database in the remaining chapters.

Open Database Connectivity (ODBC) is a database API connection standard, which is independent of the operating system and database. In order to connect to a specific **database management system (DBMS)**, you need to install a driver. ODBC will use this driver to communicate with DBMS.

Before creating our ODBC connection, we first need to install the DBMS driver. This driver will be used to communicate with the database. You don't need to worry about this driver if you have Microsoft Office installed on your machine, because the Microsoft Access driver will be installed by default. If you can't see the required Microsoft Access database driver listed in the ODBC connection wizard, then you may refer to the Microsoft site and try to reinstall it.

Another topic to take care of before starting the creation of our ODBC connection is your operating system's architecture. There are two OS architectures: 32-bit and 64-bit. So, we have two ODBC administrator applications, as you can see in the following screenshot. If your machine hardware or OS is not supporting the 64-bit version, then you will only be able to see the 32-bit version. Otherwise, you will be able to see both. We should use the 32-bit version to create our ODBC connection.

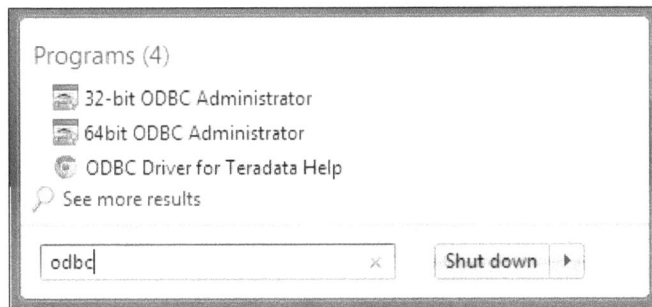

> You can change the underlying DBMS used in your ODBC connection without any negative effect on your client application.
>
> **Information Design Tool (IDT)** is a 32-bit application, so the ODBC connection will not work properly if you created the 64-bit ODBC connection instead of the 32-bit ODBC.
>
> Generic ODBC is not recommended on large-scale databases or production environments. The native DBMS driver will be faster than the generic ODBC connection. However, for training purposes, we will use ODBC to connect to the Northwind Microsoft Access database.

Now, let's start creating our ODBC connection. To create an ODBC connection to the Northwind Microsoft Access database, we need to perform the following steps:

1. Save the Northwind Microsoft Access database on a specific folder, for example, the c:\ drive.

2. Go to the **Start** menu and open **Control Panel**.

3. After that, navigate to **Administrative Tools**, and then double-click on **Data Sources (ODBC)**.

4. Then, select the **System DSN** tab, and click on the **Add...** button to add a new data source system.

5. Select **MS Access Driver (*.mdb, *.accdb)** from the driver list, as we can see in the following screenshot, and then click on **Finish**:

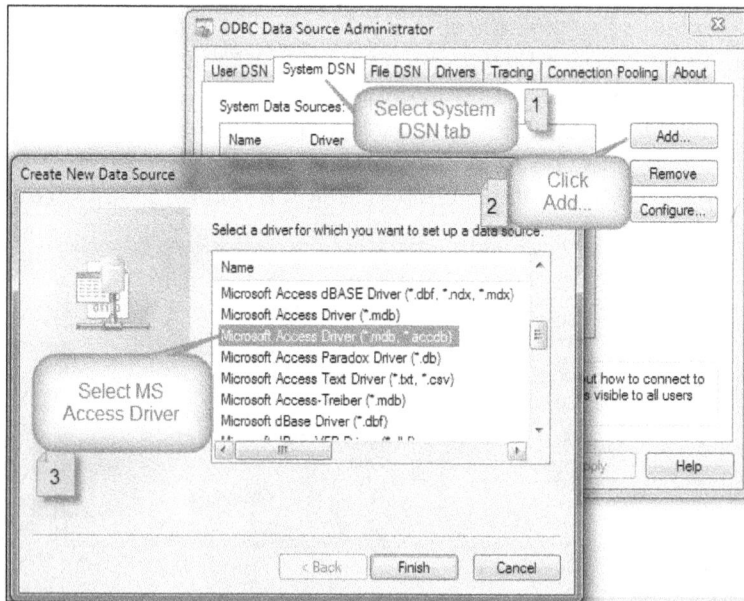

6. The configuration window will be displayed, and we should enter the Microsoft Access database name and path.

    Before we move on, let's take a look at the difference between **User DSN**, **System DSN**, and **File DSN**:

    ○   **User DSN**: This connection is stored locally, and it can be accessed only by the user who created it.

    ○   **System DSN**: This is the same as **User DSN**, but it is not restricted to its owner. It can be used by other users as well as by other system services and resources.

    ○   **File DSN**: This is a special type of connection that will save all the connection information on a flat file. This file can be shared with other users even if they are using different systems.

    The **ODBC Microsoft Access Setup** and **Select Database** windows are displayed in the following screenshot:

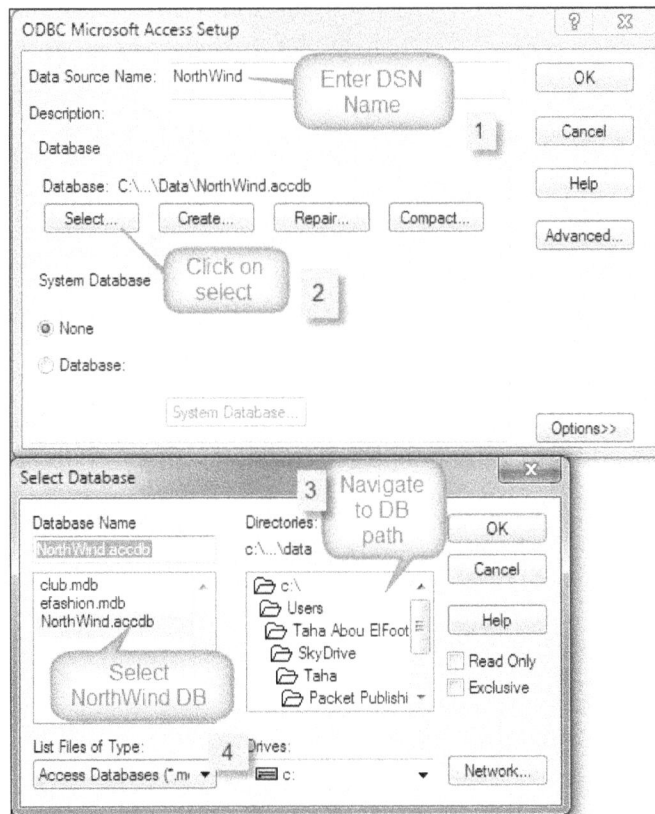

Congratulations! We completed our ODBC connection that we will use in the next chapter to build our first Universe. However, before we conclude this chapter, let's take a look on the Northwind data model, and let's try to understand the relationship between the tables that we have. This is very important because it will help us when we start working on the Universe foundation layer. This will also help us understand the specific joins between tables.

> You can find more information about the ODBC connection at `http://en.wikipedia.org/wiki/Open_Database_Connectivity`.

The Northwind data model

Now that we downloaded the Northwind Microsoft Access database and successfully created our ODBC connection, let's have a look on the Northwind data model. We can see two main contexts in the Northwind database, as shown in the following screenshot:

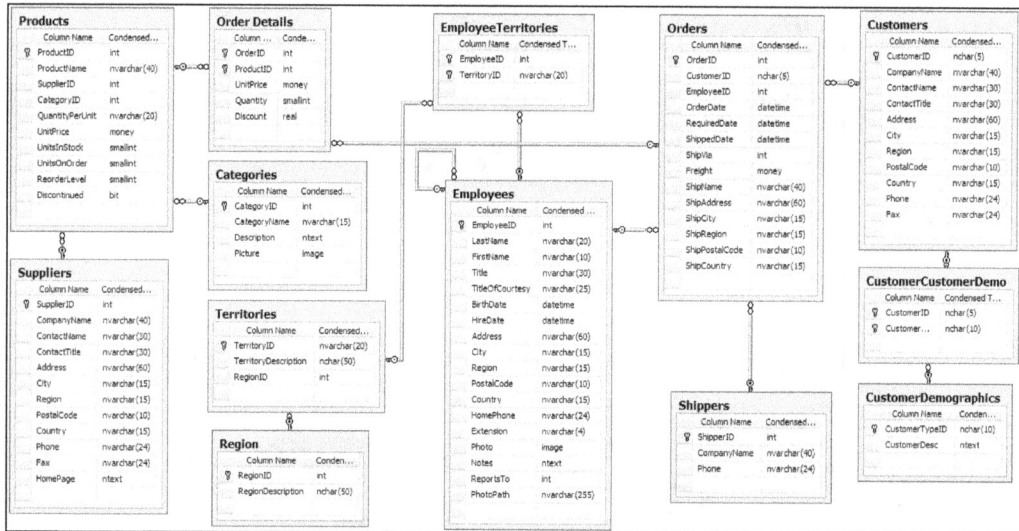

The first context is related to orders, and the other one is related to inventory. We can think of context as a subject area that covers some related information stored in some related tables. Before we go deep into the Northwind data model, let's first define some terminologies that we will use.

Dimensional modeling terminologies

We have three types of information from the business point of view:

- **Dimension**: This is an angle or point of view from which we can look at our data. Region or product is a good example. You might need to check your sales by region or by product.

- **Measure**: This is a number that represents a metric such as sales or number of purchase orders. An aggregation method should be assigned to each measure, such as sum, count, and average.

- **Attribute**: This is detailed information related to a specific dimension. It is neither a dimension nor a measure. Ship Zip/Postal code is a good example of an attribute that is part of the `Ship Address` dimension.

The following screenshot displays **Dimension**, **Measure**, and **Attribute**:

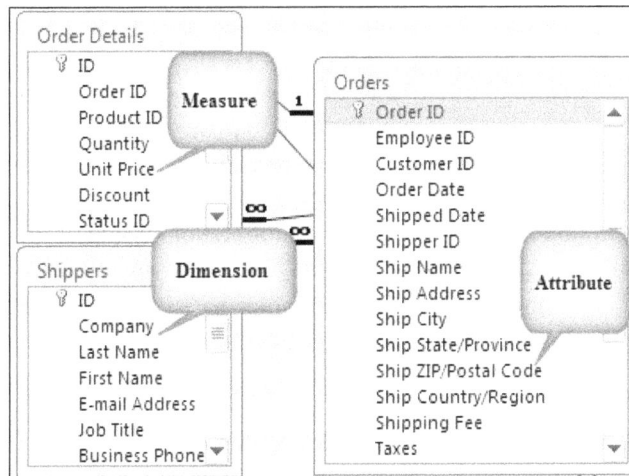

We will talk in detail about data and dimensional modeling in *Chapter 7, The Data Foundation Layer – Advanced Topics*. For now, we need to know that we have four types of tables in any data model:

- **The fact table**: This table will contain our summarized measures along with the dimensions reference keys.

- **The dimension table**: This table will store extra information about the dimension, such as the dimension's description. It will also store the dimension hierarchy if this dimension is part of a hierarchy. We shouldn't see any measure in this table.

- **The detailed table**: This is a flat table that contains dimensions, measures, and attributes in the denormalized form.

- **The mapping table**: In this table, you can find mapping (reference keys) for two fact tables.

Now, let's take a closer look at the Northwind's database.

Order information

This section will contain all information related to orders. Order information is stored in two main fact tables (Orders and Order Details) and some dimension tables such as Customer and Products. In the following table, we will go through all the tables related to order information:

Table name	Table type	Description
Orders	Fact	Information on orders, such as order date, shipping date, and employee ID
Order Details	Fact	Detailed information on orders, such as product, quantity, unit price, and discount
Invoices	Dimension	Information about invoices, such as invoice ID and date
Customer	Dimension	Detailed information about the customer, such as first name, last name, and e-mail address
Shipper	Dimension	Shipper's information, such as company name and business phone number
Orders Tax Status	Dimension	Tax information
Orders Status	Dimension	Information on the status of the order
Products	Dimension	Product information, such as product code, product description, and product supplier
Order Details Status	Dimension	Information on the status of order details

Let's have a look at the **entity-relationship diagram** (**ERD**) for this context:

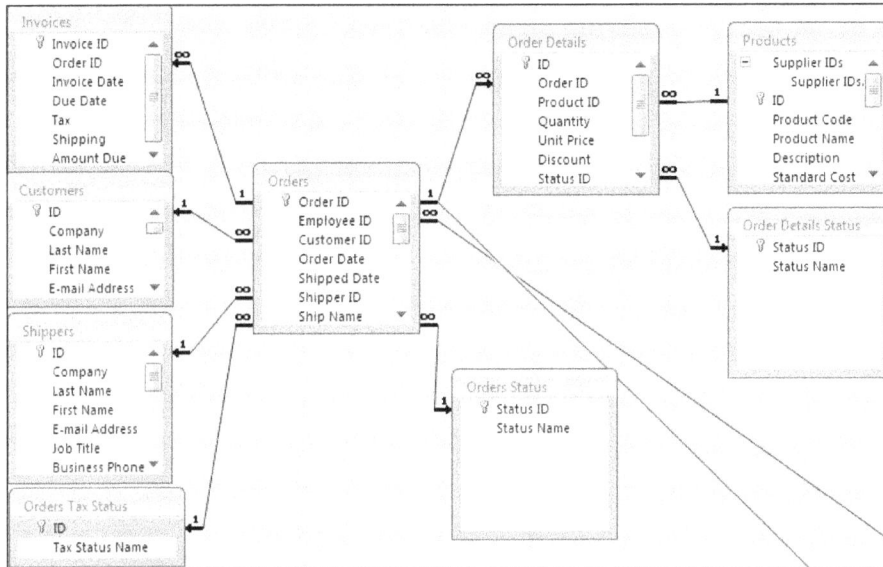

Inventory information

Now, we need to look at the other angle. Before we start selling our product, we need to maintain our inventory to know how many items are left from each product (quantity) and to make sure that our business will keep running. We also need to maintain our suppliers and purchase orders. In the following table, we will go through all the tables related to inventory information:

Table name	Table type	Description
Inventory Transactions	Fact	Inventory information, such as product ID, quantity, and transaction type
Purchase Orders	Fact	Information on purchase orders, such as supplier, submit date, and status
Purchase Orders Details	Fact	Detailed information about purchase orders, such as quantity and unit cost
Suppliers	Dimension	Supplier details and contact information
Employees	Dimension	Detailed information of employees
Products	Dimension	Product information, such as product code, product description, and product supplier
Purchase Orders Status	Dimension	Purchase orders' status
Inventory Transaction Type	Dimension	Inventory transaction type

Let's have a look at the ERD for this context:

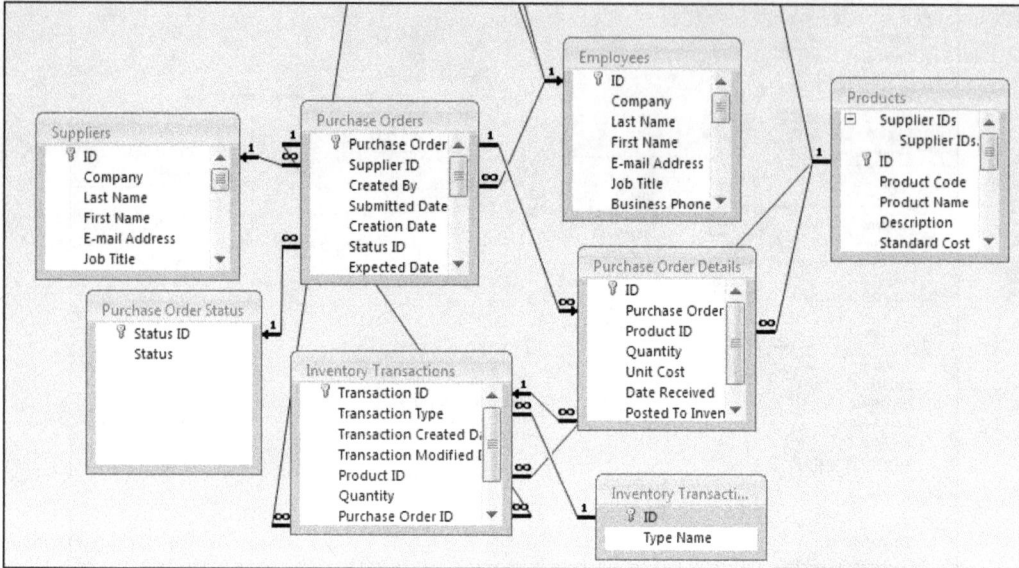

Summary

In this chapter, we analyzed a complete business case with the Northwind company's example, which could be closely related to the company's real-time problems. We talked about their reporting needs and how they initiated their own BI solution. Then, we had an overview of the BI Maturity Model, and we were able to identify that Northwind is in the initiation stage. After that, we learned how to get the Northwind sample database file and how to set up the ODBC connection on top of this database. Finally, we had an overview of the Northwind database model by introducing orders and inventory information contexts.

In the next chapter, we will build our first Universe using the ODBC connection that we created in this chapter. We will start with only one table in the Universe, and we will expand it as we are moving through the remaining chapters.

3

Creating Our First Universe

In this chapter, we will start getting our hands dirty. First, we will learn how to run SAP BO **Information Design Tool** (**IDT**), and we will have an overview of the different views that we have in the main IDT window. This will help us understand the main function and purpose for each part of the IDT main window. Then, we will use SAP BO IDT to create our first Universe. In this chapter, we will create a local project to contain our Universe and other resources related to it. After that, we will use the ODBC connection that we already created in the previous chapter to create a relational data connection. Then, we will create a simple Data Foundation layer that will contain only one table (Customers). After that, we will create the corresponding Business layer by creating the associated business objects. The main target of this chapter is to make you familiar with the Universe creation process from start to end. Then, we will detail each part of the Universe creation process as well as other Universe features while progressing through the remaining chapters.

At the end, we will talk about how to get help while creating a new Universe, using the Universe creation wizard or Cheat Sheets.

In this chapter, we will cover the following topics:

- Running the IDT
- Getting familiar with SAP BO IDT's interface and views
- Creating a local project and setting up a relational connection
- Creating a simple Data Foundation layer
- Creating a simple Business layer
- Publishing our first Universe
- Getting help using the **Universe** wizard and Cheat Sheets

Information Design Tool

The Information Design Tool is a client tool that is used to develop BO Universes. It is a new tool released by SAP in BO release 4. There are many SAP BO tools that we can use to create our Universe, such as SAP BO **Universe Designer Tool (UDT)**, SAP BO Universe Builder, and SAP BO IDT. SAP BO Universe designer was the main tool to create Universe since the release of BO 6.x. This tool is still supported in the current SAP BI 4.x release, and you can still use it to create UNV Universes. You need to plan which tool you will use to build your Universe based on the target solution. For example, if you need to connect to a BEX query, you should use the UDT, as the IDT can't do this. On the other hand, if you want to create a Universe query from SAP Dashboard Designer, then you should use the IDT. The BO Universe Builder used to build a Universe from a supported XML metadata file. You can use the Universe conversion wizard to convert the UNV Universe created by the UDT to the UNX Universe created by the IDT. We will cover this subject in detail in *Chapter 10, A Multiuser Development Environment*.

Sometimes, you might get errors or warnings while converting a Universe from .unv to .unx. You need to resolve this manually.

It is preferred that you convert a Universe from the previous SAP BO release XI 3.x instead of converting a Universe from an earlier release such as BI XI R2 and BO 6.5. There will always be complete support for the previous release.

The main features of the IDT

IDT is one of the major new features introduced in SAP BI 4.0. We can now build a Universe that combines data from multiple data sources and also build a dimensional universe on top of an OLAP connection. We will discuss this in detail in *Chapter 4, Creating the Data Foundation Layer*, and *Chapter 5, Creating the Business Layer*.

We can see also a major enhancement in the design environment by empowering the multiuser development environment. This will help designers work in teams and share Universe resources as well as maintain the Universe version control. We will talk about this subject in detail in *Chapter 10, A Multiuser Development Environment*.

For more information on the new features introduced in the IDT, refer to the SAP community network at http://wiki.scn.sap.com/ and search for *SAP BI 4.0 new features and changes*.

The Information Design Tool interface

We need to cover the following requirements before we create our first Universe:

- BO client tools are installed on your machine, or you have access to a PC with client tools already installed
- We have access to a SAP BO server
- We have a valid username and password to connect to this server
- We have created an ODBC connection for the Northwind Microsoft Access database that we already completed in the previous chapter

Now, to run the IDT, perform the following steps:

1. Click on the **Start** menu and navigate to **All Programs**.
2. Click on the **SAP BusinessObjects BI platform 4** folder to expand it.
3. Click on the **Information Design Tool** icon, as shown in the following screenshot:

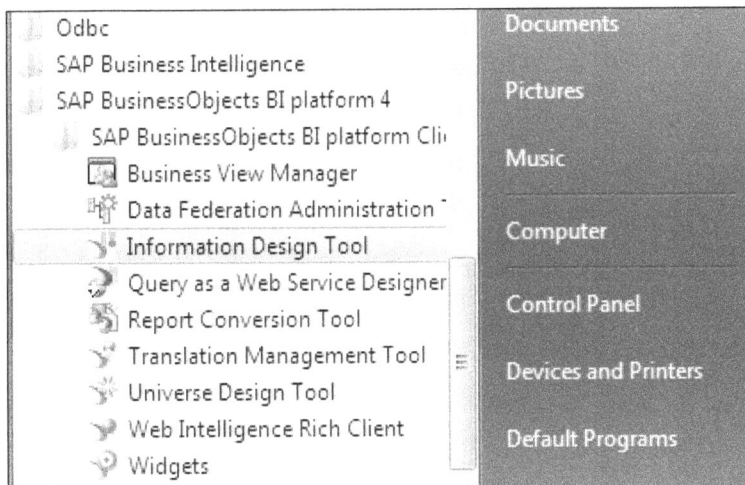

The IDT will open and then we can move on and create our new Universe.

In this section, we will get to know the different views that we have in the IDT. We can show or hide any view from the **Window** menu, as shown in the following screenshot:

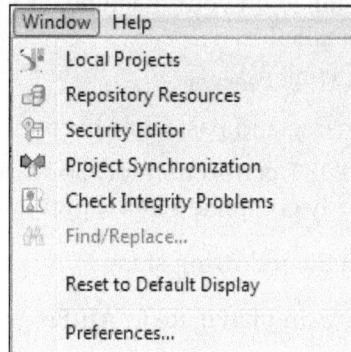

Window	Help
⌄	Local Projects
	Repository Resources
	Security Editor
	Project Synchronization
	Check Integrity Problems
	Find/Replace...
	Reset to Default Display
	Preferences...

You can also access the same views from the main window toolbar, as displayed in the following screenshot:

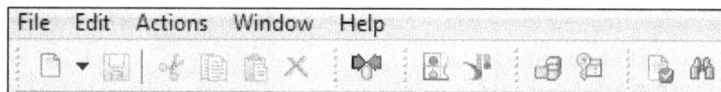

File   Edit   Actions   Window   Help

Local Projects

The **Local Projects** view is used to navigate to and maintain local project resources, so you can edit and update any project resource, such as the relation connection, Data Foundation, and Business layers from this view.

> A project is a new concept introduced in the IDT, and there is no equivalent for it in the UDT.

We can see the **Local Projects** main window in the following screenshot:

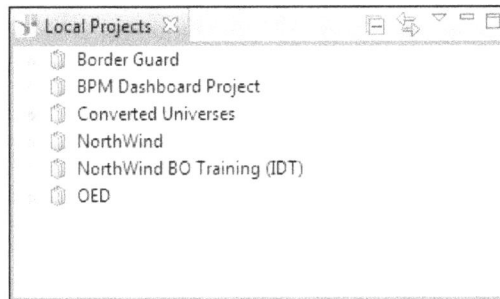

Repository Resources

You can access more than one repository using the IDT. However, usually, we work with only one repository at a time. This view will help you initiate a session with the required repository and will keep a list of all the available repositories. You can use repository resources to access and modify the secured connection stored on the BO server. You can also manage and organize published Universes. We can see the **Repository Resources** main window in the following screenshot:

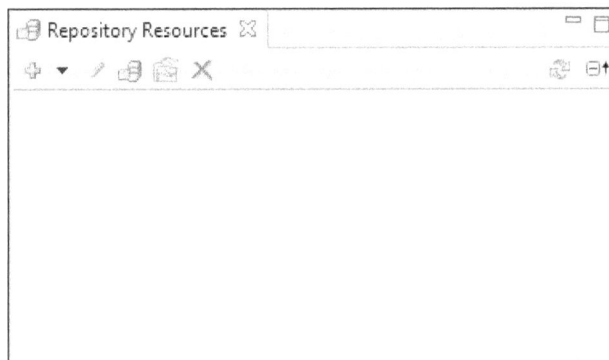

Security Editor

Security Editor is used to create data and business security profiles. This can be used to add some security restrictions to be applied on BO users and groups. We will discuss this in detail in *Chapter 9, Data Security and Profiles*.

> **Security Editor** is equivalent to **Manage Security** under **Tools** in the UDT.

We can see the main **Security Editor** window in the following screenshot:

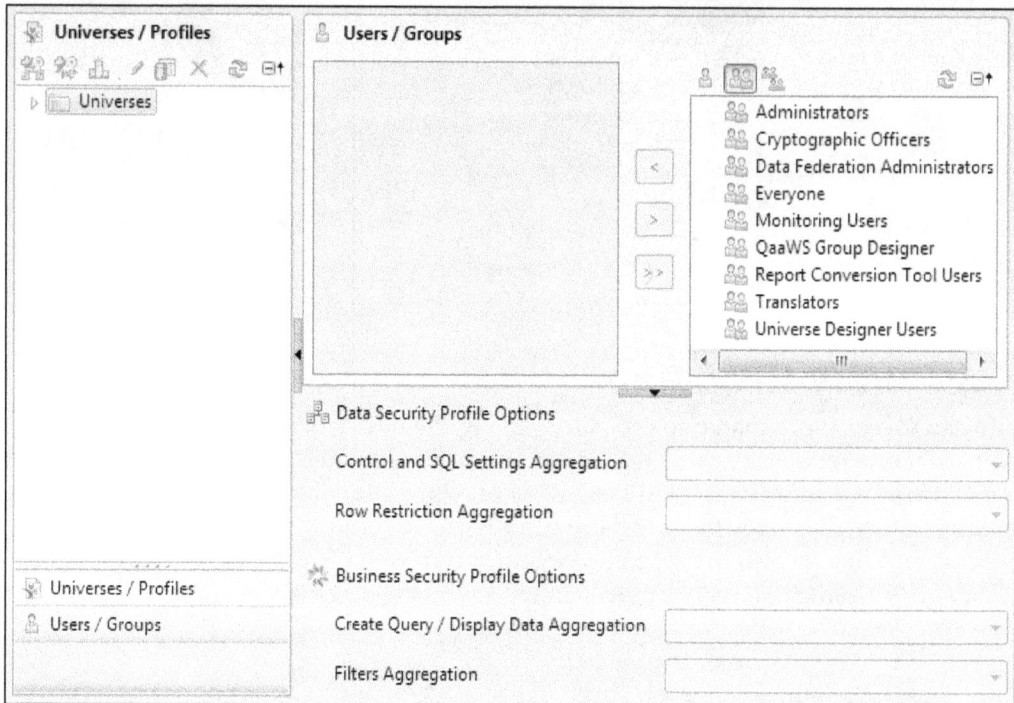

Project Synchronization

The **Project Synchronization** view is used to synchronize shared projects stored on the repository with your local projects. From this view, you will be able to see the differences between your local projects and shared projects, such as added, deleted, or updated project resources.

> Project Synchronization is one of the major enhancements introduced in the IDT to overcome the lack of the multiuser development environment in the UDT.

We can see the **Project Synchronization** window in the following screenshot:

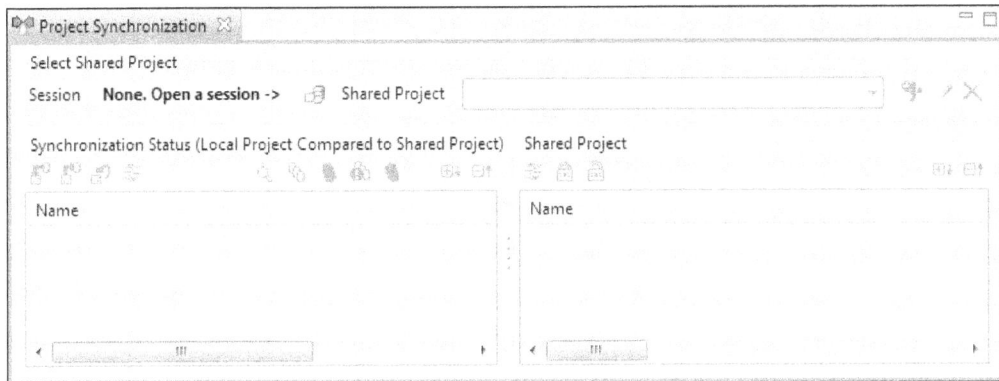

Check Integrity Problems

The **Check Integrity Problems** view is used to check the Universe's integrity.

> **Check Integrity Problems** is equivalent to **Check Integrity** under **Tools** in the UDT.

Check Integrity Problems is an automatic test for your foundation layer as well as Business layer that will check the Universe's integrity. This wizard will display errors or warnings discovered during the test, and we need to fix them to avoid having any wrong data or errors in our reports.

> **Check Integrity Problems** is part of the BO best practices to always check and correct the integrity problems before publishing the Universe.

We can see the **Check Integrity** window in the following screenshot:

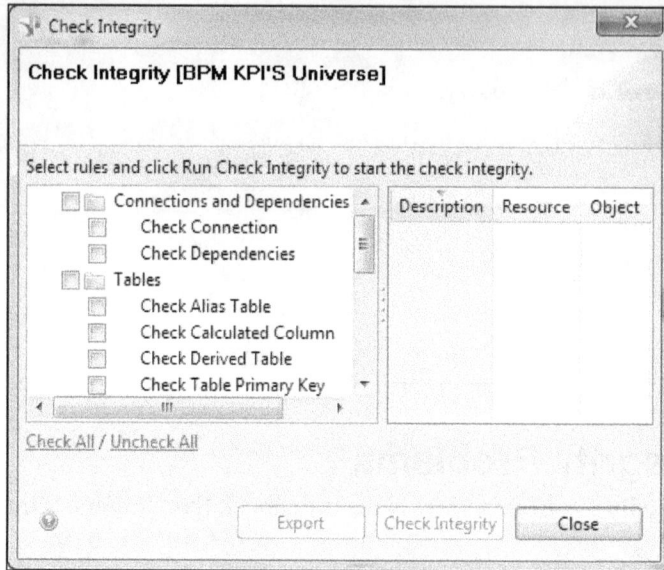

Creating your first Universe step by step

After we've opened the IDT, we want to start creating our NorthWind Universe. We need to create the following three main resources to build a Universe:

- **Data connection**: This resource is used to establish a connection with the data source. There are two main types of connections that we can create: relational connection and OLAP connection.

- **Data Foundation**: This resource will store the metadata, such as tables, joins, and cardinalities, for the physical layer.

- **The Business layer**: This resource will store the metadata for the business model. Here, we will create our business objects such as dimensions, measures, attributes, and filters. This layer is our Universe's interface and end users should be able to access it to build their own reports and analytics by dragging-and-dropping the required objects.

We need to create a local project to hold all the preceding Universe resources. The local project is just a container that will store the Universe's contents locally on your machine. Finally, we need to publish our Universe to make it ready to be used.

Creating a new project

You can think about a project such as a folder that will contain all the resources required by your Universe. Normally, we will start any Universe by creating a local project. Then, later on, we might need to share the entire project and make it available for the other Universe designers and developers as well.

This is a folder that will be stored locally on your machine, and you can access it any time from the IDT **Local Projects** window or using the **Open** option from the **File** menu. The resources inside this project will be available only for the local machine users. Let's try to create our first local project using the following steps:

1. Go to the **File** menu and select **New Project**, or click on the **New** icon on the toolbar.

2. Select **Project**, as shown in the following screenshot:

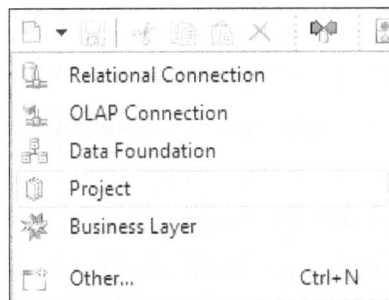

3. The **New Project** creation wizard will open.

4. Enter NorthWind in the **Project Name** field, and leave the **Project Location** field as default. Note that your project will be stored locally in this folder.

5. Click on **Finish**, as shown in the following screenshot:

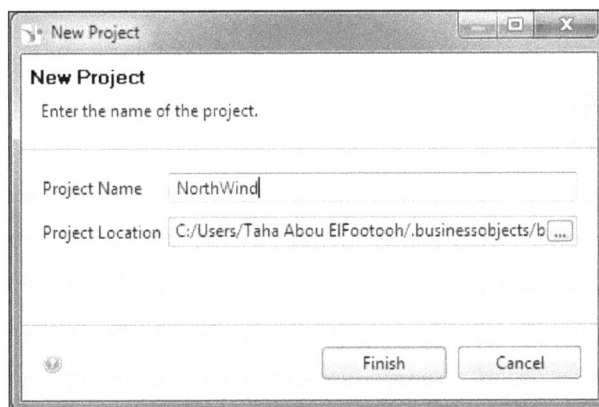

Now, you can see the NorthWind empty project in the **Local Projects** window.

> You can add resources to your local project by performing the following actions:
> - Creating new resources
> - Converting a .unv Universe
> - Importing a published Universe

Creating a new data connection

Data connection will store all the required information such as IP address, username, and password to access a specific data source. A data connection will connect to a specific type of data source, and you can use the same data connection to create multiple Data Foundation layers. There are two types of data connection: relational data connection, which is used to connect to the relational database such as Teradata and Oracle, and OLAP connection, which is used to connect to an OLAP cube.

To create a data connection, we need to do the following:

1. Right-click on the NorthWind Universe.
2. Select a new **Relational Data Connection**.
3. Enter NorthWind as the connection name, and write a brief description about this connection.

> The best practice is to always add a description for each created object. For example, code comments will help others understand why this object has been created, how to use it, and for which purpose they should use it.

We can see the first page of the **New Relational Connection** wizard in the following screenshot:

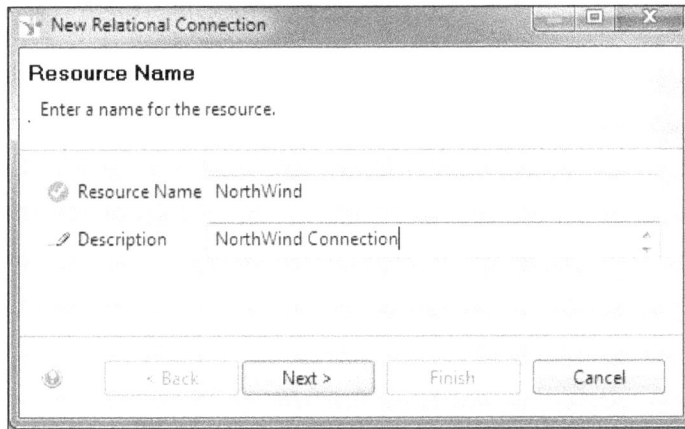

4. On the second page, expand the **MS Access 2007** driver and select **ODBC Drivers**.

5. Use the `NorthWind` ODBC connection that we already created in the previous chapter.

6. Click on **Test Connection** to make sure that the connection to the data source is successfully established.

7. Click on **Next** to edit the connection's advanced options or click on **Finish** to use the default settings, as shown in the following screenshot:

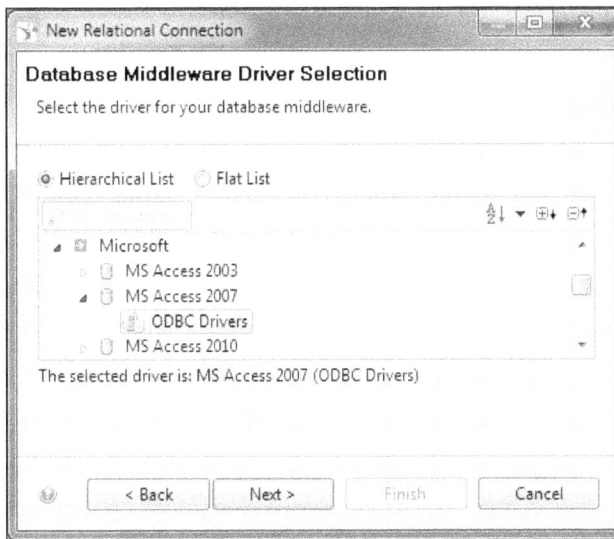

We can see the first parameters page of the MS Access 2007 connection in the following screenshot:

You can now see the `NorthWind` connection under the `NorthWind` project in the **Local Projects** window.

> The local relational connection is stored as the `.cnx` file, while the shared secured connection is stored as a shortcut with the `.cns` extension. The local connection can be used in your local projects only, and you need to publish it to the BO repository to share it with other Universe designers.

Creating a new Data Foundation

After we successfully create a relation connection to the Northwind Microsoft Access database, we can now start creating our foundation.

Data Foundation is a physical model that will store tables as well as the relations between them (joins).

> Data Foundation in the IDT is equivalent to the physical data layer in the UDT.

To create a new Data Foundation, right-click on the NorthWind project in the **Local Projects** window, and then select **New Data Foundation** and perform the following steps:

1. Enter NorthWind as a resource name, and enter a brief description on the NorthWind Data Foundation.
2. Select the **Single Source** Data Foundation.
3. Select the **NorthWind.cnx** connection.

After that, expand the NorthWind connection, navigate to NorthWind.accdb, and perform the following steps:

1. Navigate to the Customers table and then drag it to an empty area in the **Master** view window on the right-hand side.
2. Save your Data Foundation.

> An asterisk (*) will be displayed beside the resource name to indicate that it was modified but not saved.

We can see the **Connection** panel in the NorthWind.dfx Universe resource in the following screenshot:

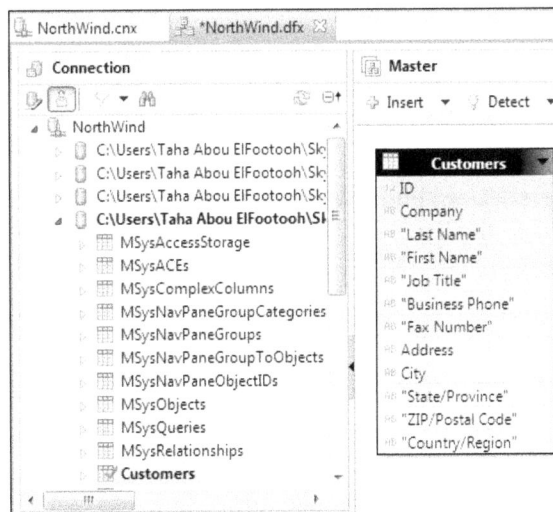

Creating a new Business layer

Now, we will create a simple Business layer based on the `Customer` table that we already added to the `NorthWind` Data Foundation. Each Business layer should map to one Data Foundation at the end.

> The Business layer in the IDT is equivalent to the business model in the UDT.

To create a new Business layer, right-click on the `NorthWind` project and then select **New Business Layer** from the menu. Then, we need to perform the following steps:

1. The first step to create a Business layer is to select the type of the data source that we will use. In our case, select **Relational Data Foundation** as shown in the following screenshot:

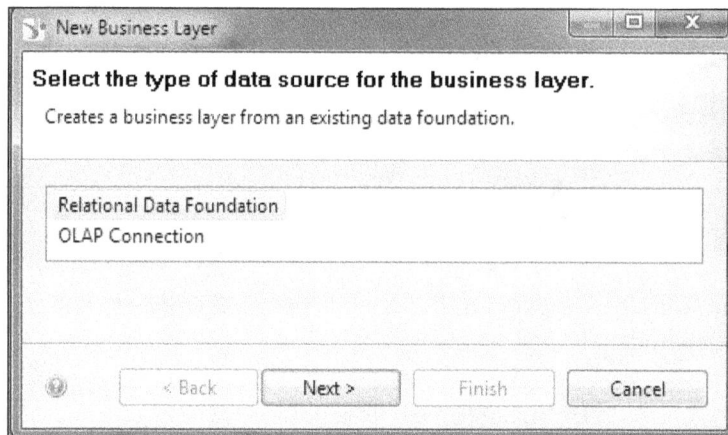

2. Enter `NorthWind` as the resource name and a brief description for our Business layer.

3. In the next **Select Data Foundation** window, select the `NorthWind` Data Foundation from the list.

4. Make sure that the **Automatically create folders and objects** option is selected, as shown in the following screenshot:

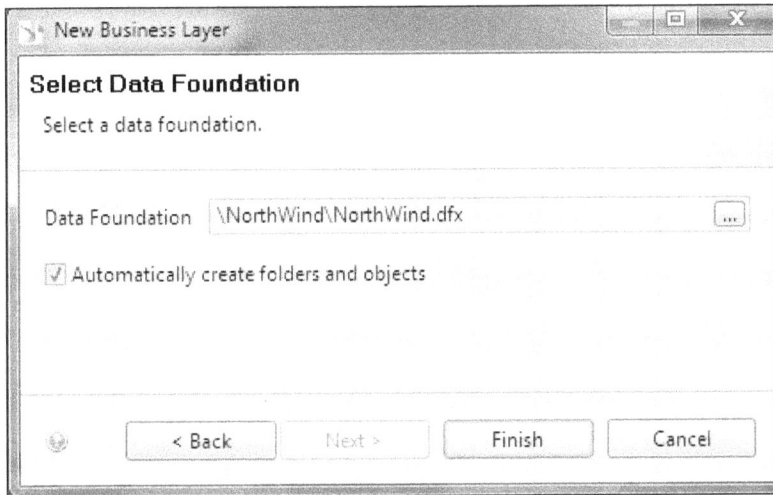

Now, you should be able to see the Customer folder under the NorthWind Business layer. If not, just drag it from the NorthWind Data Foundation and drop it under the NorthWind Business layer. Then, save the NorthWind **Business Layer**, as shown in the following screenshot:

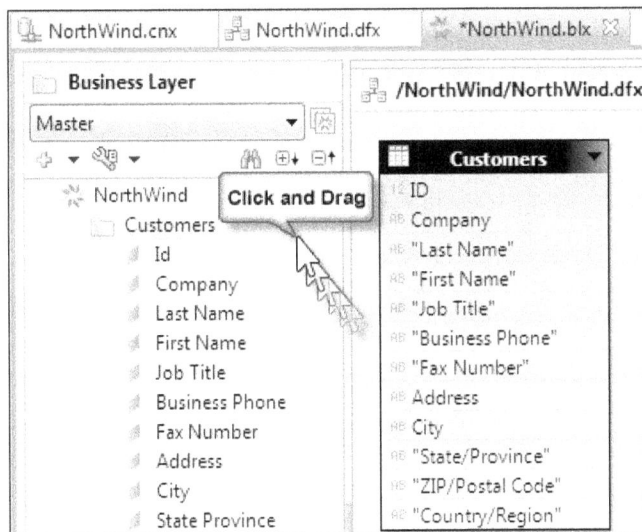

A new folder will be created automatically for the Customers table. This folder is also populated with the corresponding dimensions. The Business layer now needs to be published to the BO server, and then, the end users will be able to access it and build their own reports on top of our Universe.

If you successfully completed all the steps from the previous sections, the project folder should contain the relational data connection (NorthWind.cnx), the Data Foundation layer (NorthWind.dfx), and the Business layer (NorthWind.blx). The project should appear as displayed in the following screenshot:

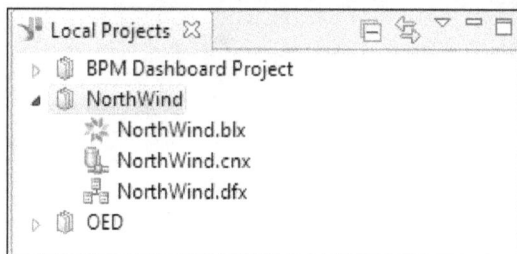

Saving and publishing the NorthWind Universe

We need to perform one last step before we publish our first simple Universe and make it available for the other Universe designers. We need to publish our relational data connection and save it on the repository instead of on our local machine. Publishing a connection will make it available for everyone on the server. Before publishing the Universe, we will replace the NorthWind.cnx resource in our project with a shortcut to the NorthWind secured connection stored on the SAP BO server. After publishing a Universe, other developers as well as business users will be able to see and access it from the SAP BO repository.

> Publishing a Universe from the IDT is equivalent to exporting a Universe from the UDT (navigate to **File** | **Export**).

To publish the NorthWind connection, we need to right-click on the NorthWind.cnx resource in the **Local Projects** window. Then, select **Publish Connection to a Repository**.

As we don't have an active session with the BO server, you will need to initiate one by performing the following steps:

1. Create a new session.

2. Type your `<system name: port number>` in the **System** field.

3. Select the **Authentication** type.

4. Enter your username and password.

We have many authentication types such as Enterprise, LDAP, and Windows **Active Directory** (**AD**). Enterprise authentication will store user security information inside the BO server. The user credential can only be used to log in to BO, while on the other hand, LDAP will store user security information in the LDAP server, and the user credential can be used to log in to multiple systems in this case. The BO server will send user information to the LDAP server to authenticate the user, and then, it will allow them to access the system in case of successful authentication. The last authentication type is Windows AD, which can also authenticate users using the security information stored inside.

> There are many authentication types such as Enterprise, LDAP, Windows AD, and SAP.

We can see the **Open Session** window in the following screenshot:

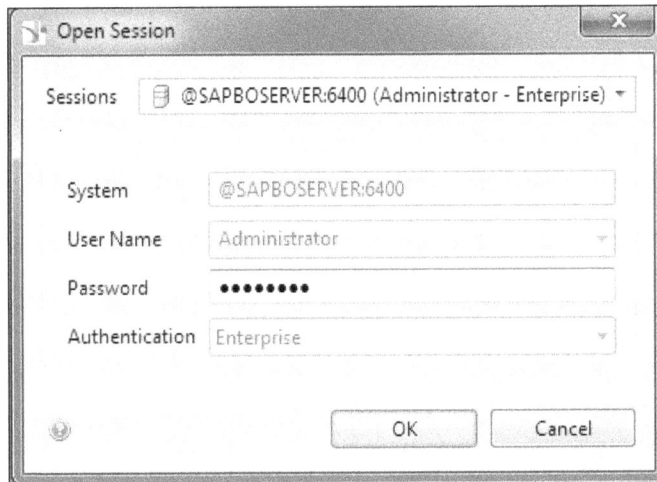

[The default port number is 6400.   ]

A pop-up window will inform you about the connection status (successful here), and it will ask you whether you want to create a shortcut for this connection in the same project folder or not. We should select **Yes** in our case, because we need to link to the secured published connection instead of the local one. We will not be able to publish our Universe to the BO repository with a local connection. We can see the **Publish Connection** window in the following screenshot:

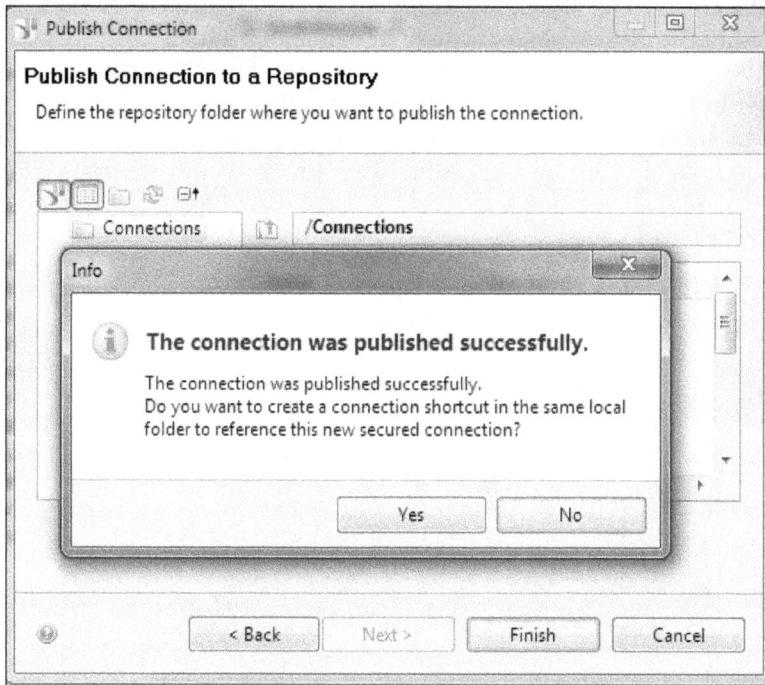

Finally, we need to link our Data Foundation layer with the secured connection instead of the local connection. To do this, you need to open `NorthWind.dfx` and replace `NorthWind.cnx` with the `NorthWind.cnc` connection. Then, save your Data Foundation resource and right-click on `NorthWind.blx`. After that, navigate to **Publish | To a Repository...**. The **Check Integrity** window will be displayed. Just select **Finish**.

We can see how to change connection in `NorthWind.dfx` in the following screenshot:

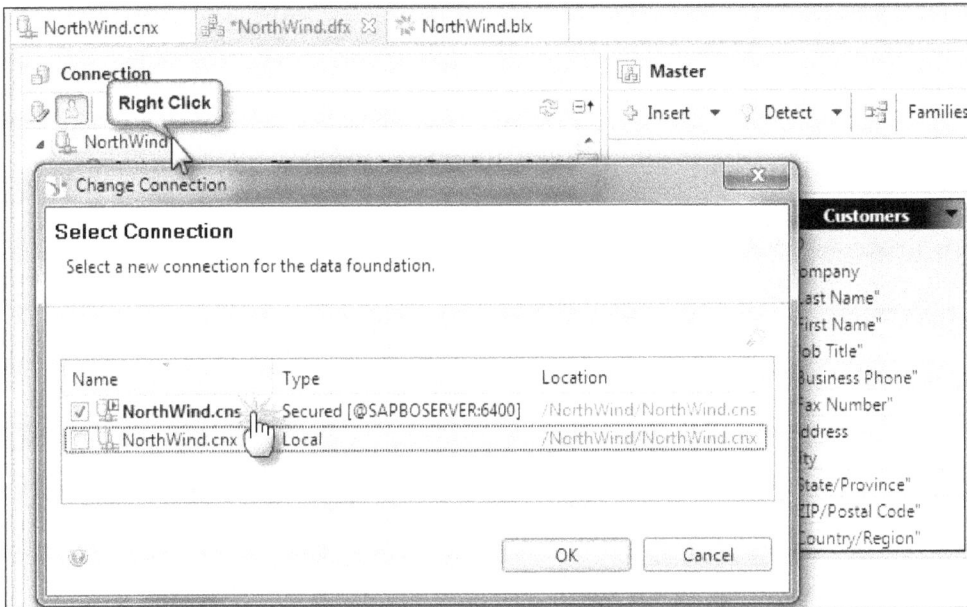

After redirecting our Data Foundation layer to the newly created shortcut connection, we need to go to the **Local Projects** window again, right-click on `NorthWind.blx`, and publish it to the repository.

Our Universe will be saved on the repository with the same name assigned to the Business layer.

Congratulations! We have created our first Universe.

Finding help while creating a Universe

In most cases, you will use the step-by-step approach to create a Universe. However, we have two other ways that we can use to create a universe.

In this section, we will try to create the `NorthWind` Universe again, but using the **Universe** wizard and Cheat Sheets.

The Universe wizard

The **Universe** wizard is just a wizard that will launch the project, connection, Data Foundation, and Business layer wizards in a sequence. We already explained each wizard individually in an earlier section. Each wizard will collect the required information to create the associated Universe resource. For example, the project wizard will end after collecting the required information to create a project, and the project folder will be created as an output. The **Universe** wizard will launch all the mentioned wizards, and it will end after collecting all the information required to create the Universe. A Universe with all the required resources will be created after finishing this wizard.

> The **Universe** wizard is equivalent to the **Quick Design** wizard in the UDT.

You can open the **Universe** wizard from the welcome screen or from the **File** menu. As a practice, we can create the NorthWind2 Universe using the **Universe** wizard:

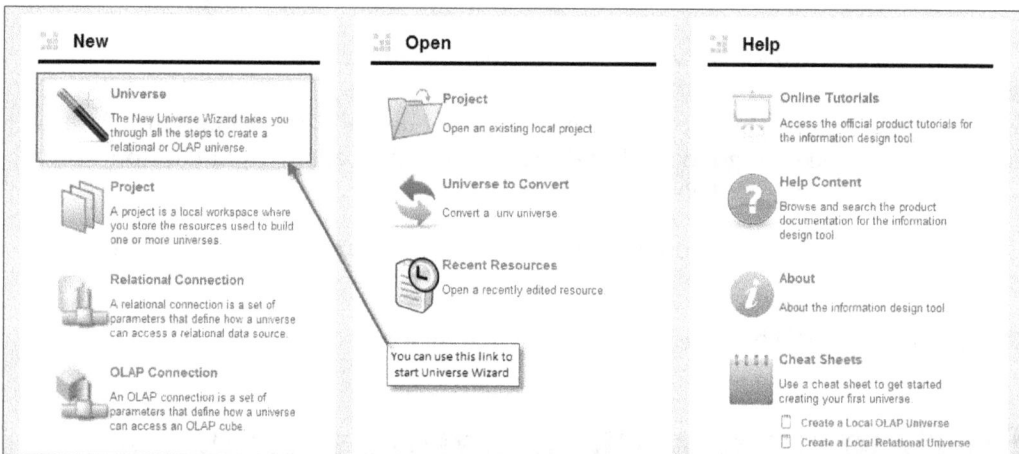

> The **Universe** wizard and welcome screen are new features in SAP BO 4.1.

Cheat Sheets

Cheat Sheets is another way of getting help while you are building your Universe. They provide step-by-step guidance and detailed descriptions that will help you create your relational Universe. We need to perform the following steps to use Cheat Sheets to build the NorthWind3 Universe, which is exactly the same as the NorthWind Universe that we created earlier in the step-by-step approach:

1. Go to the **Help** menu and select **Cheat Sheets**.

2. Follow the steps in the **Cheat Sheets** window to create the NorthWind3 Universe using the same information that we used to complete the NorthWind Universe.

3. If you face any difficulties in completing any steps, just click on the **Click to perform** button to guide you.

4. Click on the **Click when completed** link to move to the next step.

> Cheat Sheets is a new help method introduced in the IDT, and there is no equivalent for it in the UDT.

We can see the **Cheat Sheets** window in the following screenshot:

Summary

In this chapter, we discussed the difference between IDT views, and we tried to get familiar with the IDT user interface. Then, we had an overview of the Universe creation process from start to end. In real-life project environments, the first step is to create a local project to hold all the related Universe resources. Then, we initiated the project by adding the main three resources that are required by each universe. These resources are data connection, Data Foundation, and Business layer. After that, we published our Universe to make it available to other Universe designers and users. This is done by publishing our data connection first and then by redirecting our foundation layer to refer to a shortcut for the shared secured published connection. At this point, we will be able to publish and share our Universe.

We also learned how to use the **Universe** wizard and Cheat Sheets to create a Universe.

In the next chapter, we will discuss the Data Foundation layer in more detail.

4
Creating the Data Foundation Layer

This is a big chapter, so prepare a mug of your favorite coffee and make sure that you are comfortable and ready to move on.

In the previous chapter, we had an overview of the creation process of the Universe from start to end. In this chapter, we will focus on the Data Foundation layer, which is the core resource for any Universe. However, before that, we will talk about data connection, as it is the first Universe resource that we need to create. After that, we will learn how to use different functions and features provided by the Data Foundation layer.

In this chapter, we will cover the following topics:

- Working with data connections and learning the difference between the relational and OLAP connections
- Learning the difference between single-source and multisource Data Foundation
- Learning the difference between the physical database table, view, alias table, and derived table
- Populating `NorthWind` Data Foundation layer with tables, views, alias tables, and derived tables
- Understanding join cardinality and the difference between the primary key and foreign key columns
- Learning the difference between join types (equal, theta, outer, and self joins)
- Creating joins between Data Foundation objects
- Understanding the Data Foundation layer's functions, features, menus, and toolbars

- Learning how to control the Data Foundation display by inserting Data Foundation display views and modifying the visualization properties

- Getting to know actions that we can perform on a selected table

- Learning how to get more information on a selected table, such as the number of records stored inside this table or how to display sample data from it

Working with data connections

The main function of data connection is to store all the required information to access a specific data source. Each data connection will connect to a specific type of data source, and you can use the same data connection to create multiple Data Foundation layers. Data connection is like a bridge between our Universe and physical database. The data connection middleware driver is the translator that will communicate directly with the database. There are two data connection types: the relational connection and the OLAP connection.

The relational connection

We already created a relational data connection in the previous chapter, but we will talk about supported database middleware drivers that we have. Actually, you can find a driver for almost all known databases such as Oracle, MS SQL, and Teradata. You can also create a connection to the SAP database (MaxDB) and SAP HANA.

We might edit/change a driver or test a connection after we create our relational data connection. We might also use the **Show Values** function (shown in the following screenshot) to analyze our tables and data before we start creating our Data Foundation layer:

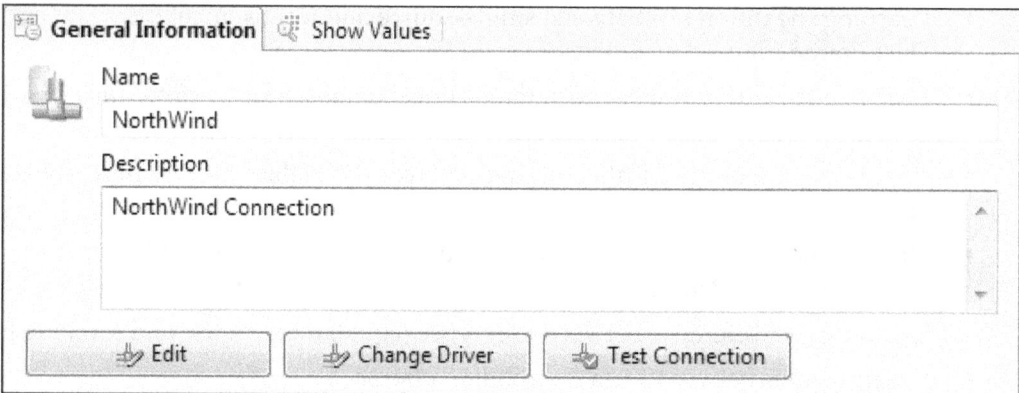

The OLAP connection

An OLAP connection is a special type of data connection. It is a star schema data model that is tailored for analytics and summary reports. We will talk in detail about data models in *Chapter 7, The Data Foundation Layer – Advanced Topics*. To create an OLAP connection, we will follow the same steps that we used to create a relational connection, but we will select a new OLAP connection instead of the new relation connection from the **New** menu.

> In the UDT, we can use the **Define New Connection** wizard (**File** | **Parameters** | **Definition** | **Connection**) to create a new relational or OLAP connection, while in the IDT, we have a separate wizard for each connection type.

Building the Data Foundation layer

The Data Foundation layer is the core resource for any Universe. Here, we will start managing our Data Foundation objects (tables, views, alias tables, and derived tables) as well as the relationship between them using joins. Data Foundation can refer to one or more data connection. You can also build as many Business layers as you wish on top of the same Data Foundation layer. We will talk in detail about each object, but let's talk first about the types of Data Foundation.

Types of Data Foundation

When we create a new Data Foundation, it will ask if we want to use a single-source or multisource Data Foundation. It is a major choice to decide and select the right type from the beginning, because in the current SAP BO 4.x, it is not possible to change it later on. There is no conversion routine that can be used to convert a single-source Data Foundation into multisource and vice versa. So, we need to know when we have to select and use single source and when we should use multisource Data Foundation; this is the aim of the upcoming sections of the chapter.

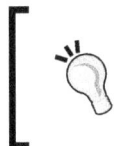

> When you convert a UNV Universe to a UNX Universe, the Data Foundation will be single source by default. You might need to rebuild your Universe if you want to convert it to multisource Data Foundation.

Now, let's have a look at the features supported by each type, which are shown in the following screenshot:

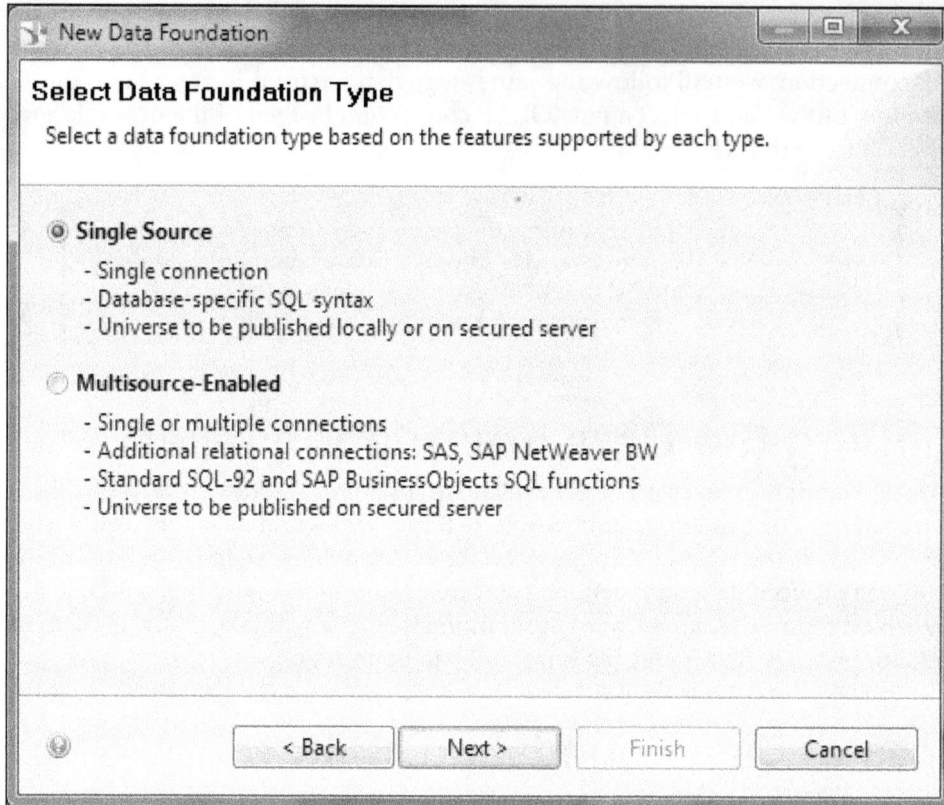

```
┌─────────────────────────────────────────────────────────────┐
│  ▶  New Data Foundation                    [ — ] [ □ ] [ X ] │
├─────────────────────────────────────────────────────────────┤
│  Select Data Foundation Type                                 │
│  Select a data foundation type based on the features         │
│  supported by each type.                                     │
│                                                              │
│  ◉ Single Source                                             │
│       - Single connection                                    │
│       - Database-specific SQL syntax                         │
│       - Universe to be published locally or on secured server│
│                                                              │
│  ○ Multisource-Enabled                                       │
│       - Single or multiple connections                       │
│       - Additional relational connections: SAS, SAP NetWeaver BW │
│       - Standard SQL-92 and SAP BusinessObjects SQL functions│
│       - Universe to be published on secured server           │
│                                                              │
│                                                              │
│  ⑦    [ < Back ]  [ Next > ]  [ Finish ]  [ Cancel ]        │
└─────────────────────────────────────────────────────────────┘
```

Single Source

Single-source Data Foundation will allow us to use only one data connection. There is no restriction on the data connection type that will be used, so we can use the relation data connection as well as the OLAP data connection. We usually use single-source Data Foundation if we are sure that we will only use one single source or if we want to use one of the following features:

- **Single connection**
- **Database-specific SQL syntax**
- **Universe to be published locally or on secured server**

Multisource-Enabled

One of the challenges that we had in the previous Universe designer tool is to build a Universe on top of two or more different databases. Sometimes, we used to create a database link to solve this, but now, this functionality is fully integrated with multisource Data Foundation in the IDT. We might use multisource-enabled Data Foundation if we want to use one of the following features:

- **Single or multiple connections**
- **Additional relational connection: SAS, SAP NetWeaver BW**
- **Standard SQL-92 and BusinessObjects SQL functions**
- **Universe to be published on secured server**

> The choice to identify the required features and suitable types for your Data Foundation layer is based on business analysis during the data modeling phase.

> The UDT can be used to create a single-data-source Universe only, while in the IDT, we can create a single or multisource Data Foundation.

In the next section, we will talk about contents that we might have in our Data Foundation, but let's first have a look at the **Data Foundation** screen. The numbers refer to the same order of topics that we will discuss in this chapter.

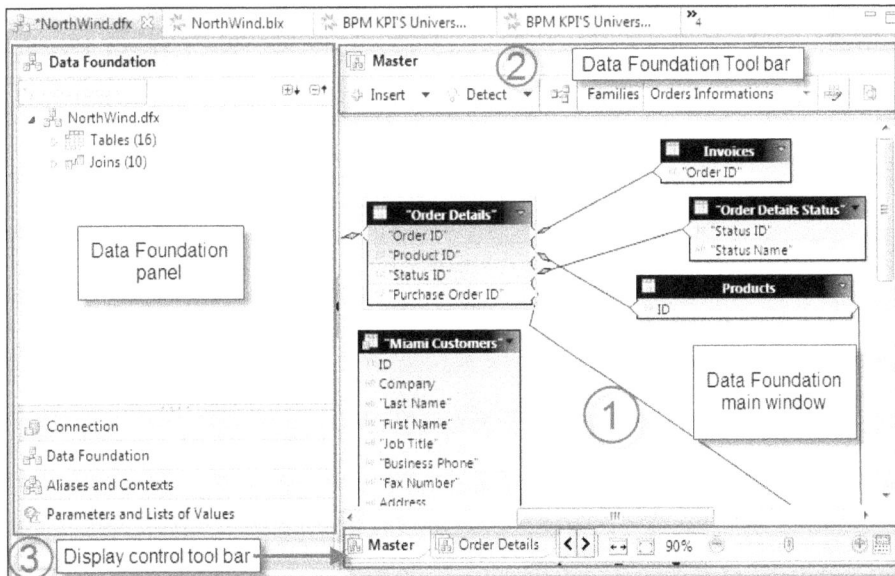

Physical tables and views

Tables and views are physical objects stored inside database schemas, and they will be the main objects that we will use to create our Data Foundation. We need to clearly understand the major differences between tables and views before we start adding them to NorthWind Data Foundation layer. The major differences are as follows:

- **Table**: This is a physical database entity that will store data.
- **View**: This is a virtual table based on a select statement that queries one or more database tables or even other database views. It will be stored in the database for later usage, and there is no data stored in a view except for materialized views.

To insert a table or a view in your Data Foundation layer, we can use one of the three following methods:

- Click on the **Insert** option
- The connection panel
- Right-click on any empty space in the Data Foundation layer

Now, let's build the Orders context in NorthWind Data Foundation layer using the following steps:

1. Right-click on any empty space in the NorthWind Data Foundation.
2. Click on **Insert** and then select **Tables...** from the menu, as shown in the following screenshot:

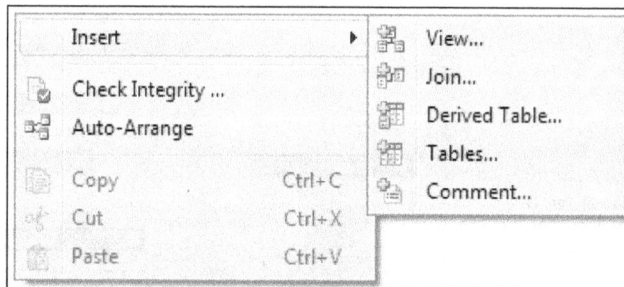

Insert	▶		View...
Check Integrity ...			Join...
Auto-Arrange			Derived Table...
			Tables...
Copy	Ctrl+C		Comment...
Cut	Ctrl+X		
Paste	Ctrl+V		

Expand NorthWind connection and then check the following tables:

- Orders
- Order Details
- Orders Tax Status

- Orders Status
- Order Details Status Invoices
- Customer
- Shipper
- Products
- Invoices

You can also do the same from the connection panel. A list of tables is shown in the following screenshot:

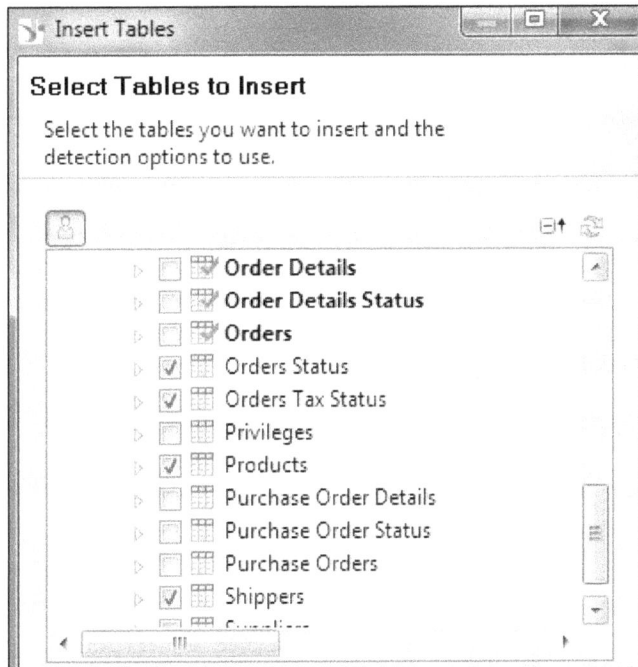

Alias tables

An alias table is a copy (alias) from a database object. We normally create an alias if we have one dimension shared among more than one fact table to avoid loops. We can create as many aliases from the shared dimension table as we want. We will talk in detail about loops and how to solve looping problems using alias tables in *Chapter 7, The Data Foundation Layer – Advanced Topics*.

To create an alias for the `Products` table, right-click on the `Products` table and select **Alias Table...** from the menu. You need to give a unique name to the alias table. Please enter the `Products_Orders_AL` name for the alias table, as shown in the following screenshot:

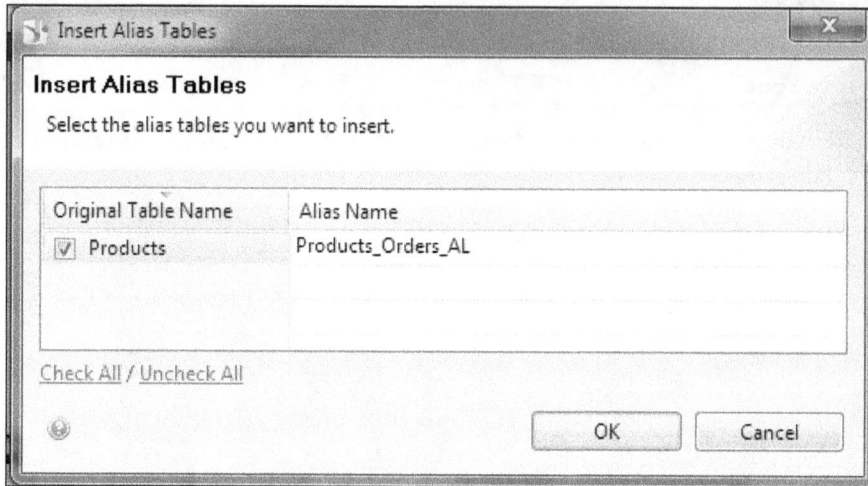

The original table name will be displayed beside the alias table name, as shown in the following screenshot:

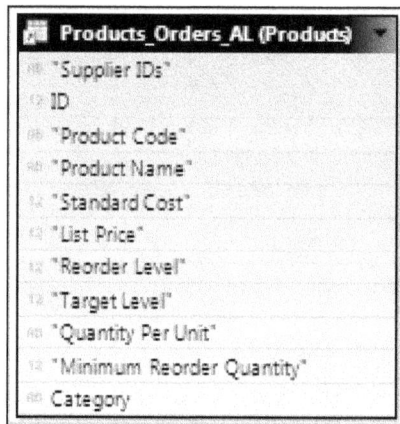

Next, we will talk about another type of object (derived tables) that we can create inside our Data Foundation.

In the UDT, we can also create and use alias tables (navigate to **Insert | Alias**) in the same way that we are using in the IDT.

In the UDT, we can display a list of aliases inside the physical layer using **List** under **Tools**, while in the IDT, we can navigate to **Data Foundation | Aliases and Contexts** to display the same list. We will discuss aliases and contexts in more detail in the upcoming chapters.

Derived tables

A derived table is another type of object that we can create inside the Data Foundation layer. It is like a database view as we need to define an SQL statement to create a derived table. The only difference between the database view and derived table is that the view is created and stored inside the database, while the derived table is stored along with Universe Metadata. This means that we need to have the right database privilege to create a database view. In most cases, we can create a derived table inside our Data Foundation if we don't have the database privilege to create the database view.

The best practice is to create the data access layer between the database and Data Foundation layer. This layer will act like an extra database layer that contains some specific views based on customer requirements. We can find the following advantages of the creation of the data access layer:

- The database administrator is able to optimize the SQL code because they are DB experts (the Universe designer usually does not know how to optimize queries' execution plans).
- The views will be maintained in one place only (the database dedicated to them). When there is a modification, you do not have to modify both the DB views and BO Universe.
- Access restrictions can be added (security). For example, we can create views to restrict specific users' access to sensitive information.
- In terms of data availability, each view will be created with "locking table X for access." This means that even when there is a write lock on the table, the user who will ask for data will not be locked, and they will not have to wait until the ETL process is finished, for example. This is the plus side, but on the other hand, it can lead to "dirty reads," so this should be discussed with the customer.

We can use derived tables in the following cases:

- When we have a complex query with advanced SQL coding
- If we don't have the database privilege to create the database view
- If we want to derive a new table from one or many database tables
- If we want to use a @Prompt function inside a table definition

Now, let's try to create a derived table. First, we need to insert the following two tables:

- Shippers
- Suppliers

Then, we will perform the following steps:

1. Expand the **Insert** menu.

2. Select **Insert Derived Table...** from the menu, as shown in the following screenshot:

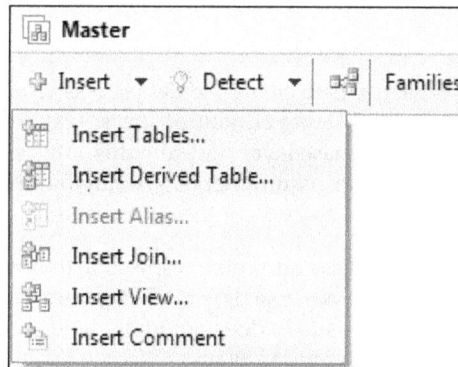

3. Then, enter the following information in the **Edit Derived Table** window:

   ○ **Name:** Vendors

   ○ **Description:** This table contains information about NorthWind's vendors. Vendor is a supplier or a shipper.

   ○ **Expression:** We will use the UNION ALL clause to combine the output of suppliers' and shippers' queries and to keep duplicate values. We need to enter the following code in the **Expression** area inside the **Edit Derived Table** window:

```
SELECT
'Shipper' as Vendor_Type,
Shippers.Company ,
Shippers.ID,
```

```
Shippers."Last Name",
Shippers."First Name"
FROM Shippers
UNION ALL
SELECT 'Supplier' as Vendor_Type,
Suppliers.Company ,
Suppliers.ID,
Suppliers."Last Name",
Suppliers."First Name"
FROM Suppliers
```

4. Click on the **Validate** button to make sure that there are no syntax errors in the SQL expression, as shown in the following screenshot:

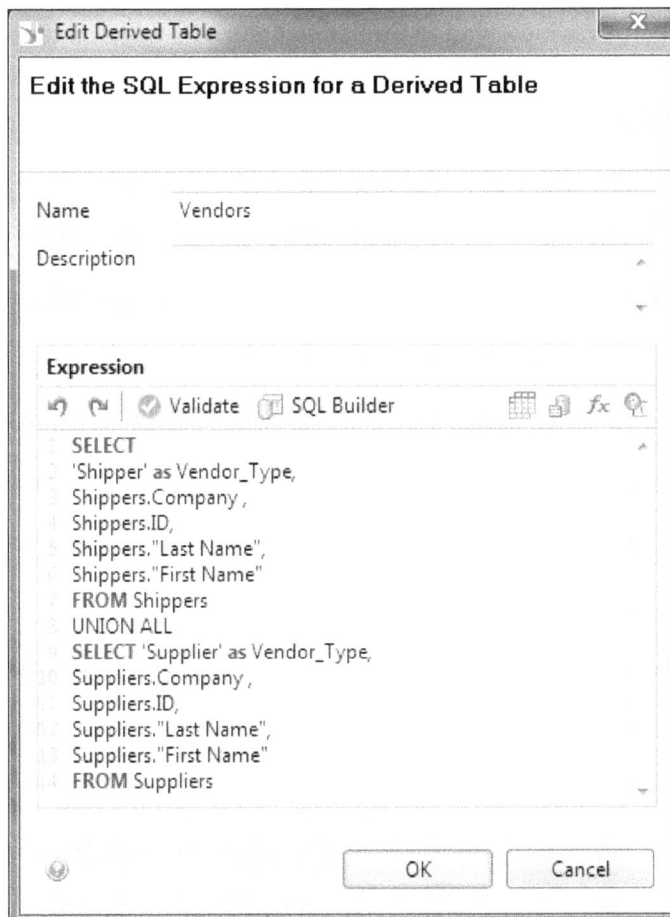

Now, we have a `Vendors` table that we can use in `NorthWind` Data Foundation layer.

Using the @Prompt functionality in a derived table

We can use the business objects' `@Prompt` functionality in the definition of our derived table. When we use any object related to this derived table, it will prompt the end user to enter the required prompt values. We can use the `@Prompt` function in the `where` or `select` clause. We will talk in detail about the `@Prompt` function in *Chapter 8, The Business Layer – Advanced Topics*.

Nested derived tables

A nested derived table is a derived table created on top of another derived table. This feature was released in BO XI 3.0, and it is also supported in the IDT. In a nested derived table, we will use one derived table to define the other one. Normally, we use nested derived tables if we want to simplify the design when we have a very complex data model. In such a case, we should build small derived tables and use them to construct the bigger one. This should make our design more readable and simple.

Now, let's try to create a nested derived table from the `Vendors` table with the following steps:

1. Insert a new derived table.
2. Type in `Vendors With Missing Information`.
3. Type in the following code in the derived table expression:

```
SELECT *
FROM @DerivedTable("Vendors")
WHERE Vendors."First Name" IS NULL
```

The following screenshot displays our **Edit Derived Table** window:

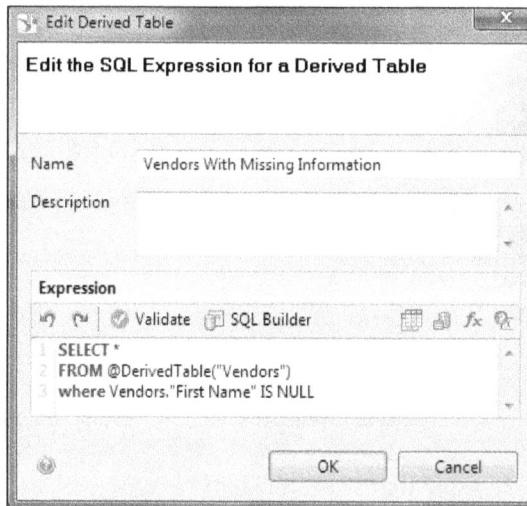

List of derived tables

For large Universes, it will be impossible to manage your derived tables if you don't have a centralized place to access them. We can use the **Data Foundation** panel to display summary information about tables and joins used inside our Data Foundation.

> In the UDT, we can navigate to **Tools | List of Derived Tables** to display a list of all the derived tables inside the physical layer, while there is no equivalent function for this in the IDT. We can use the **Data Foundation** panel to display summary information for all the existing objects (tables, alias tables, views, derived tables, and joins).
>
> In the UDT, we can also create derived tables (navigate to **Insert | Derived Table**), edit derived tables (navigate to **Edit | Edit Derived Table**), use nested derived tables, and we can also use the @Prompt function inside the derived table definition.

In the following screenshot, we can see the NorthWind.dfx summary information:

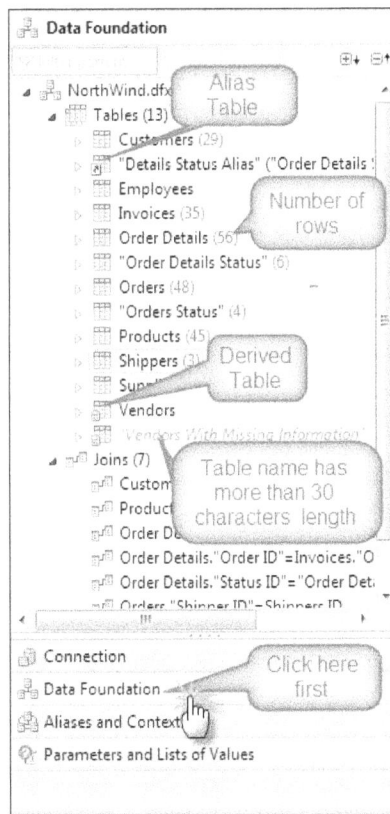

Joining tables

Joins are used to define the relationship between Data Foundation objects. A join will help us combine a table's rows using one or multiple shared columns. A **shared column** will be the primary key for one table and foreign key in another table. In this chapter, we have already added many objects, such as physical database tables, alias tables, and derived tables, to NorthWind Data Foundation. If we didn't define the relationship between these objects, the Universe integrity will not be satisfied. Indeed, the objects will not be linked, so the results will be inconsistent because of product (Cartesian) joins generated by the SQL queries.

A join will define only one relationship between two tables. For example, in NorthWind Data Foundation layer, we have a business relationship between the Orders and Customers tables. The Orders table stores all order information as well as the customer ID for the customer who completed this order. The Customers table contains detailed customer information such as customer name and address. We need to join the Customers table with the Orders table in order to be able to retrieve information from both tables in the same SQL query. Before we start creating joins, let's have a look at some important terminologies that are related to joins such as cardinality, key types, and join types.

We will use the following tables (Employees, Departments, and Age Bucket) in the examples introduced in this section, but let's find out what kind of data is stored in each table and what the relationship between them is. The Employees table contains employees' main information as well as a reference code for the corresponding department. Each employee works in one department, while each department can hold many employees. We can also see the employee's age, so we can link it with the Age Bucket table to get the age bucket for each employee. The following table shows the Employees table's structure with some sample data:

Employee ID	Employee Name	Age	Manager ID	Department ID
1	John	25	5	1
2	Julia	35	5	2
3	Alex	31	5	2
4	Amanda	40		
5	Jack	26		2

The following table shows the `Departments` table's structure with some sample departments:

Department ID	Department Name
1	HR
2	Development
3	Testing
4	Finance

Here, we can find the `Age Bucket` table with some sample data:

Age lower bound	Age upper bound	Age Bucket
18	20	18-20
21	25	21-25
26	30	26-30
31	100	Over 30

Cardinality

Cardinality is a data-modeling term that describes the relationship between tables. Cardinality can be one to one, one to many, many to one, and finally, many to many. To understand cardinality, let's take a look at the following example.

The cardinality of the join between the `Employees` and `Departments` tables is many to one. This is because each employee is working in one department only, while each department will have many employees working in it.

Key types

Each database table is a set of records (rows) along with a set of attributes (columns). Some columns are special because they have a unique nature. A **key**, also known as constrains, can be defined on a database level. If they are defined on the database, we can simply use the **Detect** option in the IDT to detect them and create joins for us.

> In Teradata, the detect function works based on the primary index definition and not on the primary key.

Now, we will discuss the key types.

A primary key

A primary key is a unique key that acts as an identifier for each record in the table. A primary key can be a single primary key if it is only one column, and it can be a composite primary key if it is more than one column. The primary key for the Employees table is Employee ID, as each record represents an employee, and for each employee, there is only one unique identifier, which is Employee ID.

> Each table can have multiple unique keys but should have only one primary key.

A foreign key

A foreign key, which is also known as a reference key, is a special column because the values stored in this column are the primary keys for another table. The Department ID column is an example of a foreign key in the Employees table, as it is the primary key for the Departments table. A foreign key is usually used to join a table with it is reference.

Note that here we are talking about general concepts. Each database will have its own way to define and handle the keys' columns. In Teradata, for example, primary keys do not exist (there is no primary key in the database tables' DDL). A physical concept, **primary indexes**, is used for data distribution. They are the columns that will be used for access and distribution of the rows of the tables among the **Access Modules Processors (AMPs)**.

> For more information on keys' implementation, refer to the RDBMS official site. The following are the website addresses for the most known vendors:
> - **Oracle**: http://www.oracle.com
> - **Teradata**: http://www.teradata.com/
> - **Microsoft SQL Server**: http://www.microsoft.com

Join types

There are many join types that we can create depending on the relation between involved tables. To define a join, we need to find out the following information:

- Right table
- Left table
- Foreign key

- Primary key
- Join operator
- Cardinality

A typical join will try to match the right table foreign key with the left table primary key using the join operator. By changing any one of the preceding parameters, we will get different types of joins.

Equal joins

An equal join is the most common join type. It will simply match each record from the right table with each record from the left one using the equals character as a join operator. In our example, we can join the Employees table with the Departments table using the following information:

Right table	Employees
Left table	Departments
Foreign key	EMPLOYEES.DEPARTMENT_ID
Primary key	DEPARTMENTS.DEPARTMENT_ID
Join operator	Equals (=)

Let's try to create an equal join in NorthWind Data Foundation layer using the following steps:

1. Go to the **Insert** icon and select **Insert Join** to open the **Edit Join** dialog box.
2. Select the Customers table from the drop-down menu under **Table 1 (NorthWind)**.
3. Select the Orders table from the drop-down menu under **Table 2 (NorthWind)**.
4. Select the ID column from the Customers table and Customer ID from the Orders table.
5. Note that the expression pane will be updated as you select columns.
6. Leave the = join operator as default.

> You can also right-click on any empty area in your Data Foundation. Then, you can select **Insert Join** from the **Insert** menu.
>
> You can also drag the primary column from the first table and drop it on the foreign key from the second table.

The next step is to set the join cardinality, but first, you need to understand the relation between customers and orders. Each order can be made by only one customer, while each customer can make many orders. Set the cardinality with the following steps:

1. Set the join cardinality to **1,n**.

2. Read the description after setting the cardinality, and make sure that the sentence is correct.

> For small tables, you can use the **Detect** button to detect the cardinality automatically.
>
> Don't use the **Detect** cardinality feature with big tables such as transaction tables in the banking or telecom industry. You might wait for ages before the detection is completed.

The **Edit Join** dialog box should look like the following screenshot:

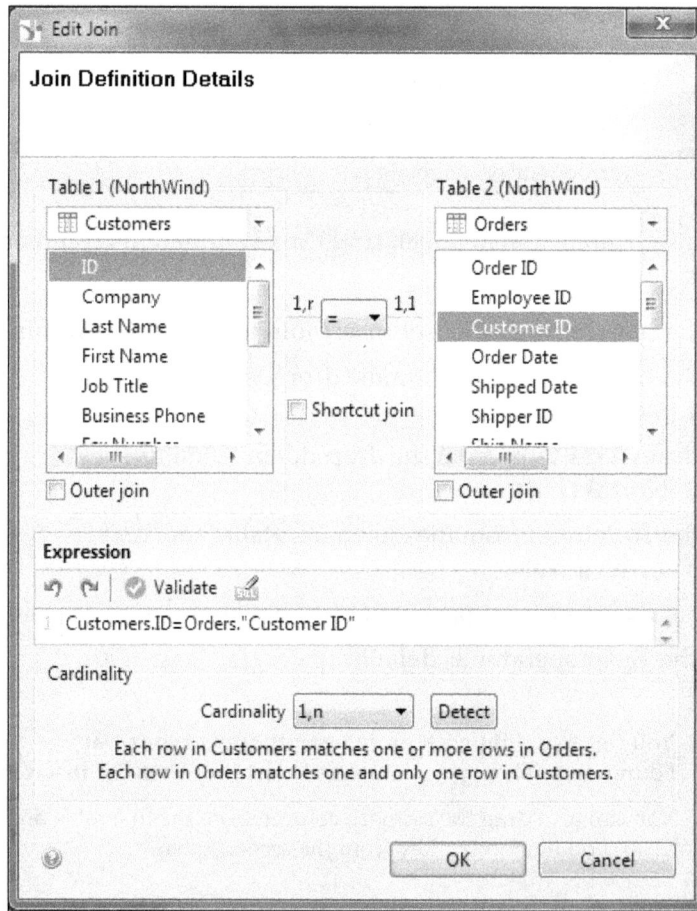

You can use **SQL Assistant** (the green SQL icon beside the **Validate** icon) to open **SQL Expression Editor**. This will assist you in building a complex expression.

In the following screenshot, we can see the **SQL Expression Editor** window:

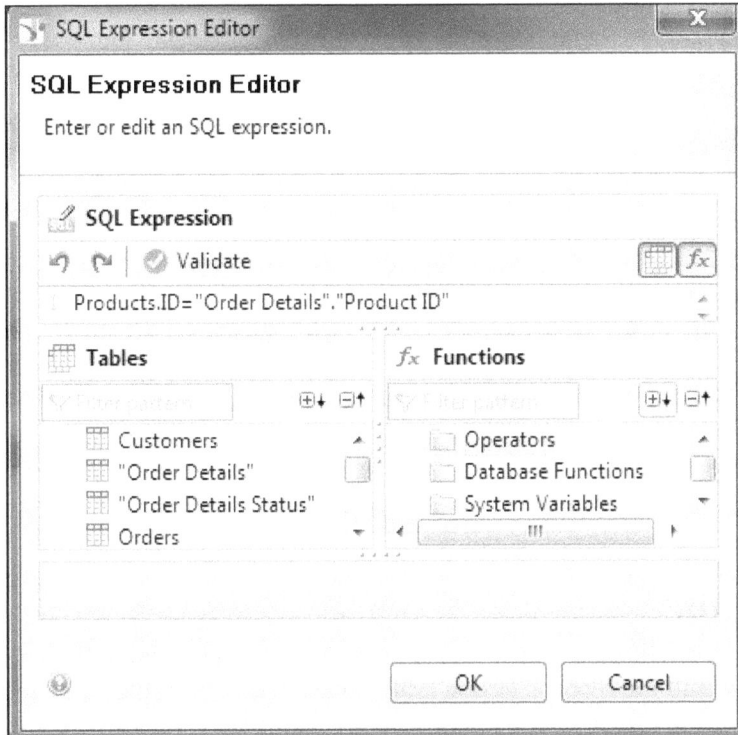

Now, as an exercise, try to complete the following joins as well:

Table1	Table1. column	Table2	Table2. column	Operator	Cardinality
Orders	Shipper ID	Shippers	ID	=	n,1
Orders	Tax Status	Order Tax Status	ID	=	n,1
Orders	Order ID	Order Details	Order ID	=	n,n

Theta joins

In a theta join, the joining operator will be BETWEEN. This operator takes two operands. We usually use this join when there is no direct match between a table's records. In our example, we will join one column from one table with two columns from the second table. In our example, we can join the Employees table with the Age Bucket table using the following expression:

```
EMPLOYEES.AGE BETWEEN "AGE BUCKET".AGE_LOWER_BOUND AND "AGE BUCKET".
AGE_UPPER_BOUND
```

> Theta joins are also known as **complex joins**. The join operation will be displayed as **Complex** when we create a theta join.

The **Complex** join will be displayed like in the following screenshot in Data Foundation:

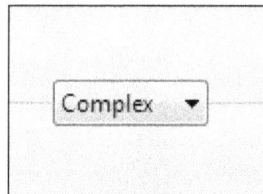

Outer joins

Using equal joins will match the exact records from both tables, but what if we want to retrieve all the records in one table, regardless of whether they have a matching record in the other table. A common example of this is if we want to list all departments along with the number of employees in each department. Using an equal join will return only the departments with employees. However, what if we have a new department with no employees assigned to it yet and we want to display this department in our query output with an empty number of employees. Here, we should use an outer join to display the new department in our query results.

Each join will define the relation between two tables. If our outer join focuses on retrieving data from the right table involved in our join, then we call this the **right outer join**. If we are focusing on the left table, then we call it the **left outer join**. We can also create a **full outer join**, which will retrieve all records from both tables.

> In Universe, we can only create either the right outer join or left outer join. If you want to create a full outer join, you might use a derived table with an SQL-specific database or use Union between the required tables to simulate a full outer join.

Now, let's get back to the NorthWind Data Foundation layer. In the Orders context, we want to create a join between the Order Details and Products tables using PRODUCT_ID. This is a simple equal join, but we will apply an outer join on the Products table side to cover the following case. What if we have a new product and there is no order issued on this product yet? What if we want to display a list of products along with the number of orders made for each one? Using only an equal join will not display the new product because there is no matching record for this product in the Order Details table. The solution is to apply an outer join on the Products table side.

We need to perform the following steps in order to create an outer join in NorthWind Data Foundation between the Order Details and Products tables:

1. Drag the ID column from the Products table and then drop it on top of the PRODUCT_ID column in the Order Details table.
2. Click on this join to open the **Edit Join** dialog box.
3. Detect the cardinality.
4. Tick the outer join checkbox under the Products table.

> You can spot outer joins (without opening the **Edit Join** dialog) by a small circle marked on the outer table side, as we can see in the following screenshot.

We can see that the Order Details and Products tables are joined in the following screenshot:

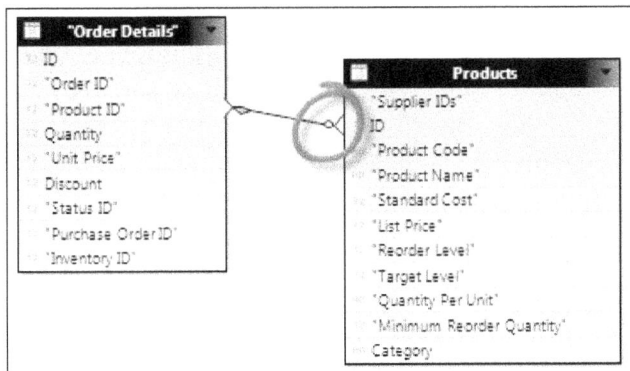

Self joins

A self join will join a table with itself. A common example of this is if we have an `Employees` table that stores all the information about employees, such as employee ID, name, department, and manager ID. In this case, an employee's manager is also an employee, and we should find the manager's details in the same `Employees` table. In this case, we will join the `Employees` table with itself by matching the employee ID with the manager ID.

> A best practice is to create an alias table from a table to join it with itself.

Data Foundation menus and functions

In this section, we will discuss useful functions and features that will help us while we are building our Data Foundation. First, we will cover the features that we can access using the Data Foundation toolbar, which is shown in the following screenshot:

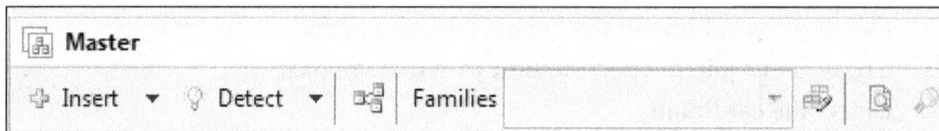

Detecting joins

Detect Joins is a nice feature that can be used in the following two cases:

- **Database Keys**: If your reference (foreign) keys are defined on the database level
- **Column Names**: If your database columns follow a standard naming convention

The **Detect Joins** feature can save a lot of time and effort if you have the data access layer with naming standards and well-defined database keys. Let's try to use the **Detect Joins** feature to create the remaining joins between tables already inserted in `NorthWind` Data Foundation with the following steps:

1. Navigate to the **Detect** icon on the toolbar under the **Master** Data Foundation.

2. Expand it and select **Detect Joins...**, as shown in the following screenshot:

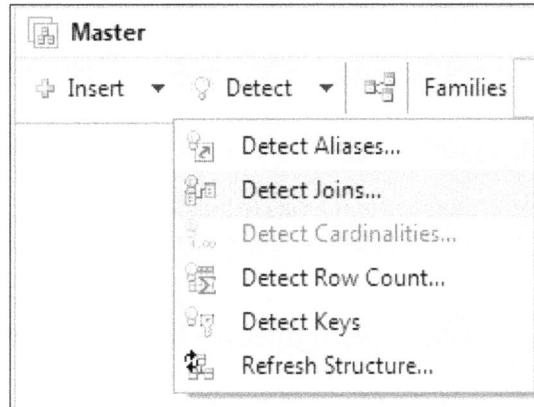

The following dialog window will open:

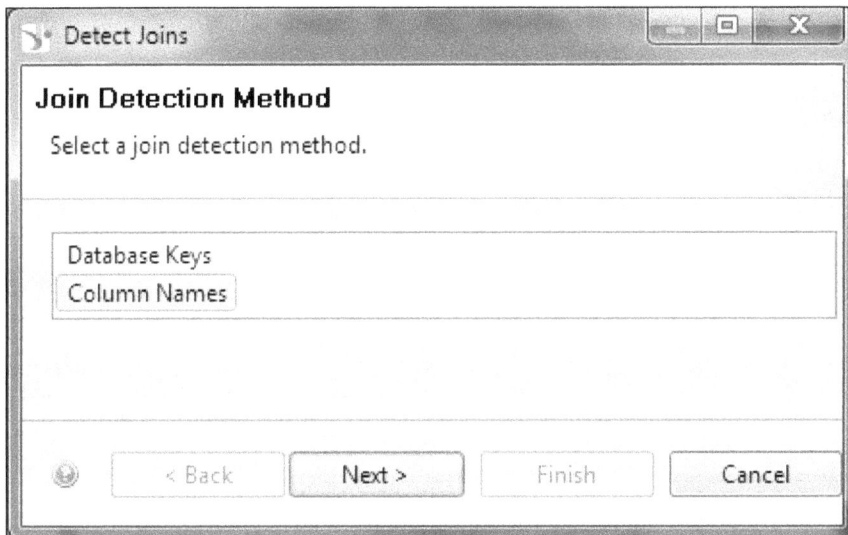

3. Select **Column Names**, as we don't have the keys defined in our NorthWind database.

The **Candidate Joins** window will display a list of joins extracted by the detection engine. We should review this list and keep only the right joins selected, as shown in the following screenshot:

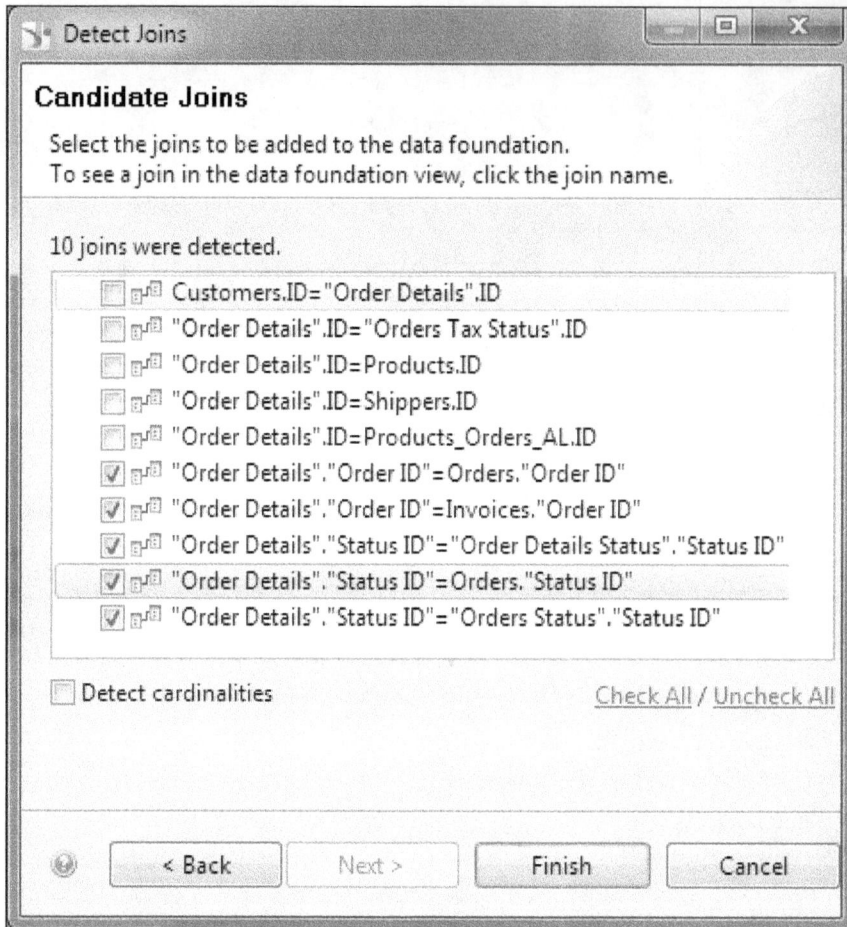

The next logical step after creating joins is to set their cardinalities, and so, we will find out how to use the **Detect Cardinalities** feature to detect join cardinality.

> We can highlight any join from the list displayed to display tables involved in this join.

Detecting cardinalities

We already discussed this before when we were creating joins between tables. **Detect Cardinalities** is a feature that can help you to detect all cardinalities on created joins with a click of a button.

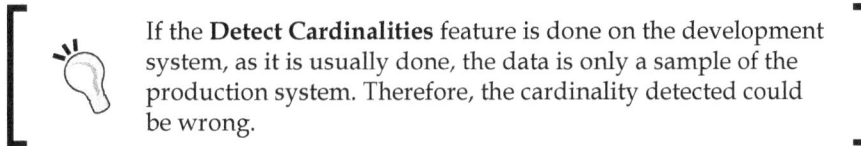

> If the **Detect Cardinalities** feature is done on the development system, as it is usually done, the data is only a sample of the production system. Therefore, the cardinality detected could be wrong.

To detect join cardinalities, perform the following steps:

1. Navigate to the **Detect** icon on the toolbar under the **Master** Data Foundation.

2. Expand it and select **Detect Cardinalities...**.

   The **Detect Cardinalities** window will open:

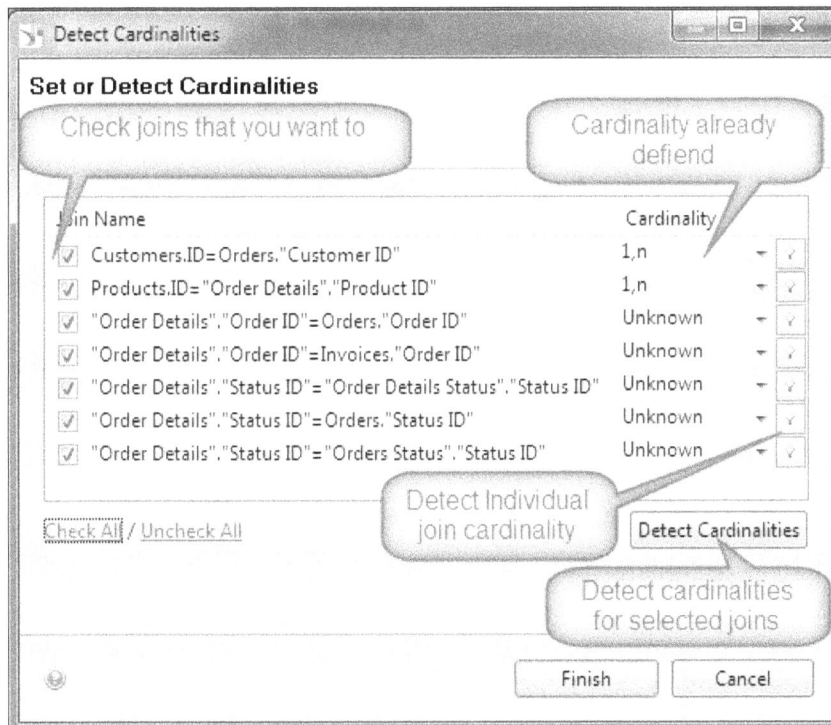

As we can see, we can detect cardinalities for all joins, or we might only select some joins that we want to detect their cardinalities. We can also individually detect the cardinality for one join.

Detecting the row count

We can use the **Detect Row Count** function to detect row counts for tables inside Data Foundation. This will give a good indicator to estimate the size of each table.

To detect the row count, perform the following steps:

1. Navigate to the **Detect** icon on the toolbar under the **Master** Data Foundation.

2. Expand it and select **Detect Row Count...**.

    The **Detect Row Count** window is very similar to the **Detect Cardinalities** window.

3. Select tables that you want to detect the row count for, or you can detect row counts for individual tables, as shown in the following screenshot:

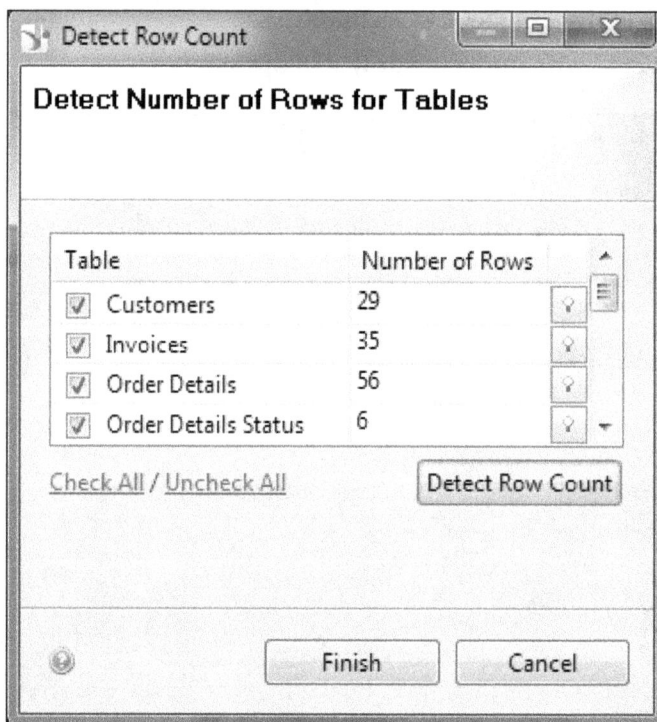

You can also detect the row count for a specific table by right-clicking on the table header and then selecting **Count Rows...** or navigating to **Detect | Row Count**, as displayed in the following screenshot:

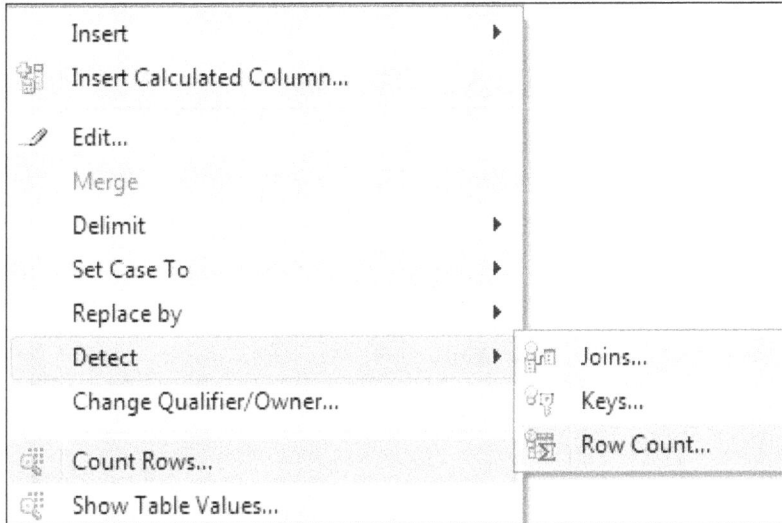

	Insert	▶	
⊞	Insert Calculated Column...		
✎	Edit...		
	Merge		
	Delimit	▶	
	Set Case To	▶	
	Replace by	▶	
	Detect	▶	⊞ Joins...
	Change Qualifier/Owner...		⊞ Keys...
⊞	Count Rows...		⊞ Row Count...
⊞	Show Table Values...		

Refreshing the structure

The **Refresh Structure** option is the last option in the **Detect** menu. We use the **Refresh Structure** feature to identify the following:

- If one of the tables inserted in Data Foundation is missing from the database
- If a table column is missing from the database
- If a table column is added on the database and needs to be added to our Data Foundation
- A modified database column

In the following screenshot, we can see the **Refresh Data Foundation Structure** window:

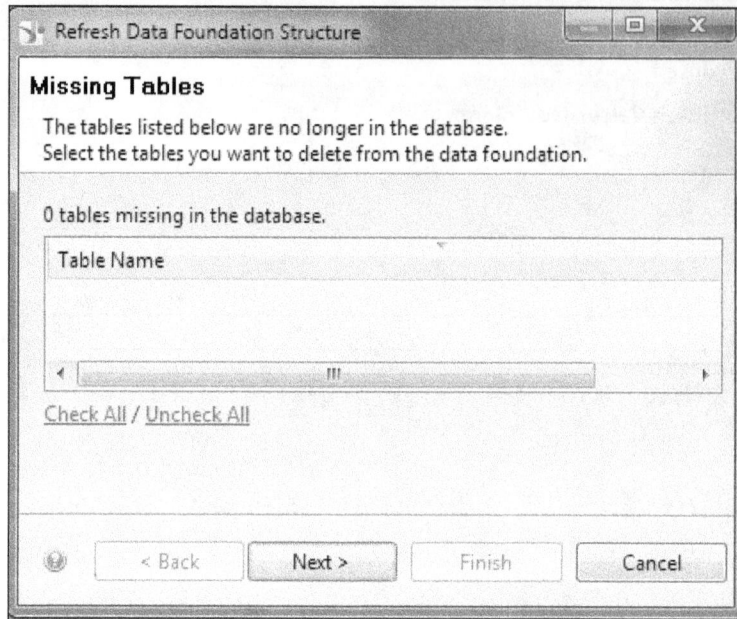

Note that in the UDT, we can navigate to **View | Refresh Structure** to refresh the Universe structure as well, but it will only refresh the table's structure and display a message to confirm "removing outdated objects". In the IDT, we can get more information about the modified objects, and we have more flexibility to decide what kind of action to take for each modified object as we already explained.

> You can also access **Refresh Structure** from the **Action** menu.
>
> It is part of the best practices to refresh the Universe structure before publishing the Universe and make it available to the business users.

Managing families

Families are a color visualization that can help developers spot related tables. We can also use families to differentiate between physical tables, views, alias tables, contexts, and derived tables. We need to create families first before we start applying them on the Data Foundation layer's objects. To create a family, we need to perform the following steps:

1. Go to the Data Foundation toolbar.

2. Click on the **Edit Families** icon.

The **Edit Families** window will open:

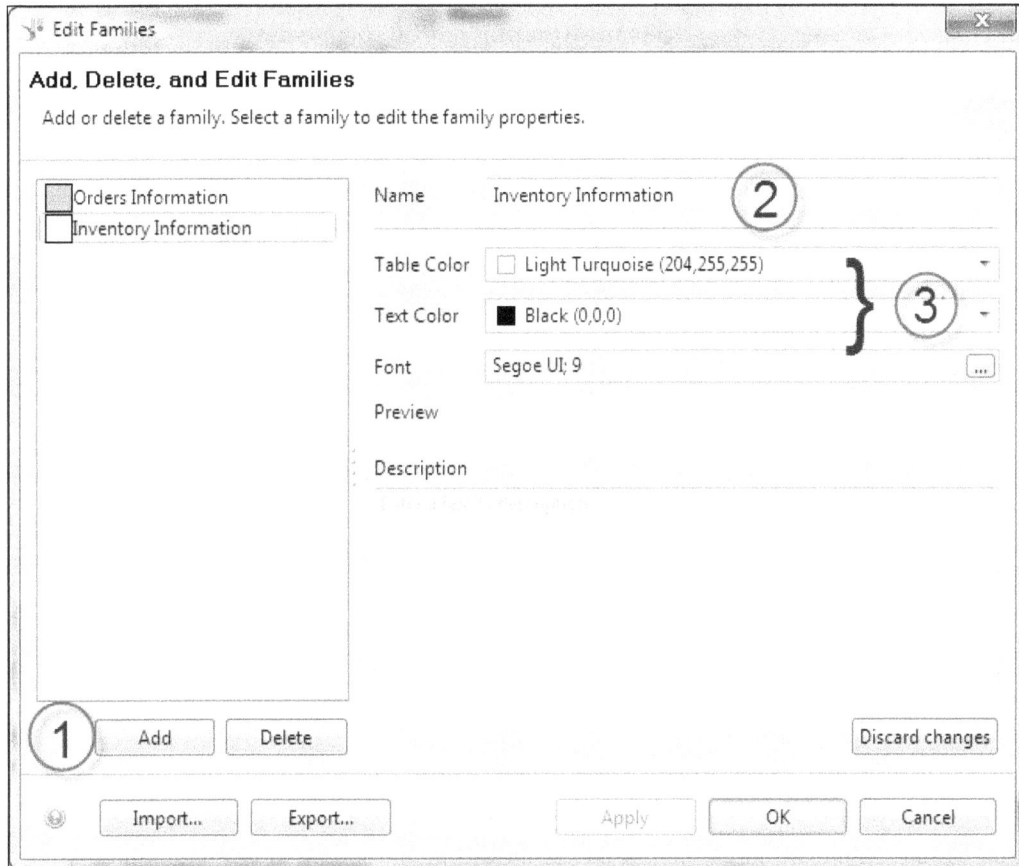

In this window, we need to perform the following steps:

1. Click on the **Add** button to add a new family.

2. Enter the family name. In our case, we need to create two families. One family will be used to mark tables related to **Order Information**, and the other one will be used to mark **Inventory Information**.

3. Enter the following family information:
   - Table color, text color, and font
   - Description about this family

4. Click on **OK** to close this window.

Note that you can also use this window to edit or delete the families that already exist.

Now, let's select all the tables in the Data Foundation, as they are all related to order information, and select the **Order Information** family to give them a special color, as shown in the following screenshot:

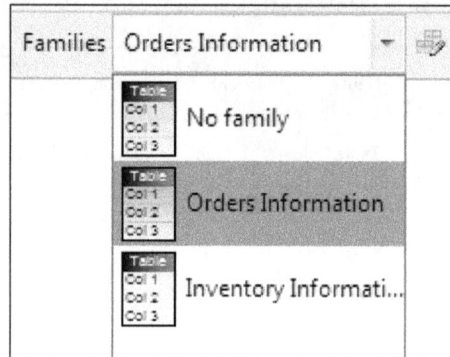

Save the view as an image

Sometimes, we might need a screenshot from our Data Foundation to include it in our design documentation, to share it in a presentation, or for any other reason. To do this, we need to simply click on **Save View as Image**. This will save the current view only. We just need to give a name to the image file and choose the preferred location.

The search panel

This is a very powerful feature that can help us search for any object in our Data Foundation. We can narrow our search results to table, column, and context. Let's try it using the following steps:

1. Click on the **Show / Hide Search Panel** icon.
2. The **Search** panel will open on the right-hand side.
3. Enter order as the search term in the **Search** box.
4. Expand the small icon beside the **Search** box and select tables.

5. Notice the results in the Data Foundation panel, and then, switch your search to columns, as shown in the following screenshot:

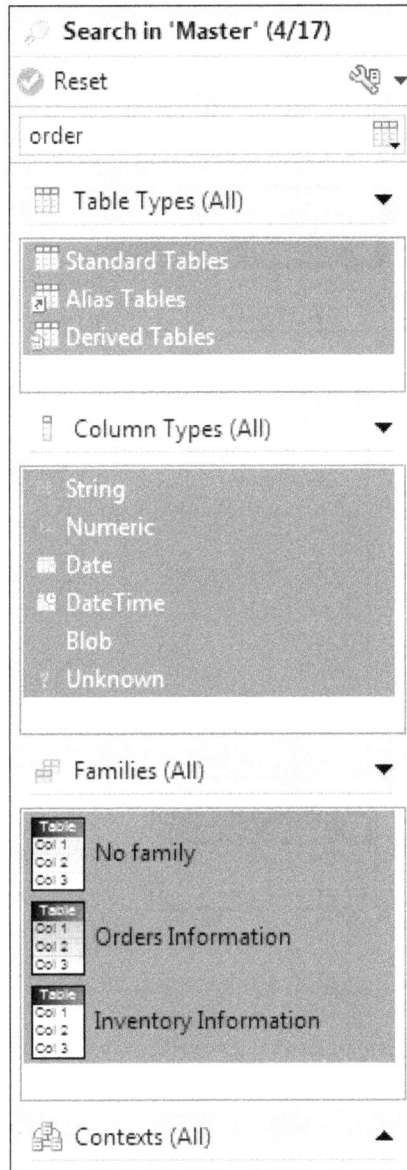

Note that search will be performed on the current active Data Foundation view.

Auto-arranging tables

This feature aims to rearrange tables on your Data Foundation layer. After we used the **Detect Joins** feature to create joins between tables, the Data Foundation looks like the following screenshot:

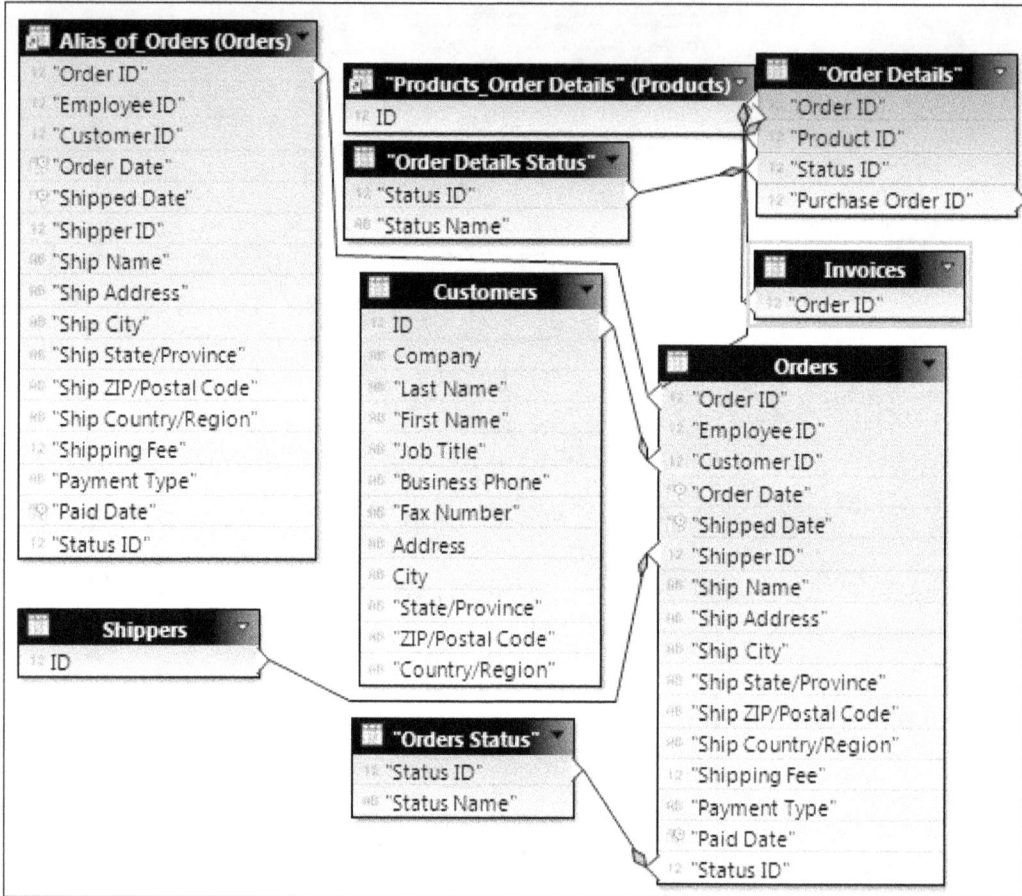

As you can see, this is a big mess, and we want to arrange our table on the foundation panel to see the relationship between the Data Foundation objects better. We can do this using the following steps:

1. Go to the Data Foundation toolbar.
2. Click on the **Auto Arrange Tables** icon.

The Data Foundation layer will look like the following screenshot:

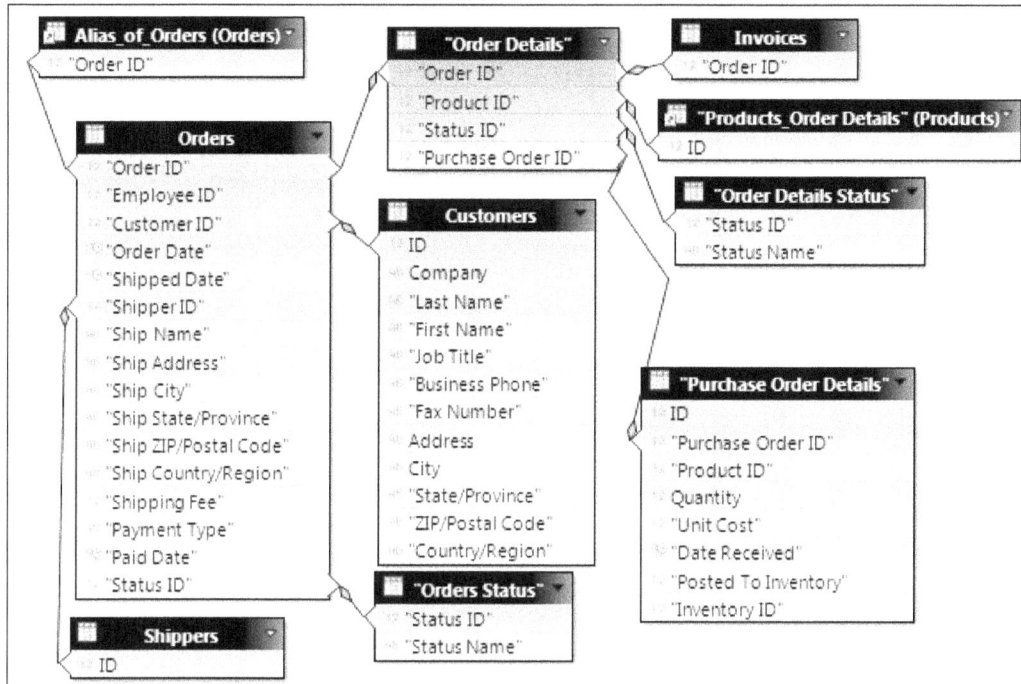

> In the UDT, we can also arrange tables (navigate to **View | Arrange Tables**) in the Universe.

Controlling the Data Foundation display

We can control the Data Foundation display area from the display control toolbar as we can see in the following screenshot:

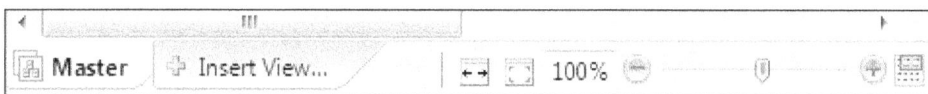

In this section, we will get to know how to perform the following actions:

- Inserting views to organize and group related Data Foundation objects to display them together
- Controlling Data Foundation screen properties such as zoom percentage and active screen area

Insert View

By default, when you create a new Data Foundation, it will start with a default view, **Master**. This view contains all the objects inserted in this Data Foundation. Sometimes, we might need to create different views to focus on some of the Data Foundation objects. This can help us while developing our Data Foundation by assigning each view to a specific developer. It can also help in large Data Foundation, which might contain up to 100 tables. To create a new view, we need to perform the following steps:

1. Click on the **Insert View** icon at the bottom.

2. Enter Order Details in the view name and description, as shown in the following screenshot:

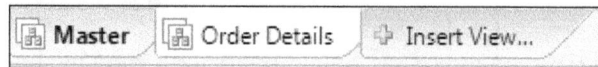

3. Now, select the following tables and right-click on one of them. Then, select the Order Details view from the **Add to View** list.

> The Data Foundation view is totally different from the database view. We just use it to enhance visualization.
>
> You can also select the tables that you are concerned about. Then, right-click and navigate to **Insert | View**.
>
> In the UDT, one or more Universe designers can display the Universe, but only one can modify it at a time. In the IDT, we can work in a collaborative way and more than one designer can work in the same Universe.

Data Foundation visualization

Display control functions exist to enhance our Data Foundation visualization. For a big Data Foundation, we might not see all tables in the **Data Foundation** window and might need to use the control visualization function to enhance our ability to see objects inside our Data Foundation. This is a typical zooming bar that is available in many applications. We can zoom in (**+**) and out (**-**) or simply write the zooming percentage directly in the zoom percentage box. We can also select to fit our Data Foundation to screen or rest the screen size, as shown in the following screenshot:

Data Foundation object manipulation

In this section, we will get to know all the functions and features that we can apply using the pop-up menu that is displayed by right-clicking on any Data Foundation object. By the Data Foundation object, we mean a table, view, alias table, or derived table.

When you right-click on any table placed in Data Foundation, we will able to see a menu divided into four sections.

Insertion

This is the first section in this menu, and we can use it to insert the following:

- An alias table based on the selected table
- A derived table from the current selected table
- A Data Foundation view from the current selected table/tables

The **Insert** menu and its options are shown in the following screenshot:

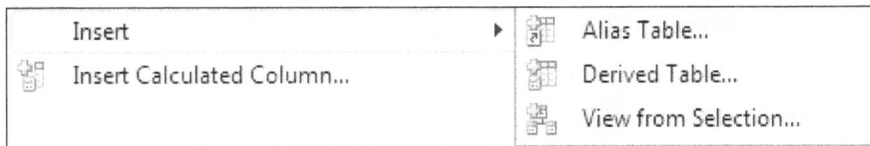

	Insert	▶	Alias Table...
	Insert Calculated Column...		Derived Table...
			View from Selection...

Note that if we select the **Derived Table...** option, it will create a derived table with the `select` statement that will display (`Select *`) all the columns in the selected table. Later on, we can edit the expression for the derived table and customize it as per our needs.

The second option is to create a calculated column. This option will allow us to create a calculated column from the current existing columns in the selected table. We have the employee's first name and last name in the `Employees` table, and we want to create a new column, `Full Name`, based on the two columns mentioned earlier. So, let's try to create a calculated employee's `Full Name` column with the following steps:

1. Right-click on the `Employees` table.
2. Select the **Insert Calculated Column** option.
3. The expression editor will open, but you can only use it and select from the columns currently available in the selected table.

4. Use the **Concat** function to create the employee's `Full Name` column by concatenating the first name, space, and last name, as shown in the following screenshot:

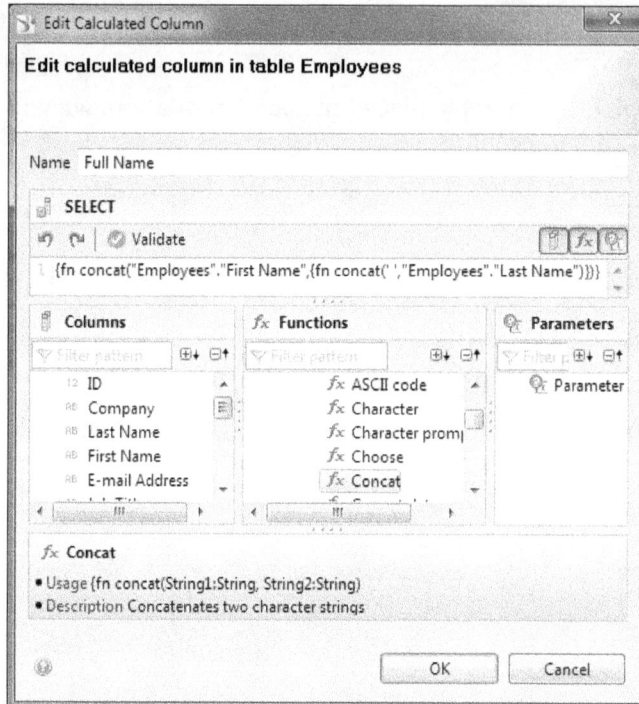

The inserted calculated column should look like the following screenshot in the Data Foundation view:

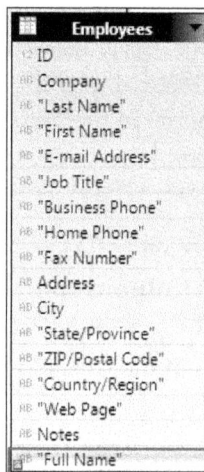

Table manipulation

In this section of the menu, we have options that we will use to manipulate the selected table/tables. Some options will be dimmed or disabled if they are not applicable to perform the action using the selected table(s). For example, the **Merge** option is disabled in the following screenshot because this option is only available when two or more tables are selected:

Add to View...	▶
✎ Edit...	
Merge	
Delimit	▶
Set Case To	▶
Replace by	▶
Detect	▶
Change Qualifier/Owner...	

Add to View

We can use the **Add to View** function to add the currently selected table(s) to one of the already existing Data Foundation views. This differs in selection from the insert view, which we discussed in the previous section, because this will create a new view, while this **Add to View** option will use the existing views.

Edit

This option can be used to perform one of the following actions based on the selected table type. If the selected table is a derived one, then this option will open the **Edit Derived Table** window. If the selected table is a physical one, then this option will open the **Edit Table** window. We can use the **Edit Table** window to perform the following actions:

- Select or deselect a column. This option might be very helpful if we have some empty or unused columns and we just don't want to see them again in our table. Note that this option will just hide and show a column, and there in no impact on the real database table.

- Change the column data type. This also has nothing to do with real columns stored in the database. This will change only the table metadata stored in the Data Foundation layer. We need to note that it is not recommended that you change the data type for the imported physical database column, while we can do this for the newly added calculated columns.
- Define the primary and foreign keys.

The **Edit Table** window is displayed in the following screenshot:

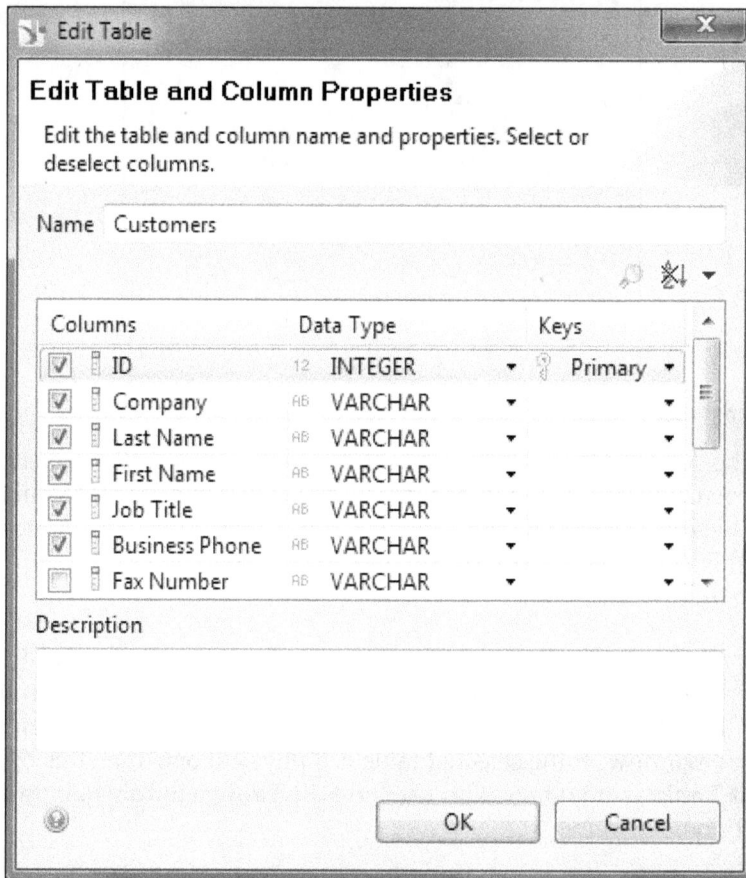

Merge

The **Merge** option can be used to merge two or more tables into one table. This option will be implemented based on joins created between selected tables, and this is as if we created a derived table to replace the selected tables. This is the same as the **Derived Table** option under **Replace by**, which we will discuss shortly.

Delimit

By default, there are certain characters that you are not allowed to use in table names and columns in the database. The space character is a good example as we can't use it in table and column names, but we can use it in alias names if we delimit it. The Data Foundation layer displays the delimited table's alias name, such as `Order Details`, to indicate that this is a delimited name, but we can change this by selecting **No** from the **Delimit** menu. If the table name is one word or doesn't contain any unsupported characters, then delimiting the table name will not have any effect, as shown in the following screenshot:

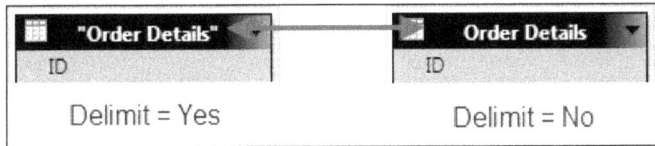

Set Case To

This option can help us change the case display for tables and column names. It has no effect on actual physical tables, and really, it's just a matter of display. We can set our case to be lowercase or uppercase.

You can set the case to display one of the options shown in the following screenshot:

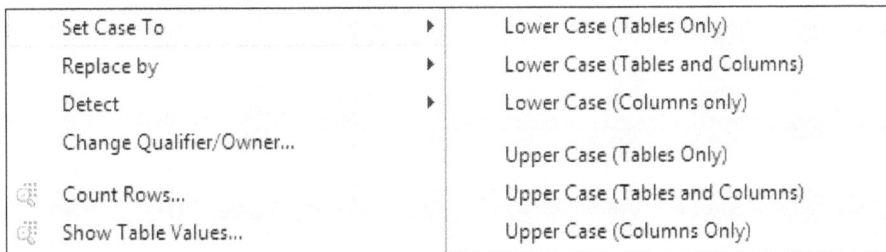

The result should be like the following screenshot if we set the **Set Case To** option to **Lower Case (Tables and Columns)** and apply this on the Orders table:

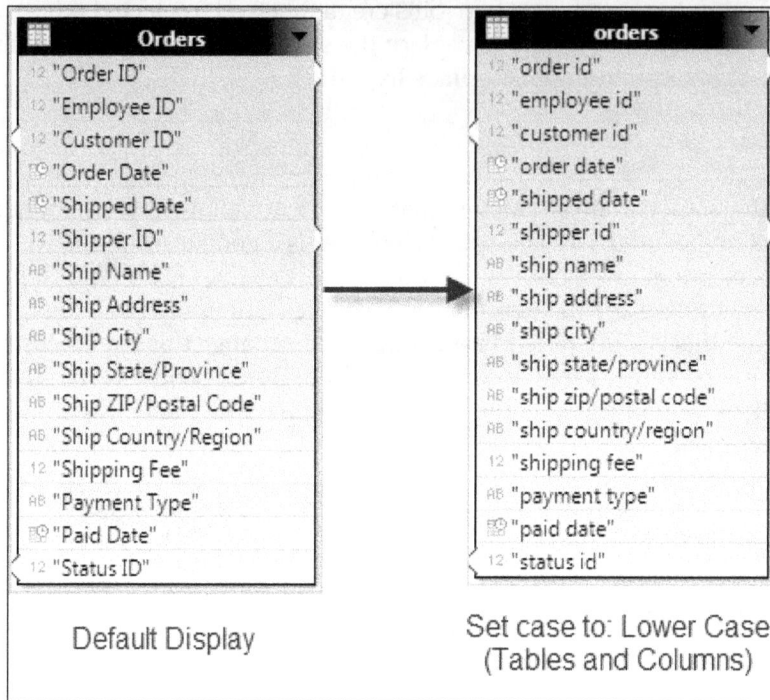

Default Display

Set case to: Lower Case (Tables and Columns)

Replace by

We can simply use the **Replace by** option to replace the currently selected tables with one of the following tables:

- A derived table
- An alias table
- Another database table

The **Replace by** option is displayed in the following screenshot:

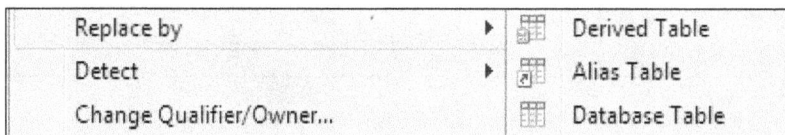

In the next section, we will talk about the **Detect** menu for a selected table.

> The only difference between the **Derived Table** option under **Replace by** and the **Merge** option is that the **Merge** option needs two or more tables as an input, while the **Derived Table** option under **Replace by** can only accept one table as an input.
>
> The **Replace by** option can be used to replace a table with another table in the same database. You can't replace an Oracle table with an MS SQL one unless you have a multisource Data Foundation.

Detect

We already went through all the options available here. This is just another place to access them. Note that this function will act only on the selected table. Like the **Detect** option from the Data Foundation toolbar, it will not act on all Data Foundation tables. The **Detect** option is shown in the following screenshot:

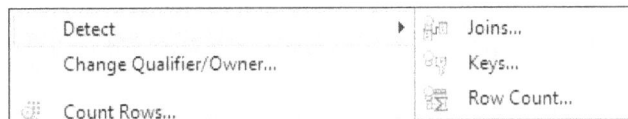

Detect	▶	Joins...
Change Qualifier/Owner...		Keys...
Count Rows...		Row Count...

Change Qualifier/Owner

We can use the **Change Qualifier/Owner...** option to redirect our table to read from another database or schema. Normally, this happens if we have only one BO installation that will be used for development as well as production while we have two databases: one for development and the other one for production. In this case, we might refer to the development database during the development phase of our Universe. After that, we should redirect our Universe tables to the production database by changing the qualifier and owner to point to the production database. The **Change Qualifier/Owner...** window is shown in the following screenshot:

Change Qualifier /Owner

Change Table Qualifier/Owner

Enter or select a new owner and qualifier for the table.

| Qualifier | | ... | ☐ Delimit |
| Owner | | ... | ☐ Delimit |

OK   Cancel

Note that the table structure should be the same on both qualifiers.

The table's values and display

This is the third section in the menu that will be displayed when you right-click on any object in the Data Foundation layer. We can get more information about the selected table, such as how many records are stored inside this table, and display a sample of records stored in this table using this section of the menu. We can also use this section to get more information about related objects. Finally, we can also control the display of the selected table. The options of this section are displayed in the following screenshot:

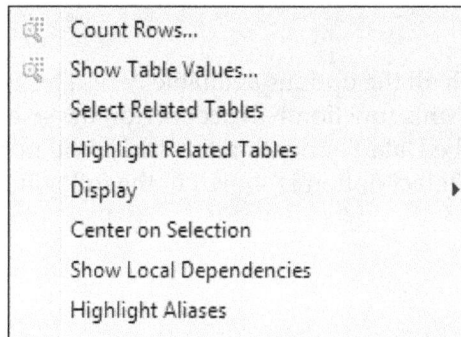

Count Rows...
Show Table Values...
Select Related Tables
Highlight Related Tables
Display ▶
Center on Selection
Show Local Dependencies
Highlight Aliases

Count Rows

We can use the **Count Rows...** option to get the row count inside the selected table. For example, we will get 48 rows when we select the **Count Row...** option while the Orders table is selected, as shown in the following screenshot:

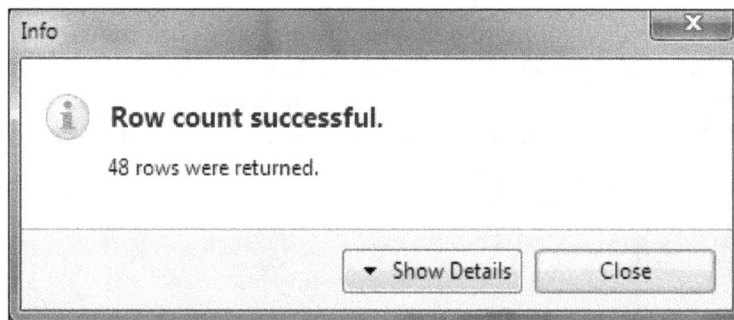

Info

ⓘ **Row count successful.**

48 rows were returned.

▼ Show Details   Close

In the UDT, we can also display the number of rows in a table by navigating to **View | Number of Rows in Table**.

Show Table Values

We can use the **Show Table Values...** option to get an idea about the data stored inside the selected table by displaying a sample of 200 records of data stored inside this table.

This is a very powerful option that can help us analyze and explore data. You can use it to find your distinct values in each column, and you might also add filters and use the expression editor to write database queries.

Let's try to explore the **Show Table Values...** feature together using the following steps:

1. Right-click on the `Orders` table, and then, select **Show Table Values...** from the drop-down menu.

2. We can now see all the records as we have only 48 rows in the `Orders` table.

3. Take a look and try to understand what the nature of the data stored in each column is.

4. Use **Add Filter** to add a filter on the `ship city` column.

5. The column filter pane will be displayed.

6. Try to filter on `Chicago`.

7. Click on **Save As File** to save the results to the local CSV file.

The `Orders` table will look like the following screenshot:

Now, let's try to analyze the data that we have in the `Orders` table with the following steps:

1. Click on **Distinct Values** to get more insight about the data stored.

2. Select the `ship city` column and see how data is distributed along different cities, as shown in the following screenshot:

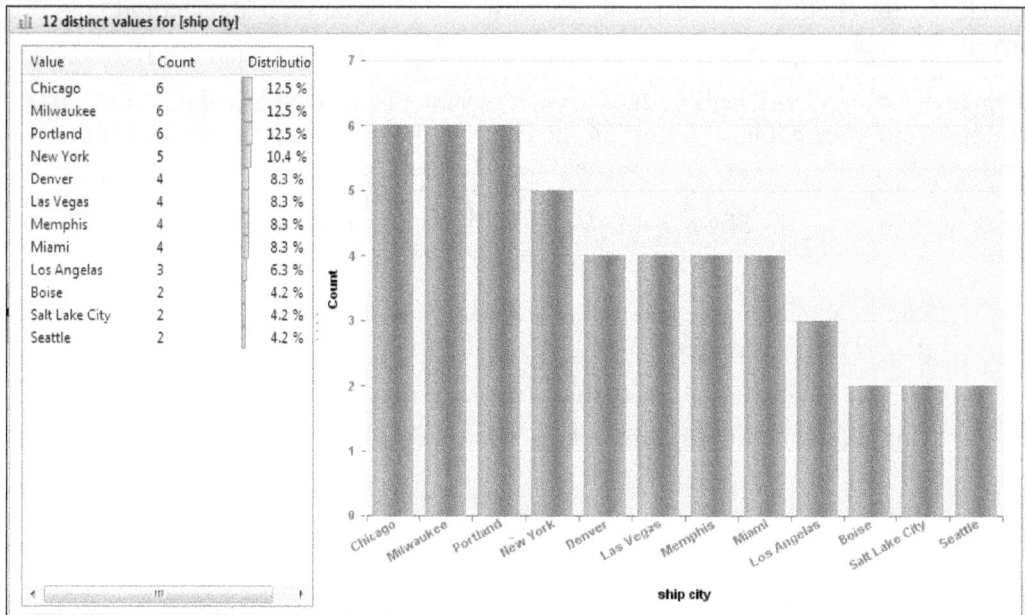

In the UDT, we can also display table values by navigating to **View | Table Values**.

> As an experimental BO developer, we used one of the database clients, such as Oracle SQL Developer, to trace and test our foundation layer. We also used to analyze our database tables using such tools. However, now, we can perform almost all these functions using the **Show Table Values...** option.

Select Related Tables

The **Select Related Tables** option will help you select the current table as well as all tables related to it with a single click. We can see that the following list of tables will be selected as well if we used this option from the menu on the right-hand side of the `Orders` table:

- `Customers`
- `Shippers`
- `Order Details`
- `Order Status`

All the related tables are selected in the following screenshot:

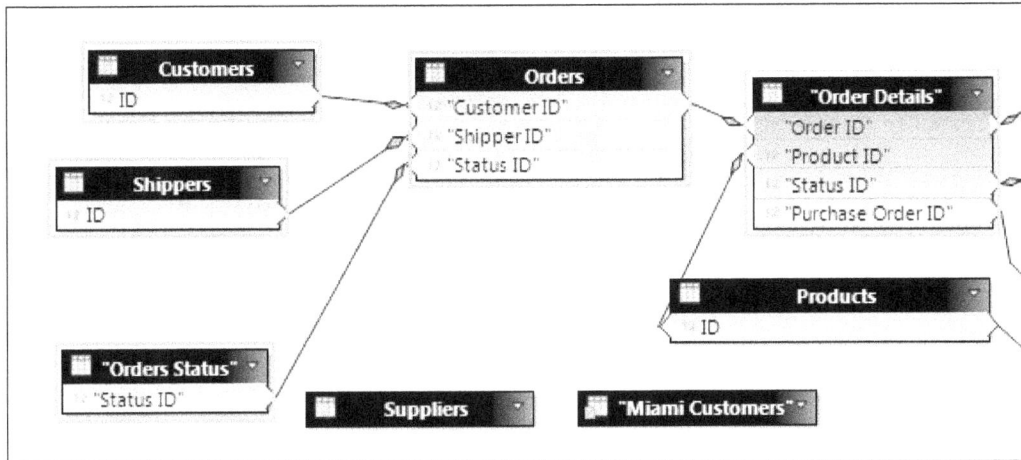

Highlight Related Tables

This is exactly the same as **Select Related Tables**, but this option will just highlight the related tables by hiding all other tables. It will also just highlight the tables without selecting them.

Select the `Orders` table and try to find the difference between the **Select Related Tables** and **Highlight Related Tables** options.

Display

There are three display modes for Data Foundation tables. We can switch between them as per our need. The display modes are shown in the following screenshot:

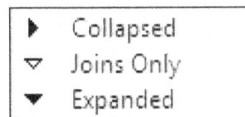

The list of display modes is as follows:

- **Collapsed**: This view will display only the table name
- **Joins Only**: This view will display the table name as well as any column used to join this table with the other table
- **Expanded**: This view will display the table name as well as all the columns in this table

Centre on Selection

The **Centre on Selection** option will help us see the selected table in the middle of the Data Foundation area.

Show Local Dependencies

We can use the **Show Local Dependencies** option to find out all the Business layer model objects that depend on the selected table. We can use this option by performing the following steps:

1. Right-click on the Customers table.

2. Select **Show Local Dependencies**.

3. A list of dependent Business layers is displayed.

4. Select NorthWind.blx, as shown in the following screenshot:

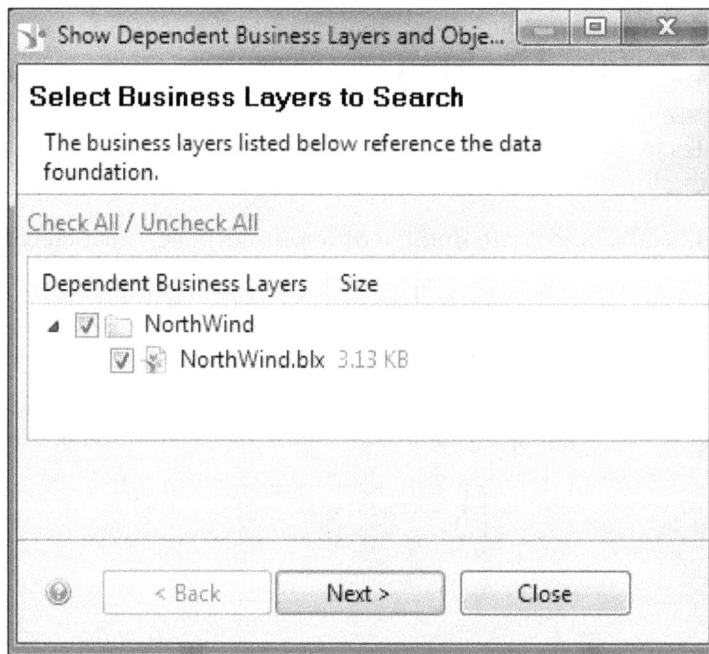

5. Click on **Next** to display the **Show Dependent Business Layer and Objects** window. Then, select the `Job Title` column from the **Tables and Columns** section. You can see that only the dimension is linked to this column, as shown in the following screenshot:

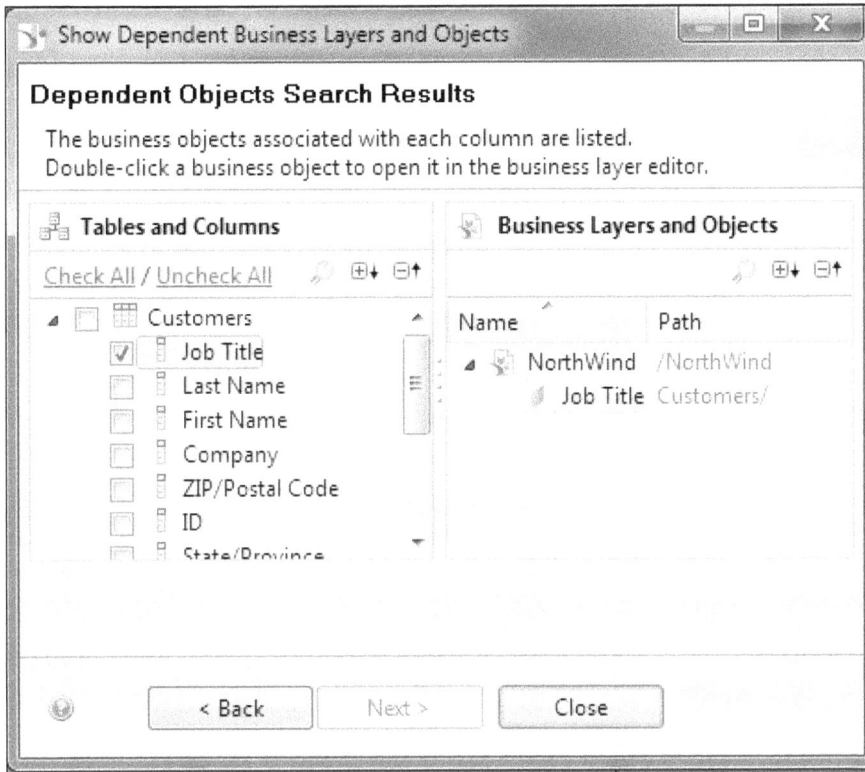

This feature is very useful to do a BO Universe audit and impact analysis, if, for example, you want to delete a specific column and if you want to make sure that there are no Business layer objects depending on this column.

Highlight Aliases

The **Highlight Aliases** option is the same as the **Highlight Related Tables** option, but this option will highlight alias tables, which are created, based on the selected one.

The table's basic functions

We can use options in this section of the menu to cut, copy, paste, and delete a selected table. These basic options are shown in the following screenshot:

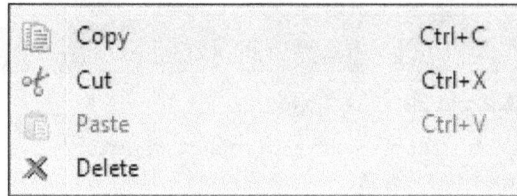

	Copy	Ctrl+C
	Cut	Ctrl+X
	Paste	Ctrl+V
	Delete	

You can use known keyboard shortcut keys to perform the corresponding function without the need to open this menu. For example, *Ctrl + C* can be used to copy an object, while *Ctrl + V* can be used to paste it.

Summary

In this chapter, we described Data Foundation functionalities in detail. We also went through BO objects (alias and derived tables) that we can add to our Data Foundation layer. After that, we learned how to join our objects. Finally, we saw a detailed description of almost all functions, options, and features that we can access from the Data Foundation layer.

In the next chapter, we will talk about creating the Business layer and populating it with business objects.

5

Creating the Business Layer

In the previous chapters, we learned how to create a data connection and Data Foundation. In this chapter, we will learn how to create a Business layer on top of the `NorthWind` Data Foundation layer. The Business layer is the most important resource in our Universe project. This is because it is shared with end users so that they can access and interact with this layer. You can think about this layer as if it is our final delivery product. If it is well designed and developed, end users will use and adopt it; otherwise, they will ignore it. This is why the Business layer should be user friendly and business oriented. Remember that the main idea of the entire Universe is to segregate between complex technical contents and business terminologies, by providing information to the end users in an easy way.

The Business layer is the gate to our Universe, and this is why we need to give it high attention. It is a very critical part and key success factor of the BI adoption within our organizations.

In this chapter, we will find out how the development of the Business layer starts. Then, we will get to know the basic panels that we have in the layer window. Next, we will learn how to create main building blocks for the Universe layer; these building blocks are layer objects (dimension, measure, attribute, and filter). In this section, we will talk in detail about each object's properties and how to configure them. After that, we will discuss the functions and features available in each layer window panel. Finally, we will take a look at the Universe properties.

In this chapter, we will cover the following topics:

- The Business layer's requirements and best practices to develop an efficient Universe
- The Business layer's interface functions and features
- How to create and configure the layer's main objects (dimension, measure, attribute, and filter)

Gathering requirements

We need to recall together what we already discussed in *Chapter 2, Aligning BI Solutions with Business Demands* (business case description for the Universe in the book). We need to gather and analyze requirements before we start any BI implementation. The requirements need to be **SMART** to lead the project to success; otherwise, the business needs could be misunderstood and lead the project to fail. The term SMART is explained as follows:

- **Specific**: Significant and simple
- **Measurable**: Meaningful
- **Achievable**: Appropriate and acceptable
- **Relevant**: Realistic and reasonable
- **Time bound**: Time framed and time limited

The requirements-gathering process is part of the initiation phase of any project, and this process needs to be completed before starting the following phases:

- **Planning**: This will help give an accurate estimate about the required time and budget to complete the project.

- **Design**: This is the critical part for our Universe's Business layer. We need to translate the gathered requirements into logical concepts to start the design phase. In the design phase, we need to complete data analysis and requirements mapping.

- **Execution**: We can't start the development phase if we really don't know what we are going to develop. This is why we need to complete and agree on business requirements first.

- **Testing**: Each requirement should be documented along with its acceptance criteria. These criteria will be agreed to by both teams, business and supplier, before starting the implementation and will be used to approve and accept the end deliverable. In our case, this might be a manual report generated by the business to pass the testing phase. This will certify the Universe behind the report as well if the test succeeded, but it will require investigation in the case of failure.

The Business layer's main window

In this section, we will try to get familiar with the **Business Layer** window. Like the **Data Foundation** window, the **Business Layer** window is divided into three main subwindows (panels). You can use the small black arrows marked in the following screenshot to expand and hide any of the windows. This gives us full control to adjust the space and focus on what we really want to see on the screen at any moment. Usually, developers need to change views and toggle between windows, but we can also see them all together. This is one of the main advantages of the IDT, which is built on top of the Eclipse framework, a very powerful and organized development framework environment. We can see the **Business Layer** window in the following screenshot:

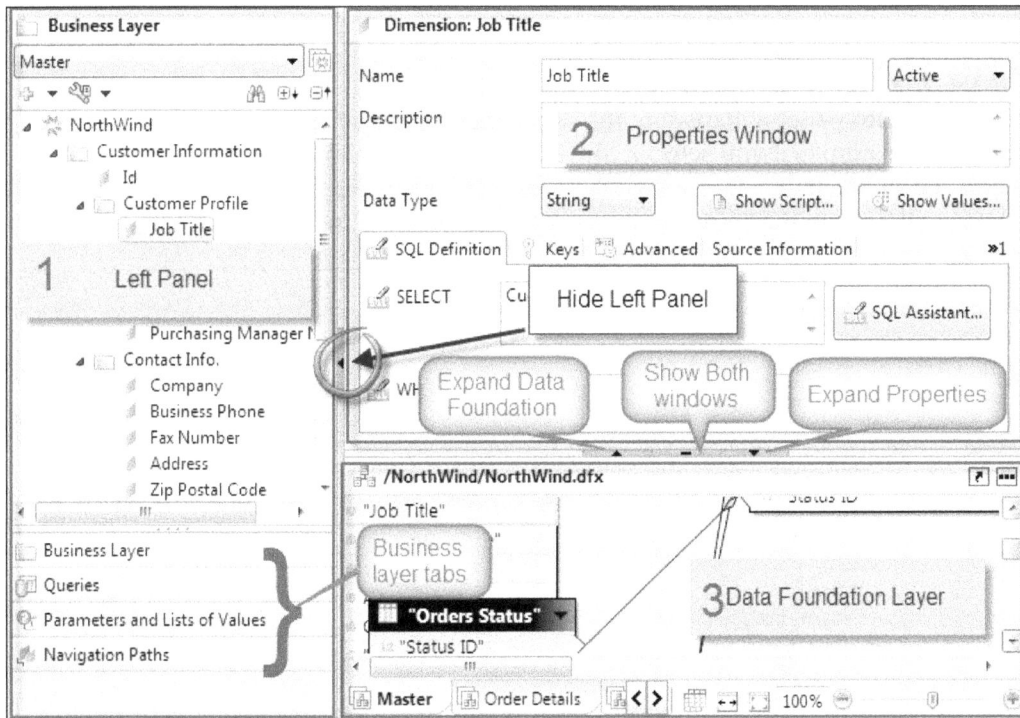

The left panel

We can select one of the following tabs at the bottom of the left panel:

- **Business Layer**: We use this tab to create folders and the Business layer objects that will be visible to the end user.

- **Queries**: In this tab, we can create queries using objects in the Business layer. Usually, we use this tab to analyze data and test our Universe. We will talk about this in detail in *Chapter 6, Testing Your Universe*.

- **Parameters and Lists of Values**: In this tab, we can create a reusable list of values that will be used to fill filters or user prompts.

- **Navigation Paths**: In this tab, we will build and customize our navigation paths formerly known by hierarchy. We can use navigation paths in the report drill mode to navigate through data, and drill up and down through navigation paths. This is a very powerful feature that will help end users analysis data and get the required information.

We will talk in detail about each tab in the upcoming sections of this chapter.

The Properties panel

The **Properties** panel will display the properties for the selected object from the left panel. For example, if you select a dimension, then the dimension properties will be displayed in this panel. If you switch to another object, let's say the Business layer, then it will display the Universe properties, as shown in the following screenshot:

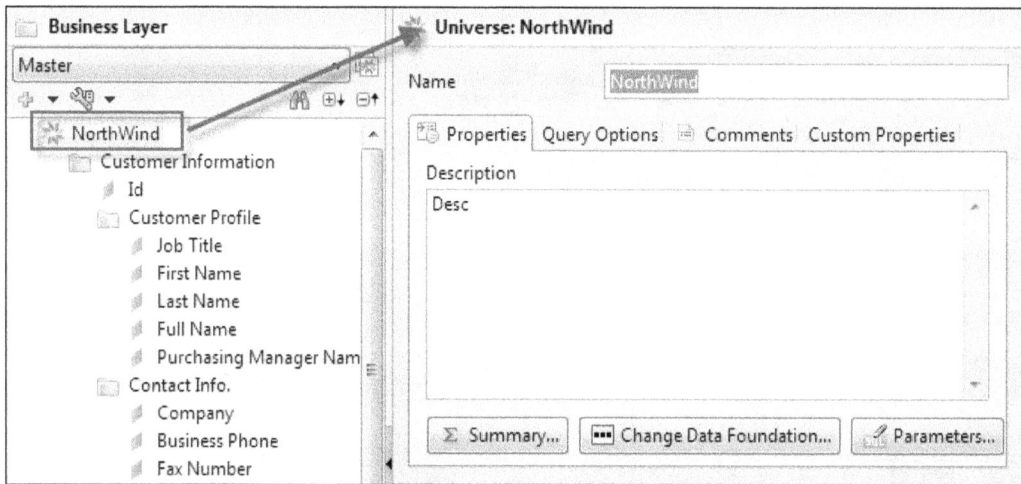

The Data Foundation panel

The **Data Foundation** panel will display the Data Foundation layer used to create the current Business layer. Remember that we need to specify a Data Foundation layer while creating any Business layer.

The first step of business objects creation could be to drag-and-drop tables from the **Data Foundation** window into the **Business Layer** window. As a result, all the created objects will be qualified as dimensions, and you have the choice to change and convert them to measures or attributes.

The only two functions that we can access from this window are:

- **Open Data Foundation**: This is a shortcut to open the Data Foundation file. This will save time as you will not need to go to the local folder window, search for the project folder, and then navigate and open the Data Foundation file. The **Open Data Foundation** icon is shown in the following screenshot:

- **Change Data Foundation**: We can use this option to change the Data Foundation file that is currently being used.

> If you already created objects in your Business layer on top of the current Data Foundation file, you might lose your work and need to remap everything again if you selected a wrong Data Foundation file.

As we can see in the following screenshot, a list of all Data Foundation resources stored in the currently selected project will be displayed. You can start typing in the **Select a Data Foundation** textbox to narrow the size of the displayed list, or you can select it directly from the list below it. As we have only one Data Foundation resource associated with the current project, we will see only **/NorthWind/ NorthWind.dfx**, as shown in the following screenshot:

In the next section, we will start with the **Business Layer** tab on the left panel.
We will have an overview of the available features and functions, such as the
following ones:

- Creating and managing business views
- Using the search panel
- Inserting new business objects into the Business layer

After that, we will discuss in detail business objects' types that we can insert into our
Business layer, along with all the properties that can be configured for each type.
We will cover the following remaining tabs under the left panel in *Chapter 8,
The Business Layer – Advanced Topics*:

- **Queries**
- **Parameters and Lists of Values**
- **Navigation Paths**

Business Layer

The **Business Layer** tab is the first tab that we have on the **Business Layer** window's
left panel. We will use the **Business Layer** tab to create business objects that will
be used by end users. Before we start talking about business objects, let's have an
overview of the functions available on this tab. The **Business Layer** tab is shown in
the following screenshot:

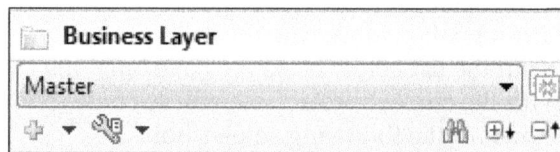

Managing Business layer views

Business layer views are the same as Data Foundation views. We use them to
organize our Business layer by grouping related objects together and reducing the
number of displayed objects. We have the default master view that will hold all the
created objects typically like the master Data Foundation view. The Universe end
user will be able to see the created views and use them.

This feature helped us solve one of the biggest challenges that we were facing in the UDT when we have one Universe used by many business departments. Each department is interested in some specific objects that are related to their business, and they usually wish to see their own objects. This feature helped avoid confusion and simplified navigation. Imagine that we have a Universe that contains 100 objects, and there is a department that is interested only in 10 objects. It would be a nightmare to let them search for their objects in the entire Universe.

This feature was the magical solution, and now you can create multiple views that will serve multiple perspectives. Each view will focus on a specific business area and will deliver the exact required information.

> Business layer views are a new feature introduced in the IDT, and there is no equivalent for it in the UDT.

Let's try to create a Business layer view with the following steps:

1. Click on the **Manage Views** icon.
2. Click on **New**.
3. Type `Orders` in the **Name** field.
4. Select the following folders:
   - `Customer Information`
   - `Orders`
   - `Order Details`

We can see the **Edit Business Layer View** window in the following screenshot:

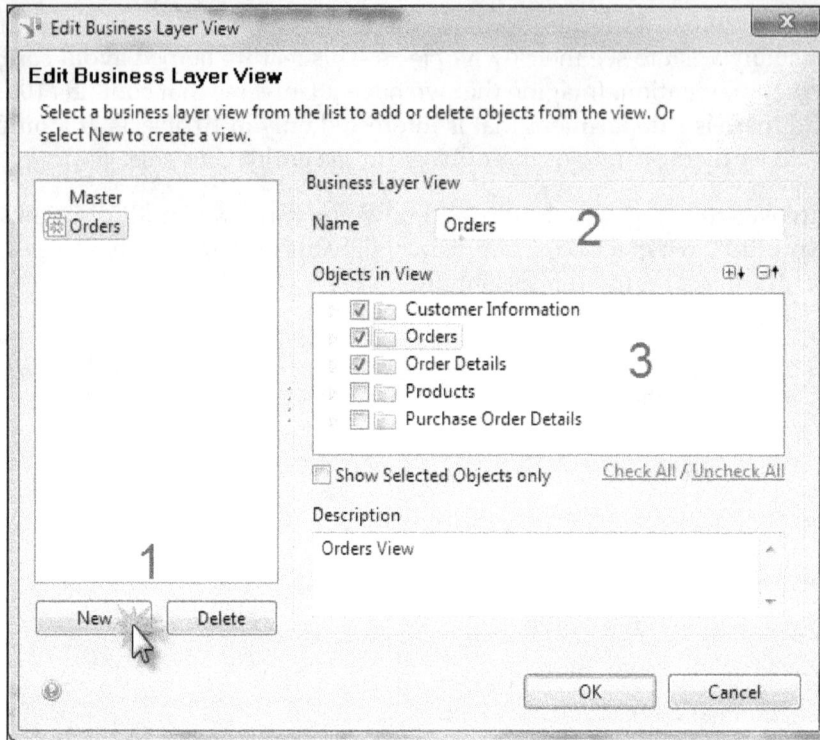

5. Now, go to the **Business Layer** pane and select the Orders view. Note that we can see only those objects and folders that we selected to define this view, as shown in the following screenshot:

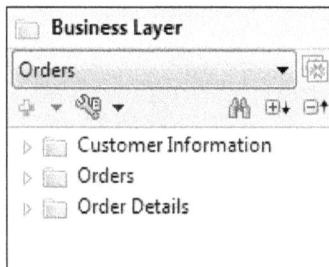

Showing/hiding the search panel

The search panel is a wonderful feature that can help us find and search for objects. We can use the following features as well:

- Filter and narrow the search for a specific object type, as shown in the following screenshot:

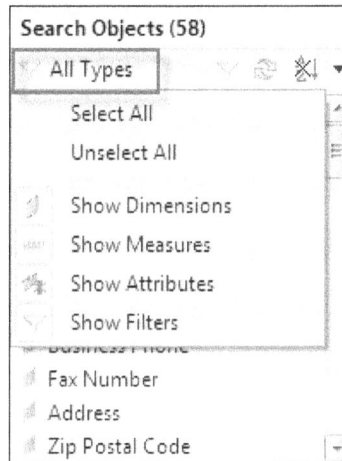

- Sort objects in ascending or descending order
- Search for objects by name, as shown in the following screenshot:

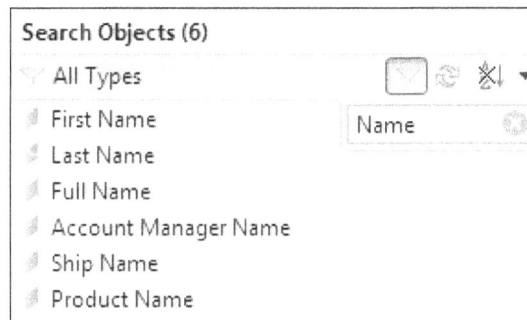

Expand and collapse all

The expand all and collapse all shortcuts can help you toggle between the expand all and collapse all views. Expand all will show all objects and expand all folders, while collapse all will collapse all folders and display only those folders that are in the root.

Display Options

There are two options under **Display Options**:

- **Show All Objects**: This option is the default one, and all objects will be displayed regardless of their status.
- **Hide Non-Active Objects**: This option will display only the active objects. This means that the hidden and deprecated objects will not be displayed.

The following screenshot shows **Display Options**:

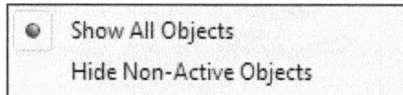

⦿	Show All Objects
	Hide Non-Active Objects

Inserting objects

The **Insert Object** menu is the main menu that we will use to insert new objects into our Business layer. We can insert new folders, dimensions, attributes, measures, and filters. The menu list will be updated based on the currently selected object from the Business layer. So, we can insert a subfolder if we have currently highlighted a folder, while we can only create a new attribute if a dimension is highlighted. The **Insert Object** menu list is shown in the following screenshot:

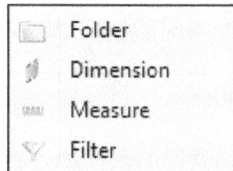

🗀	Folder
🗊	Dimension
📶	Measure
▽	Filter

Business objects

Business objects are the main building blocks of the Universe's Business layer. They are used as reporting items that will be selected by end users to create their own reports and perform analysis. The main idea of the Universe, as we discussed earlier, is to abstract the technical and complex IT-related part from the simple and informative business part. At the end, we don't want to see our business users confused about the right objects to choose while they are creating their reports. The best practices to define business objects are as follows:

- Objects' names must have a clear business meaning supported with a description to avoid any misunderstanding or misuse.

- The information is categorized and grouped in folders based on their business relation.

- Business users can navigate and find the required information.

- Only the information that is included in the business requirements and required by the business users should be available in the Universe's Business layer view. The most common mistake made by BO developers is to create the Business layer that contains all the information available in the database.

> Based on my experience, it is a big mistake to make all information available to end business users. This will confuse them and complicate the entire thing. This will end up in a big failure to the BI initiative, because business users are not able to search for their specific required information in the big Universe that contains all the **data warehouse** (**DWH**) information.

Now that we have discussed the importance of business objects and agreed on the high-level best practices that we should follow in order to create robust Universes, let's talk about the available business objects' types, which are as follows:

- Folders
- Dimensions
- Attributes
- Measures
- Filters

Folders

Folders are not really business objects. They are just containers to group and organize related objects together based on their business relations. For example, we can create a folder to group all customer-related information.

We can create nested subfolders to organize information inside parent folders. So, we can create a folder that will contain all the demographic information such as content, country, city, and region under the Customers folder to ensure better navigation for the information listed in our Business layer.

> It is not recommended that you build nested subfolders beyond four levels. This might confuse end business users.
>
> Folders in the IDT are equivalent to classes in the UDT.

To create a folder, open the `NorthWind` Business layer that we already created in *Chapter 3, Creating Our First Universe*, and perform the following steps:

1. Rename the `Customers` folder to `Customer Information`.

2. Right-click on the `Customer Information` folder, and then navigate to **New | Folder** to create the following subfolders:

    ○ `Customer Profile`

    ○ `Contact Info`

    ○ `Demographic Info`

The following screenshot displays the **Folder** option:

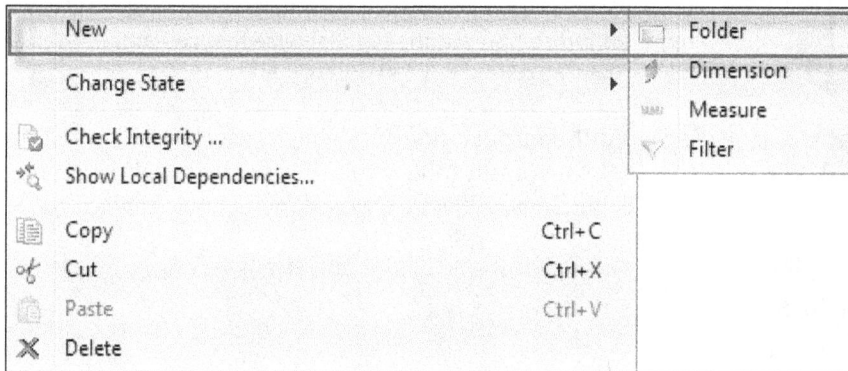

New	▶	▢	Folder
		⑂	Dimension
Change State	▶	ᴹᴱᴬ	Measure
🔲 Check Integrity ...		▽	Filter
⁺🔍 Show Local Dependencies...			
📋 Copy	Ctrl+C		
✂ Cut	Ctrl+X		
📋 Paste	Ctrl+V		
✖ Delete			

You can also insert a new object or folder using the green plus icon in the top-left corner of the **Business Layer** window, as shown in the following screenshot:

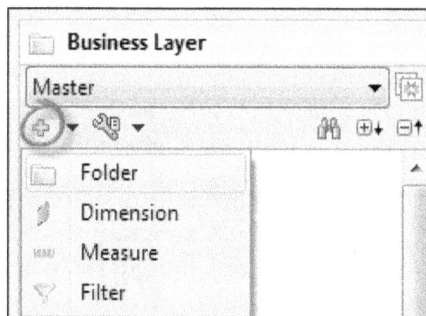

🗀 **Business Layer**		
Master	▼	🔳
⊕ ▼ 🔑 ▼	🔍 ⊞↓ ⊟↑	
🗀 Folder	▲	
⑂ Dimension		
ᴹᴱᴬ Measure		
▽ Filter		

Add the business objects to the corresponding folders based on the following table:

Folder names	Objects
Customer Information	Id
Customer Profile	Job Title
	First Name
	Last Name
Contact Info	Company
	Business Phone
	Fax Number
	Address
	Zip Postal Code
Demographic Info	City
	State Province
	Country Region

The Customer Information folder should look like the following screenshot:

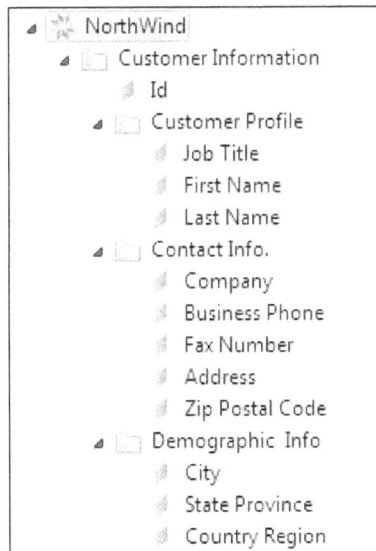

Finally, we need to discuss the **Folder** properties panel before we move to the next section. Let's select the Customer Information folder and check what the available options are.

We should be able to:

- Edit or change the folder name in the **Name** field
- Change the folder status to one of the following:
    - **Active**: End users will be able to see the folder
    - **Hidden**: Only BO Universe developers will be able to see this folder
    - **Deprecated**: The folder is marked or flagged to be deleted
- Write a brief description about this folder in the **Description** field
- Check the folder content and change the order of objects inside this folder

The **Folder** properties panel is shown in the following screenshot:

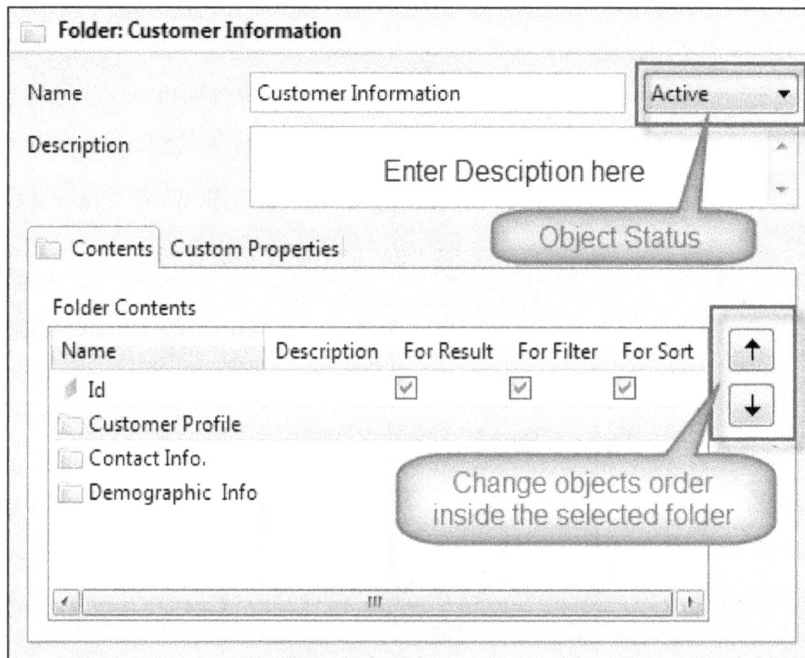

We can consider the following while creating folders:

- Don't forget to add the folder description. A **Description** field is associated with almost every Universe resource or object.

- You can right-click on the object to change the object status for multiple objects at the same time, as shown in the following screenshot:

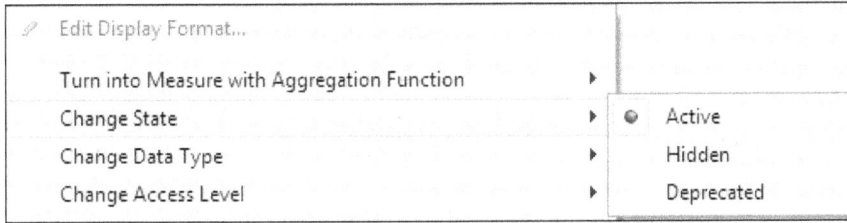

Edit Display Format...		
Turn into Measure with Aggregation Function	▶	
Change State	▶	● Active
Change Data Type	▶	Hidden
Change Access Level	▶	Deprecated

Dimensions

Dimension is an angle from which, for example, we can look at information from the perspectives of product, region, and time. To make it easier, we can think about dimension as a reporting item that we can use to group and summarize information. As an example, we can analyze our sales (measure) for each region (dimension).

We can create a dimension using one of the following methods:

- Select a folder, click on the **Insert Object** icon, and select a new dimension.

- Drag the required database column from the foundation layer area in the bottom and drop it in the required destination folder.

- Drag the entire database table and drop it in the **Business layer** panel. This will create a dimension for each column in this table. Note that it will insert all the table's columns as dimensions by default, and you need to convert measure objects manually. We already used this method in *Chapter 3, Creating Our First Universe*, to create the Customers folder in the NorthWind Business layer while we were creating our first Universe.

We will use the same methods described earlier to create measures and attributes as well. However, before we move on and start the next section, let's have an overview of the dimension's available properties with the following step:

1. Select the First Name dimension from the Customer Information folder. We can see the following properties on the properties panel on the right-hand side.

> If the properties panel is not displayed, then you can show it by expanding the **Properties** icon.

Main properties

We can access the following main properties and attributes of our dimension:

- **Name**: In this field, we can specify the dimension's name.

- **Status**: In this field, we can set the selected dimension's status. The dimension status is the same as the folder status (**Active**, **Hidden**, and **Deprecated**), which we discussed earlier.

- **Description**: We should write a brief description about the dimension in this field. This description will be visible to the end users.

- **Data Type**: The data type of the dimension will be extracted from the corresponding database column's data type. We should not change this for dimensions that map to database columns, but we will use these properties when we create a new dimension based on a complex SQL function. In such a case, it will be difficult to detect the dimension's data type, so the Universe developer should set it manually.

We have the following data types:

Data Type	Description
String	Alphanumeric values
Long Text	We use this for database columns with big size such as comments and remarks
Numeric	Integers, floats, and decimals
Boolean	True or false values
DateTime	Date and time such as 24-Feb-1981 and 5:30:12 AM, respectively
Date	Only the date part, such as 24-Feb-1981
Blob	Binary large object (images, audio, or multimedia)

> DateTime is a new data type introduced in the IDT, and there is no equivalent for it in the UDT.

You can right-click to change the object's data type for multiple objects at the same time. We can see the **Change Data Type** menu in the following screenshot:

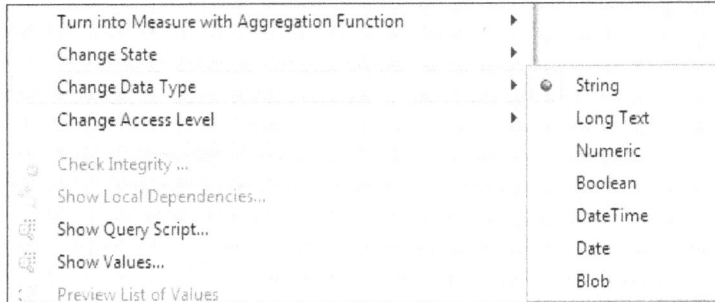

Turn into Measure with Aggregation Function	▶	
Change State	▶	
Change Data Type	▶	⊙ String
Change Access Level	▶	Long Text
Check Integrity ...		Numeric
Show Local Dependencies...		Boolean
Show Query Script...		DateTime
Show Values...		Date
Preview List of Values		Blob

We can see the properties of the `First Name` dimension in the following screenshot:

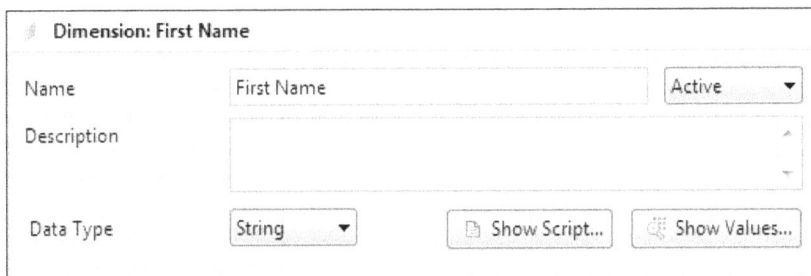

Dimension: First Name		
Name	First Name	Active ▼
Description		
Data Type	String ▼	☐ Show Script... ⊞ Show Values...

We can also use the following two functions:

- **Show Script**: This function will open **Query Script Viewer**, and it will display the SQL code used to generate the selected dimension. It is very useful in case of complex dimensions that use database-specific SQL functions. The **Query Script Viewer** window is shown in the following screenshot:

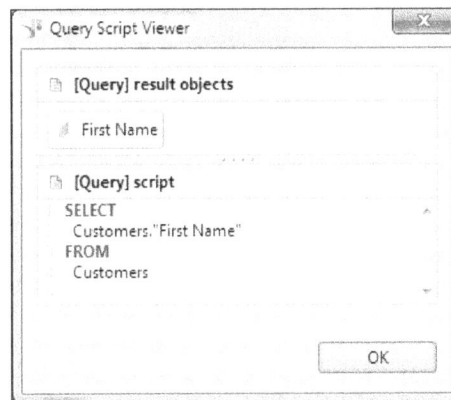

```
Query Script Viewer                              X

[Query] result objects

   First Name

[Query] script
   SELECT
      Customers."First Name"
   FROM
      Customers

                              OK
```

- **Show Values**: This is one of the new features available in the IDT. We didn't have something like this in the UDT, and we used to create SQL-select statements using any database client tool to perform such analysis. Now it is available here, and you can perform the required analysis by just clicking on this button.

We need to perform such analyses to find out how many distinct values are stored in this dimension. This will help us decide if we create a list of values for this dimension or not. We can also find out how many table's records are associated with each dimension value. We already discussed this feature in detail in *Chapter 4, Creating the Data Foundation Layer*. You can see the output of **Show Values** for the First Name dimension in the following screenshot:

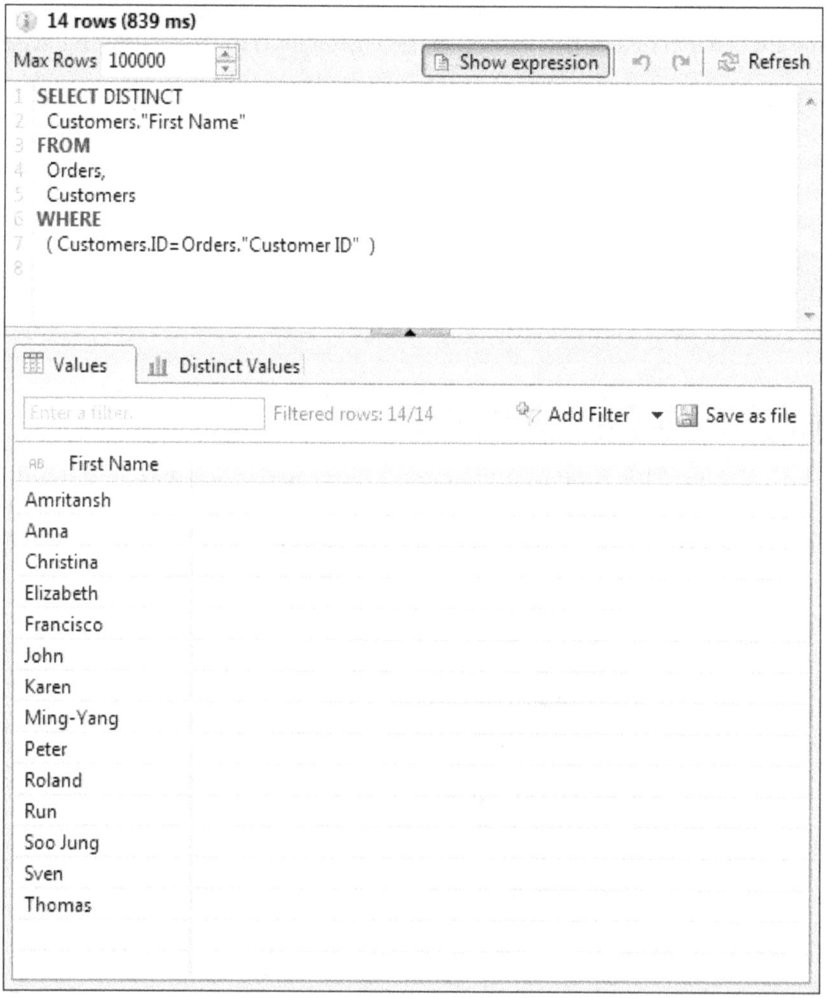

SQL Definition

In the **SQL Definition** tab, we will define our dimension and control the SQL statement that will be generated when we select this dimension to be displayed in the report.

We have the following properties that we can set:

- **SELECT**
- **WHERE**
- **Extra Tables**

These properties are shown in the following screenshot:

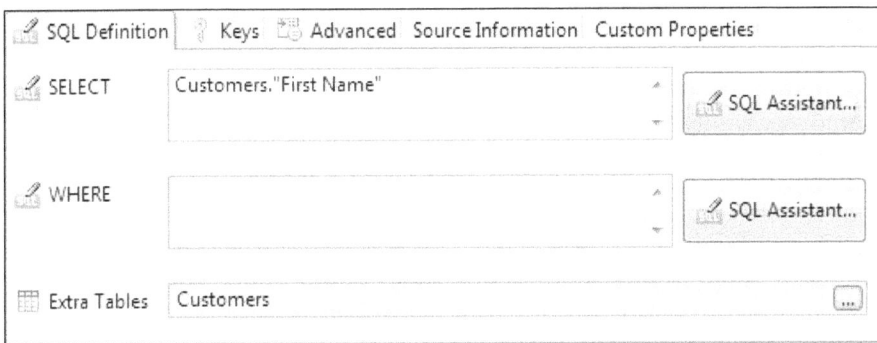

In the upcoming sections, we will talk about each property in more detail.

The Select property

By default, the **SELECT** property will be the SQL definition that should be used to generate the selected dimension. If the dimension is just a simple mapping to a database column, then you will find the column mapping in the **SELECT** property.

Let's select the Job Title dimension and open the dimension property panel, as shown in the following screenshot:

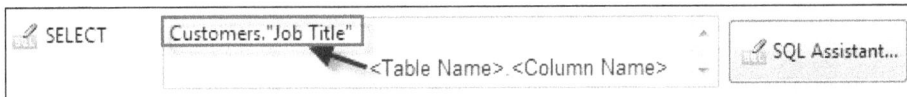

We can use **SQL Assistant** to create complex dimensions. This will open **SQL Expression Editor**. Let's try to create the customer's Full Name dimension with the following steps, as we don't have a database field to display the customer's full name:

1. Select the Customer Profile folder under the Customer Information folder.

2. Create a new dimension, Full Name.

3. Navigate to the **SQL Definition** tab and click on **SQL Assistant....**

4. Navigate to the **Functions** panel and type Concat in the filter box.

5. Select the **Concat** function to concatenate First Name and Last Name.

6. We need to use another **Concat** function to concatenate a space between First Name and Last Name.

> The **Concat** function is a specific MS Access SQL function to concatenate two strings. Other RDBMSes can have different syntaxes.

We can see the **SQL Expression Editor** window for the Full Name dimension in the following screenshot:

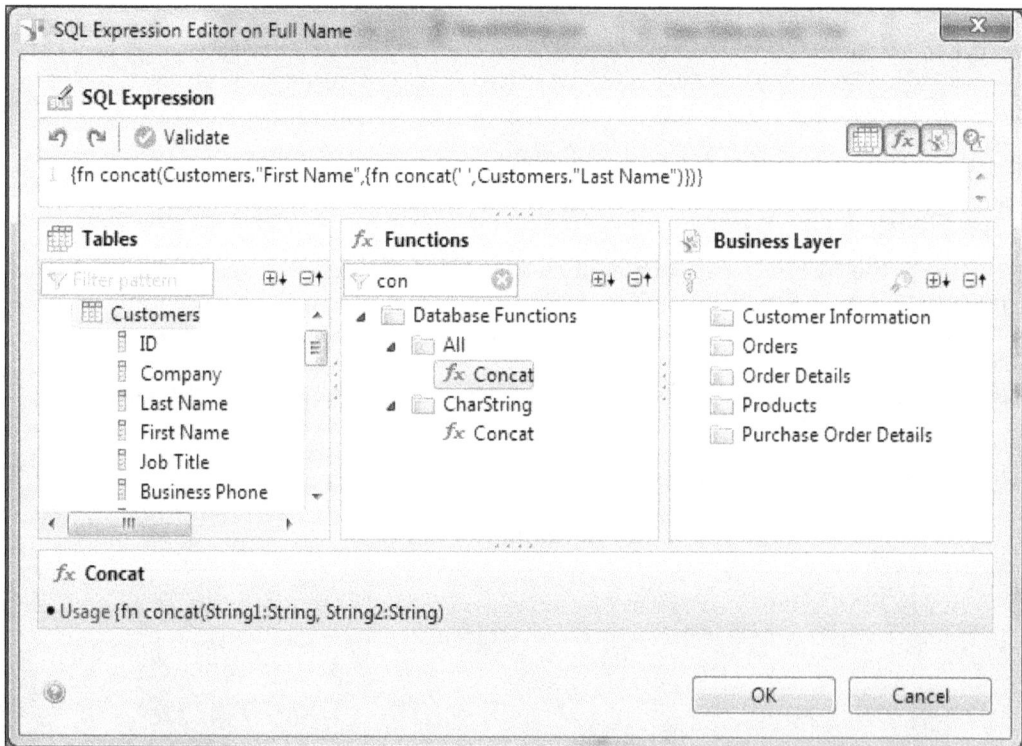

The Where property

Sometimes, we create a customized dimension that requires using some specific filters in order to produce the expected results. For example, let's create a new customized `Purchasing Manager` dimension, which displays the first and last names of the customers of the `Purchasing Manager` job with the following steps:

1. Create a new `Purchasing Manager` dimension.

2. Use the same `Select` definition for the `Full Name` dimension.

3. Add the following expression to the `Where` definition:

```
@Select(Customer Information\Customer Profile\Job Title)
='Purchasing Manager'
```

When we add this filter to the `Where` clause, this filter will be added automatically to the `where` condition of the generated SQL statement whenever we select this dimension. This functionality plays the same role as the BO filter object. Indeed, the user should be aware that adding a `where` clause to the object will automatically add this condition each time the dimension will be used. Some objects can become incompatible among themselves.

The Extra Tables property

By default, the generated SQL statement for any dimension will select only from the base database table. However, what if you want to enforce one of the database joins if this dimension is selected? We can see the default table for the `First Name` dimension in the following screenshot:

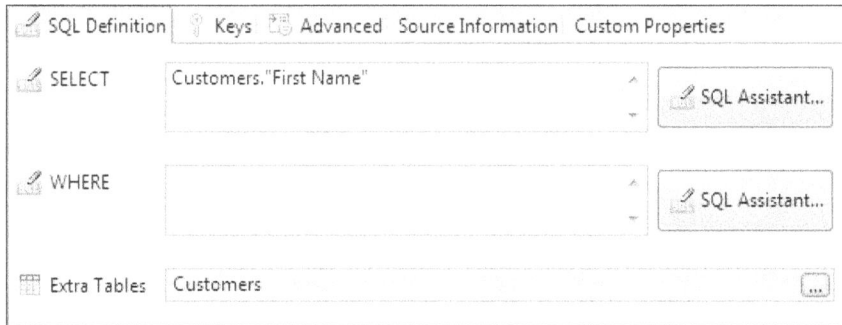

One common situation can occur when you maintain your security profiles in a database table and join this table with the main fact table in the Universe: the end user can still see all the records in the fact table if he didn't select anything from the security table. The only way to enforce security is to force the database join between the fact and security tables.

Let's try this together with the following steps:

1. Select the `First Name` object from the `Customer Profile` folder.

2. Then click on **Show Script**.

    We can see only one `Customers` table in the `From` clause of the generated SQL statement. This is because the `First Name` dimension is mapped to the `First Name` column, which got stored in the `Customers` table, as we can see in the following screenshot:

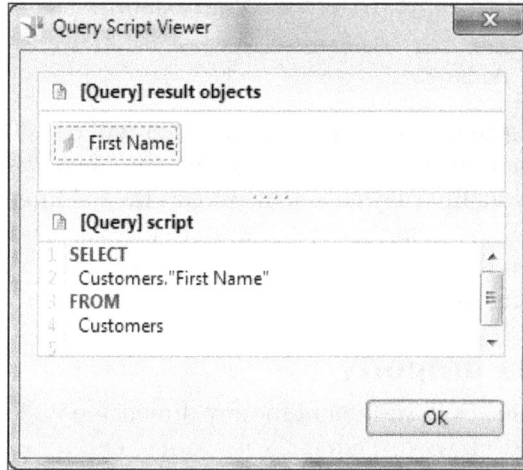

3. Now click on **Extra Tables** and select the `Orders` table from the list, as we can see in the following screenshot:

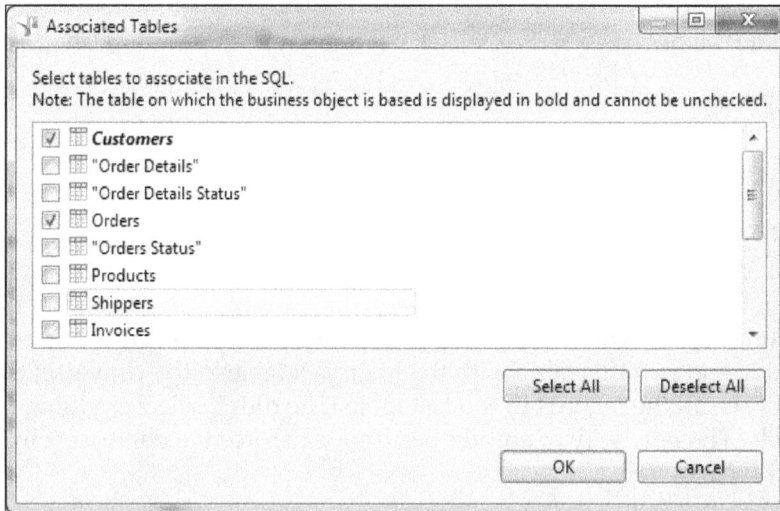

The **Extra Tables** field will display the selected tables, as we can see in the following screenshot:

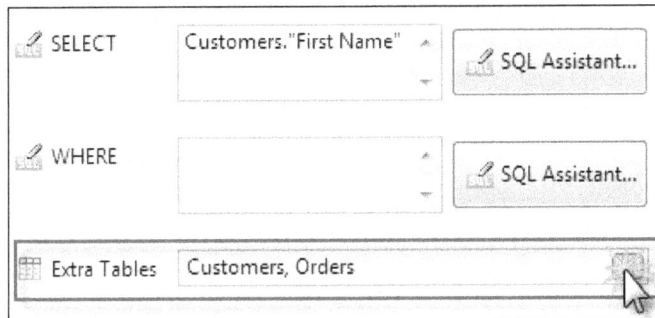

4. After that, check the generated SQL after we select the `Orders` table.

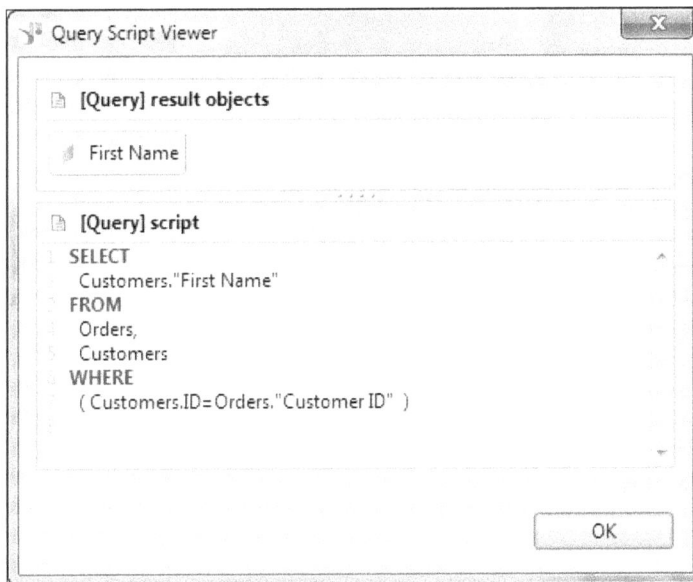

Keys

We can use the **Keys** tab to create primary and foreign keys. These keys will help the Universe SQL query engine generate performance-tuned and optimal SQL queries. This feature is known as **index awareness**, and we will talk about it in detail in *Chapter 8, The Business Layer – Advanced Topics*. The following screenshot displays the **Keys** tab:

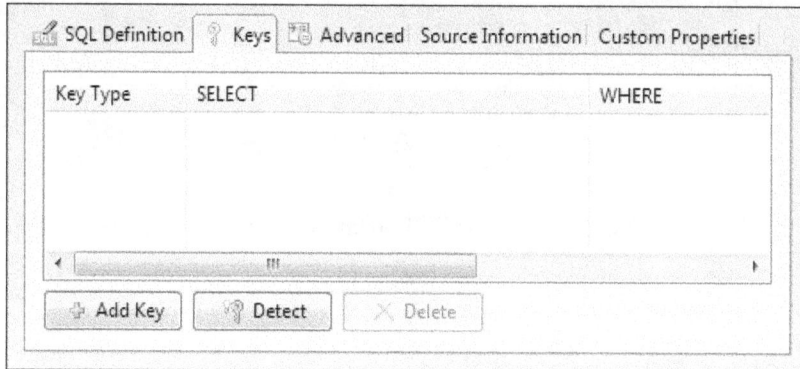

Controlling advanced properties

In this section, we can control advanced properties for our dimensions such as access levels, list of values, and usage. We can open advanced properties for the selected object by clicking on the **Advanced** tab to access the following advanced properties:

- **Access Level**
- **Object can be used in**
- **Database Format**
- **List of Values**
- **Display**

The **Advanced** tab is shown in the following screenshot:

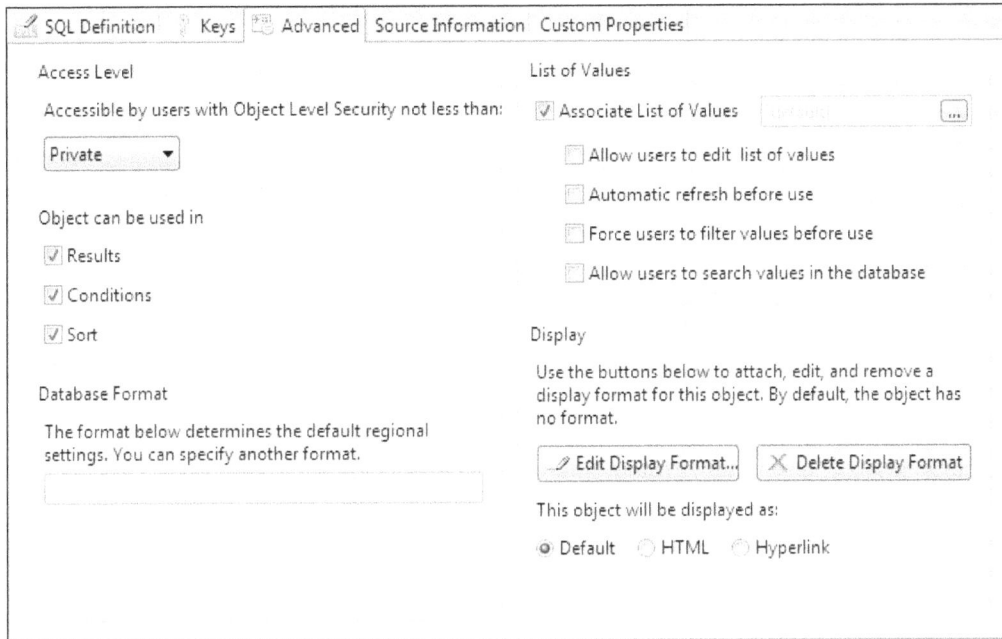

Let's go deep and talk in detail about each topic.

Access Level

The **Access Level** option will set the access level of the selected object. Only end users with the right access level will be able to see and use this object. We can set the user access level from the **Central Management Console** (**CMC**) administration window while we assign a Universe to a user or user group. We can see the **Access Level** section in the following screenshot:

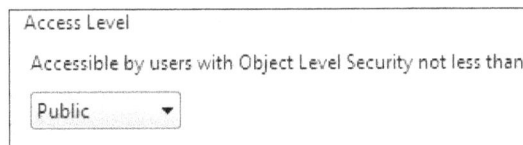

We can see the relationship between the object access level and user access level in the following table:

		User Access Level				
		Private	Confidential	Restricted	Controlled	Public
Object Access Level	Private	✓				
	Confidential	✓	✓			
	Restricted	✓	✓	✓		
	Controlled	✓	✓	✓	✓	
	Public	✓	✓	✓	✓	✓

As we can see, there are five access levels. Private is the highest access level, while public is the lowest one. End users can see objects at the same object access level assigned to them as well as objects at lower access levels; for example, if we have a user with controlled access level, then he or she can see controlled and public objects only.

> By default, both the object access level and user access level are public.
>
> You can use the right-click menu to change the object access level for multiple objects at the same time.

We can see the right-click menu for **Change Access Level** in the following screenshot:

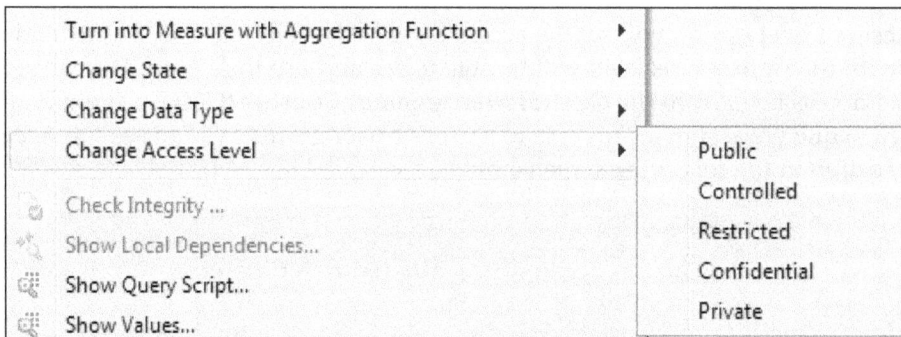

Turn into Measure with Aggregation Function ▸
Change State ▸
Change Data Type ▸
Change Access Level ▸ | Public
  | Controlled
Check Integrity ... | Restricted
Show Local Dependencies... | Confidential
Show Query Script... | Private
Show Values...

Objects can be used in

Any object can be used in one of the following places:

- **Results**: Object can be added to the query results area to be displayed in the report

- **Conditions**: Object can be added to the query filter pane to restrict output results
- **Sort**: Object can be used in the sort dialog to order query results

As we can see, we can allow the selected object to be used in multiple places. For example, for security reasons, the business could ask to anonymize the customer names. So, it makes no sense to put these objects in **Conditions**, because the names returned are the real customer ones. The **Objects can be used in** section is shown in the following screenshot:

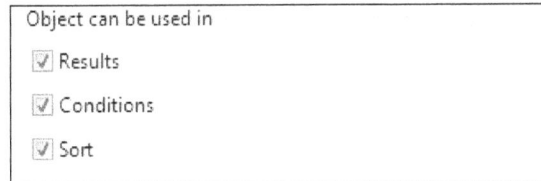

```
Object can be used in
  ☑ Results
  ☑ Conditions
  ☑ Sort
```

Note that by default the object is allowed to be used anywhere (**Results, Condition,** and **Sort**).

Database Format

Each object will inherit its database format from the corresponding database column type and from the default regional settings. We can change this if we want to enforce a custom or specific format. This format will overwrite the database one. For example, we can set the date format to DD-MM-YYYY instead of the default database format, MM-DD-YYYY.

We will not be able to apply this on one of the dimensions available in the NorthWind Universe, because we build it on top of the Access database. The **Database Format** section is shown in the following screenshot:

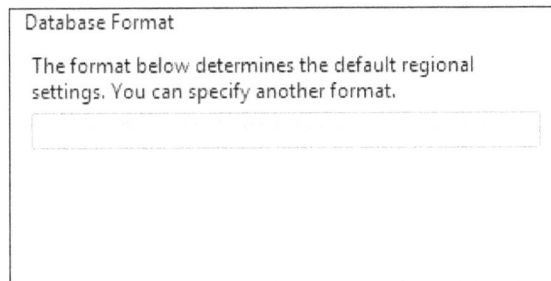

```
Database Format
  The format below determines the default regional
  settings. You can specify another format.
```

This option is usually used with DateTime objects.

List of Values

The list of values can be displayed to the end user to select the associated prompt values instead of manually writing them. Usually we assign **list of values (LOV)** to dimensions such as region, gender, and product. It is not recommended that you associate LOV with measures or attributes. It is also not recommended that you associate LOV with a dimension that has more than 100 distinct values such as account numbers in the banking industry or transaction codes in the telecommunications industry because of the query response time, which could be important. We should also assign LOV to dimensions that are moving very slowly in time (one to five new values by year), such as Region (new regions will not appear each day) or Gender (which will not change). In the case of Product, it depends on the industry; but for retail, for example, new products could appear each week or day. The **List of Values** section is shown in the following screenshot:

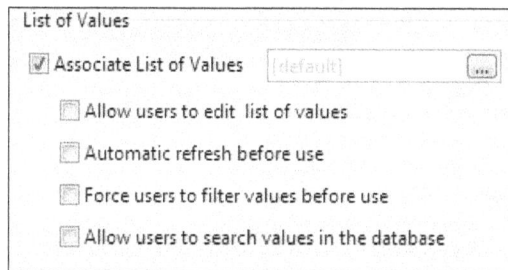

```
List of Values

 ☑ Associate List of Values     [default]          [...]

     ☐ Allow users to edit  list of values

     ☐ Automatic refresh before use

     ☐ Force users to filter values before use

     ☐ Allow users to search values in the database
```

We will talk about LOV options in detail in *Chapter 8, The Business Layer – Advanced Topics*.

Display

Using the **Display** option, we can control the following:

- Creation or deletion of the display format for the selected dimension
- How data will be displayed by this object

The **Display** section is shown in the following screenshot:

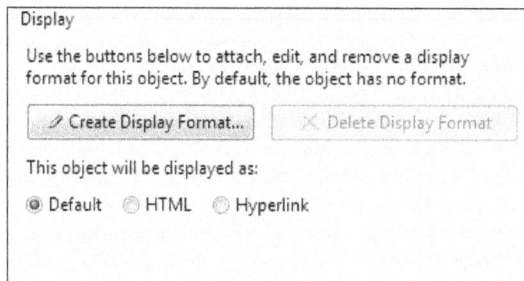

```
Display

Use the buttons below to attach, edit, and remove a display
format for this object. By default, the object has no format.

 [ 🖉 Create Display Format... ]    [ ✕ Delete Display Format ]

This object will be displayed as:

 ◉ Default   ○ HTML   ○ Hyperlink
```

Creating the display format can save a lot of the report-development time. We can use this feature if there is a specific format that we will always apply to a specific object. Let's assume that we have a measure to report annual profit, and we always apply the following format steps to this measure in all reports:

1. Format it as a number with two decimal digits.
2. Use thousand separators.
3. Prefix it with the dollar sign ($).

The annual profit should be displayed as $1,250,060.20.

Now, as we didn't create any measure yet, let's try to practice this and apply a specific display format to the `Business Phone` dimension with the following steps:

1. Navigate to the `Business Phone` dimension.
2. Go to the **Advanced** properties tab.
3. Click on **Create Display Format…**.

The following window will be displayed:

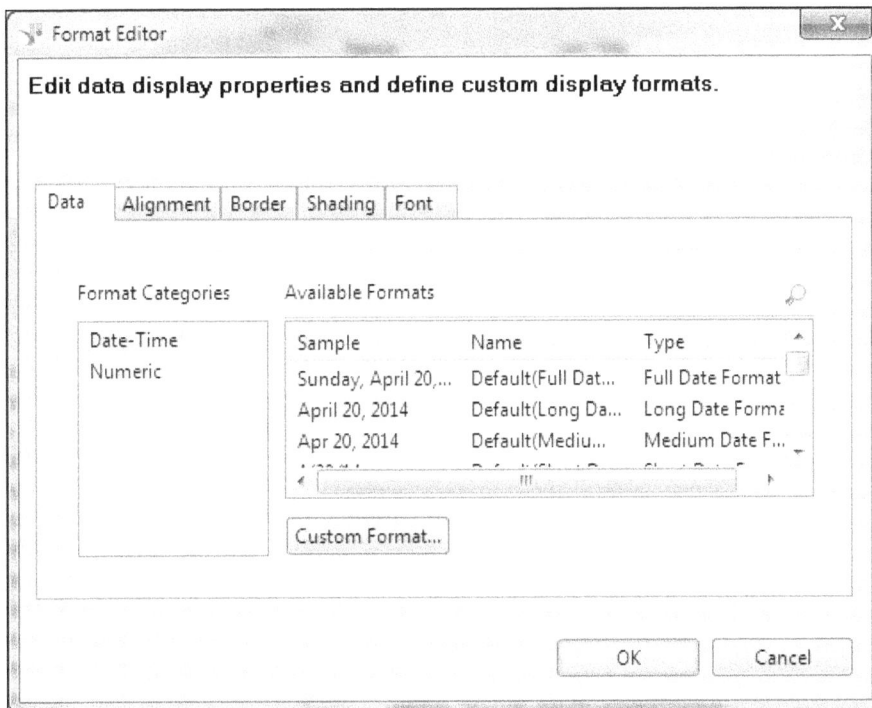

As we can see, we can control the following format properties from this window:

- **Data**: Here, we can select the data format category. There are two main categories: **Date-Time** and **Numeric**. We can use this tab to change the **Date-Time** or **Numeric** format based on the object type. So, we will create the custom format ((000)000-0000) to display Business Phone in the standard format ((123)555-0100) as we can see in the following screenshot:

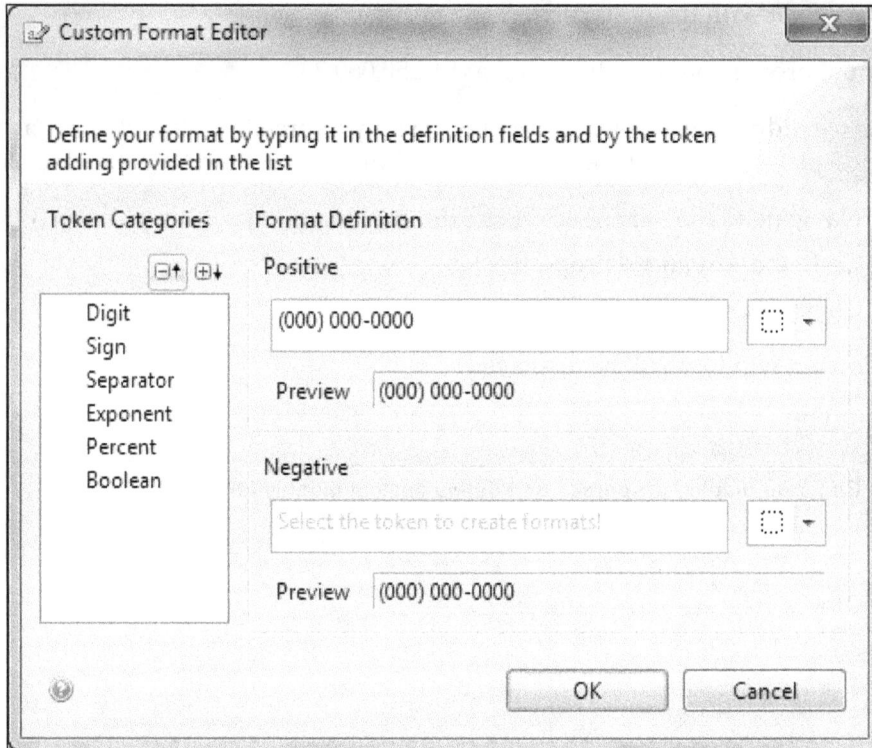

You can press *F1* while the **Custom Format Editor** window is active, or click on the **Help** icon in the bottom-left corner for more information on **Custom Format Editor** and **Format Definition**.

- **Alignment**: We can use this tab to set alignment and spacing. We can also preview changes before we apply and use them in the created display format. We can see the **Alignment** tab in the following screenshot:

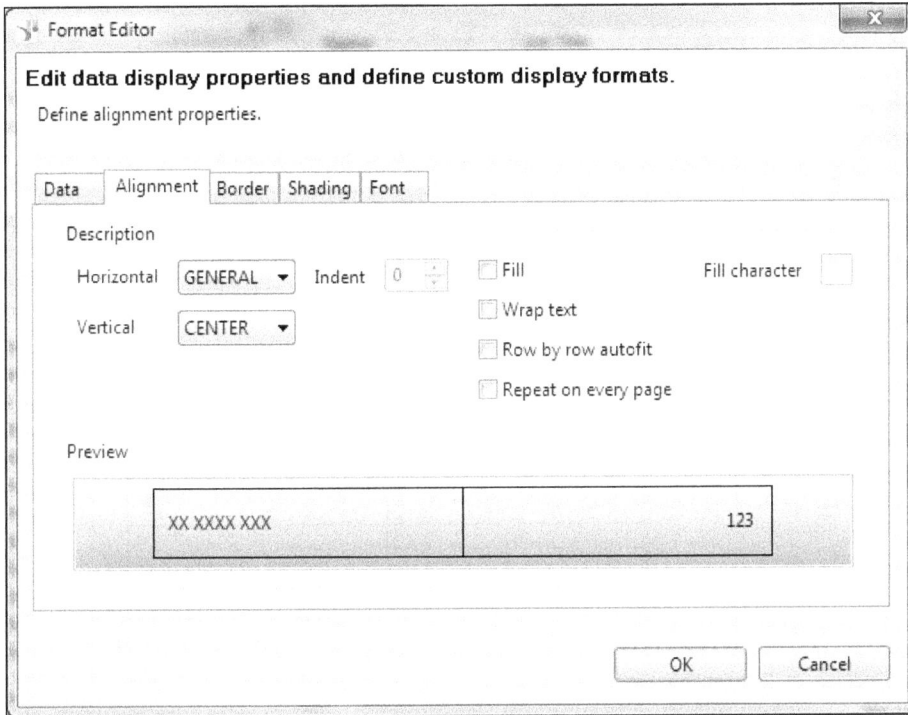

As First Name is a string object, we will use the following settings:

Property	Value
Horizontal	Left
Vertical	Center
Wrap text	Checked

The **Preview** window has two parts to show the selected **Alignment** options on strings as well as numbers.

- **Border**: In this tab, we can control the container cell's borders. Container cell is a report cell that will be used to display the selected dimension. We can control the cell's border line color as well as line style. We can see the **Border** tab in the following screenshot:

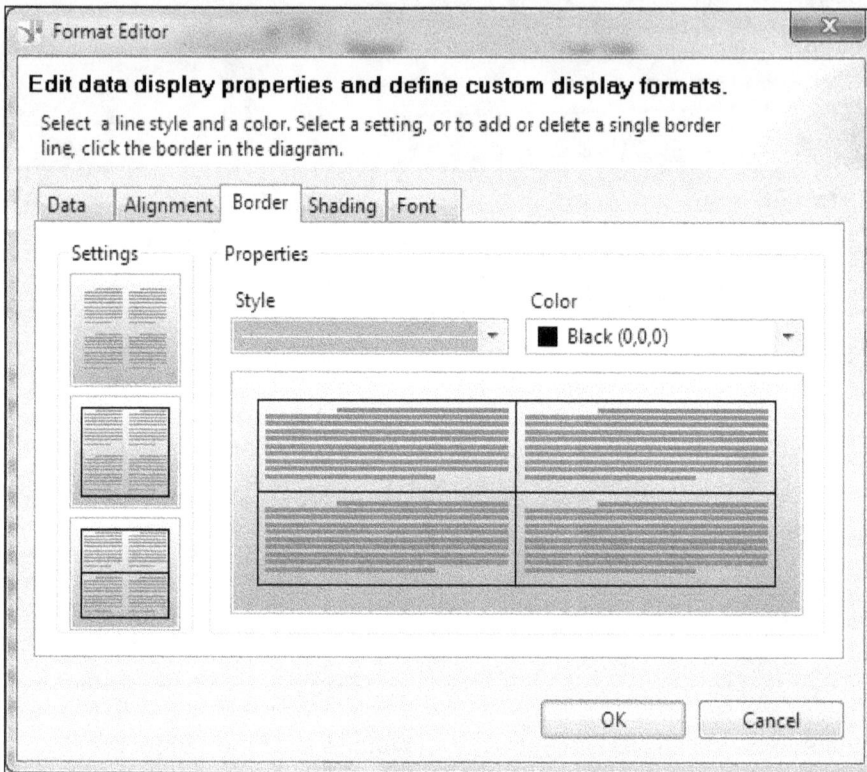

- **Shading**: We can use this tab to control shading and fill options for the container cell. We can set the following shading properties:
    - **Foreground Color**
    - **Background Color**
    - **Fill Style**

We can preview our shading selections in the **Preview** pane, as shown in the following window:

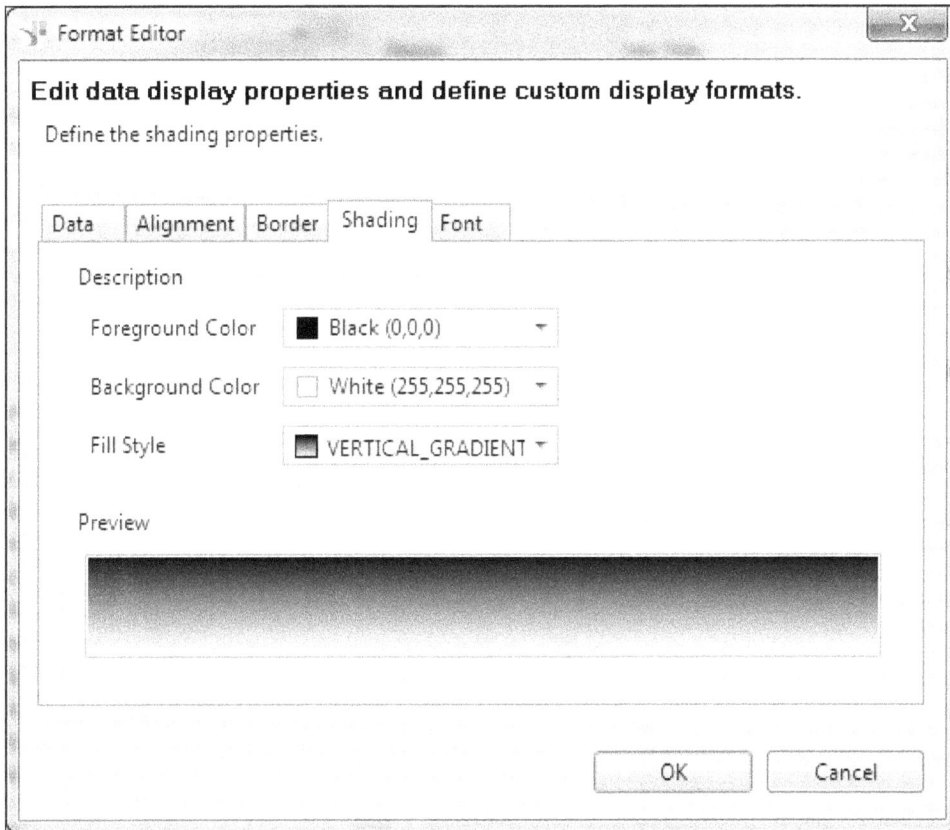

- **Font**: We can use this pane to control and set font options. We can see the **Font** tab in the following screenshot:

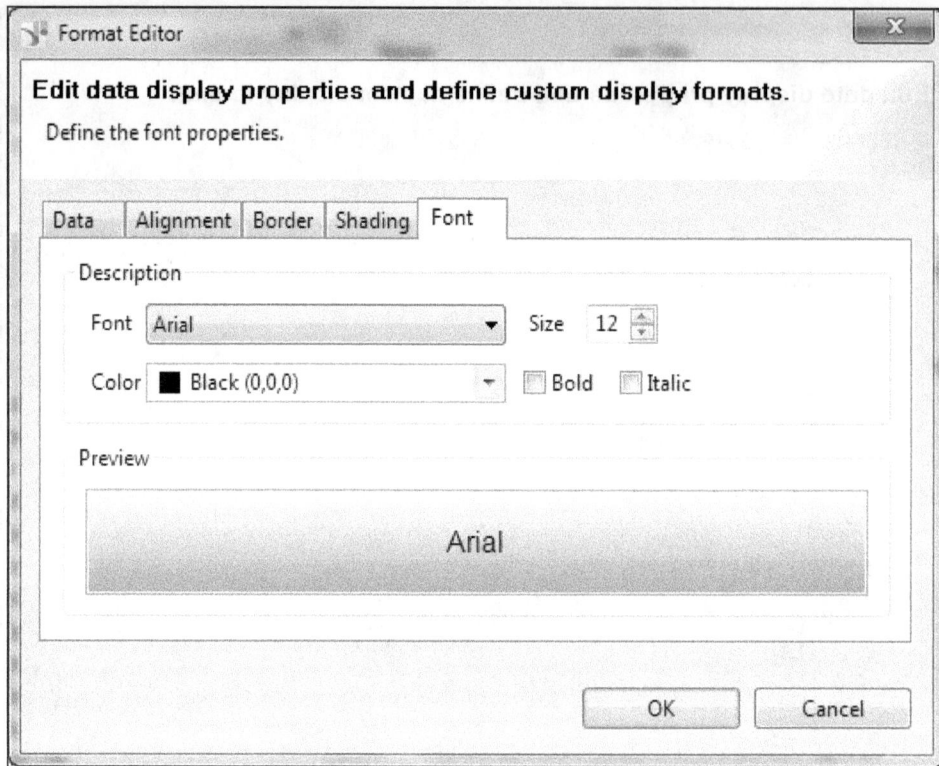

The second part of the display area in advanced object properties is to set the display type of the selected object. We can choose one of the following available options:

- **Default**: This will display normal data as retrieved from the generated SQL statement for the selected dimension.
- **HTML**: This will interpret the affected dimension as HTML. We can use the HTML code (`<b> text </b>` to display text in bold) inside this dimension, and this will take effect when this dimension is displayed in the report.
- **Hyperlink**: This will interpret the dimension data as a hyperlink. We usually use this option if we want to link one report with another or when we have a dimension such as `Customer Website` or `Company Site`.

We can see these display options in the following screenshot:

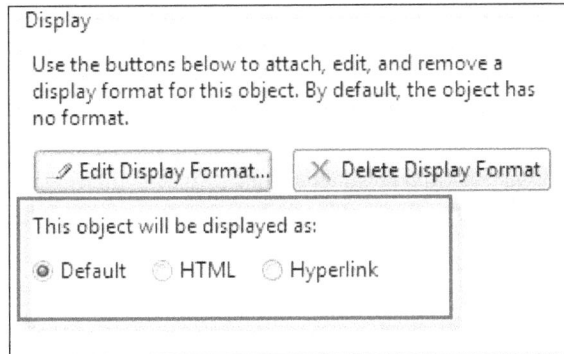

Source Information

We use the **Source Information** tab to document source information along with each business object. This is technical information and will not be visible to end users. This information will also not be a part of the Universe PDF documentation. We can add the following source information

- **Technical Information**
- **Mapping**
- **Linage**

These fields can be entered manually or can be integrated with SAP BusinessObjects Information Steward 4.0 – Metadata Management. This tool is a web-based application that can be used to track metadata information. You can find more information on how to integrate it with SAP BusinessObjects in order to trace the metadata information automatically for BusinessObjects on the SAP official website at `http://www.sap.com`. We can see the **Source Information** tab in the following screenshot:

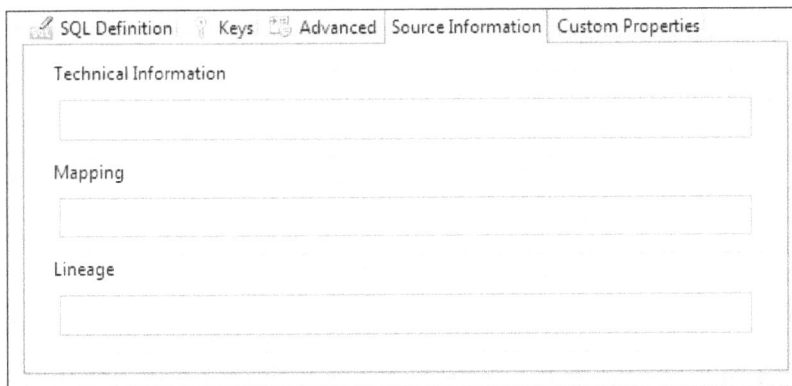

Custom Properties

Custom Properties is also another place to communicate between Universe developers. We can use the **Custom Properties** tab to add extra additional properties for the dimension that will not be visible to end users. We can see some customized properties for the First Name dimension in the following screenshot:

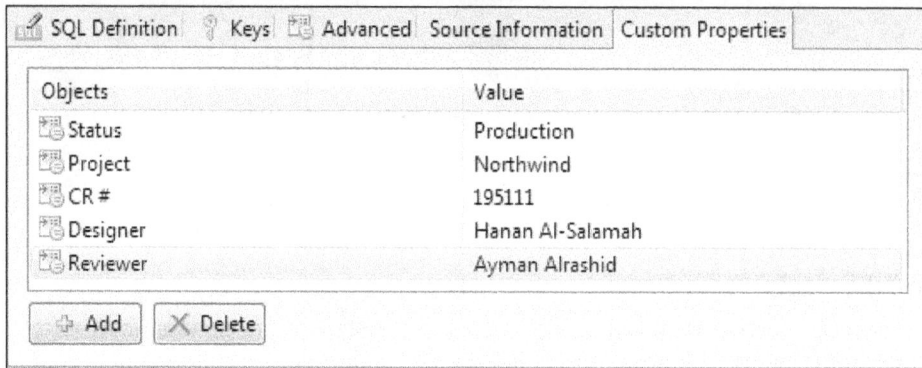

SQL Definition Keys Advanced Source Information Custom Properties	
Objects	**Value**
Status	Production
Project	Northwind
CR #	195111
Designer	Hanan Al-Salamah
Reviewer	Ayman Alrashid
⊕ Add ✕ Delete	

Now, as we completed all the properties that we can configure for a dimension object, we will talk in the next part about other business objects that we can create under our Business layer, such as attributes, measures, and filters. We will notice that most of the properties described in this section are also applicable for other business objects. So, in the following sections, we will discuss only specific or new properties.

> The **Custom Properties** feature is a new feature in the IDT, and there is no equivalent for it in the UDT.

Attributes

An attribute object is a special property for a dimension. Each attribute is linked to a dimension as it is detailed information that is somehow related to the parent dimension. Let's take Address for example. The Address dimension is a dimension that can have many detail attributes, some of which are as follows:

- Area/district
- Street name/number
- Zip/postal code

Attribute properties are exactly the same as dimension properties, and we can control attribute properties in the same manner that we used to control dimension properties. Note that attributes can't be used in the navigation paths, so we can't use them in drill down analysis in BO reports. We also can't merge attributes at the report level. This is why we need to take care while creating attribute objects and consider the two situations mentioned earlier.

> Attribute objects in the IDT are equivalent to detail objects in the UDT.

Now, let's try to create the `Zip Code` attribute for the `Address` dimension with the following steps:

1. Navigate to the `Contact Information` folder under the `Customer Information` folder.

2. Right-click on the `Address` dimension and navigate to **New** | **Attribute**.

3. Use the following information to define our new attribute:

Property	Value
Name	`Zip Code`
Dimension	`Address`
SELECT	`Customers."ZIP/Postal Code"`

We can see the new `Zip Code` attribute in the following screenshot:

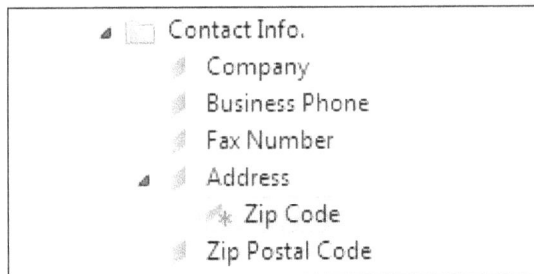

Measures

A measure is any number that represents an amount or count. We use aggregate functions with the measure object to tell the SQL engine how to aggregate this measure values.

Let's try to create some measures in the NorthWind Universe with the following steps:

1. Drag the Orders table from the **Data Foundation** pane to the **Business Layer** panel under the Customer Information folder.

2. Right-click on Shipping Fees and select **Turn into Measure with Aggregation Function**.

3. Select **Sum** from the list, as shown in the following screenshot:

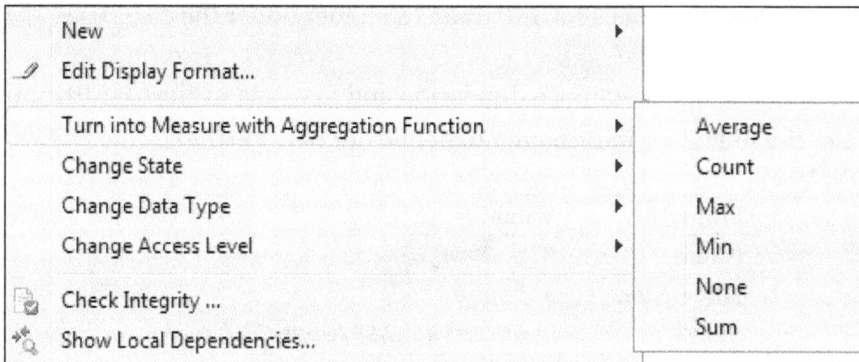

New ▶	
✐ Edit Display Format...	
Turn into Measure with Aggregation Function ▶	Average
Change State ▶	Count
Change Data Type ▶	Max
Change Access Level ▶	Min
	None
▤ Check Integrity ...	Sum
⚒ Show Local Dependencies...	

Now, let's try to create a new derived or calculated measure. We want to create a measure to display the total number of orders. We can do this with the following steps:

1. Select the Orders folder and click on the **Insert** icon.

2. Navigate to **New | Measure**.

3. Type Number of Orders in the **Name** field.

4. Type the following expression in the **SELECT** field:

   COUNT (Orders."Order Id")

5. Validate the expression and close the window.

The Number of Orders measure should be displayed in the following screenshot:

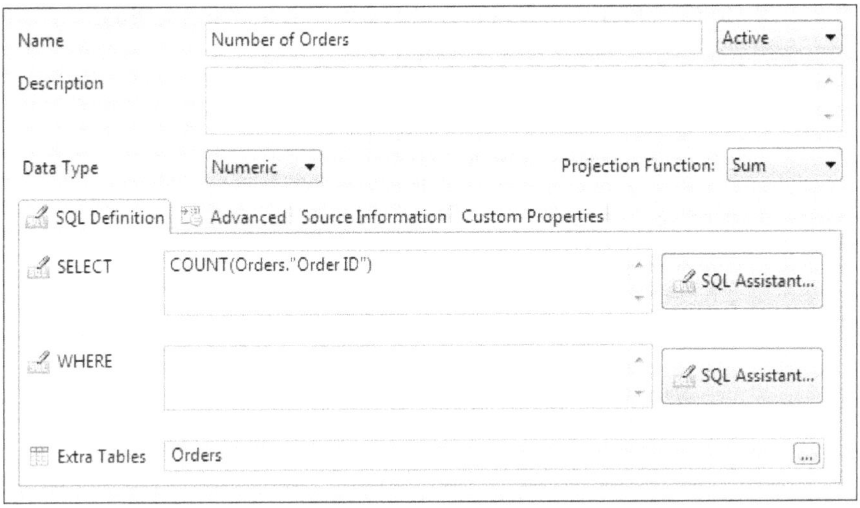

Difference between the database and projection functions

The database function is the aggregate function that we use inside the Select field while we are defining our measures. This aggregate function can be one of the following:

- **Sum**
- **Count**
- **Max**
- **Min**
- **Average**

The aggregation function is mandatory to reduce the number of records retrieved from the database. The generated query based on the aggregated measure will be optimized and include the group by clause. This will ensure the following:

- Reduce the query results' size and decrease the load on the network, because the data transferred between the database and application servers is minimized

- Reduce the application server processing time, as it will only process a small amount of data

Let's try to do an example:

1. Navigate to the Queries panel from the left window in the Business layer.

2. Create a new query, which is described as follows:

    ◦ Orders | Ship Name

    ◦ Orders | Number of Orders

These dimensions are shown in the following screenshot:

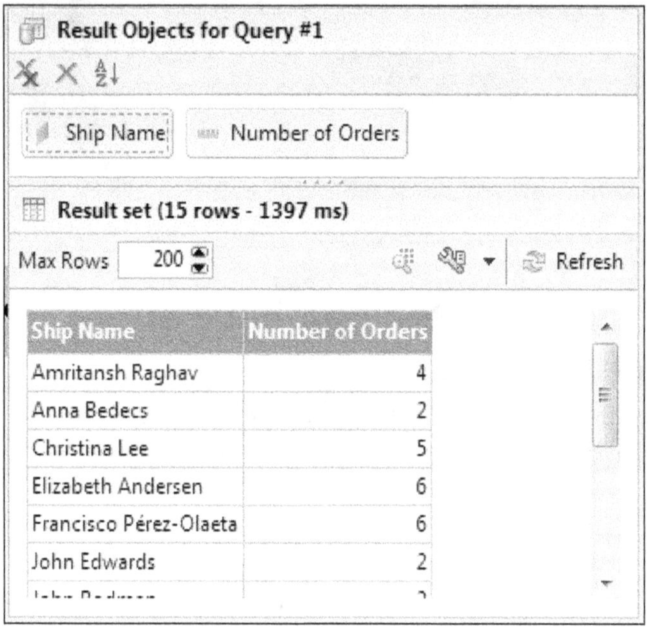

As you can see, only 15 records are retrieved from the database because we used the **COUNT** aggregation function. Before we remove the aggregation function and check the behavior, let's have a look at the generated SQL statement from the query shown in the following screenshot:

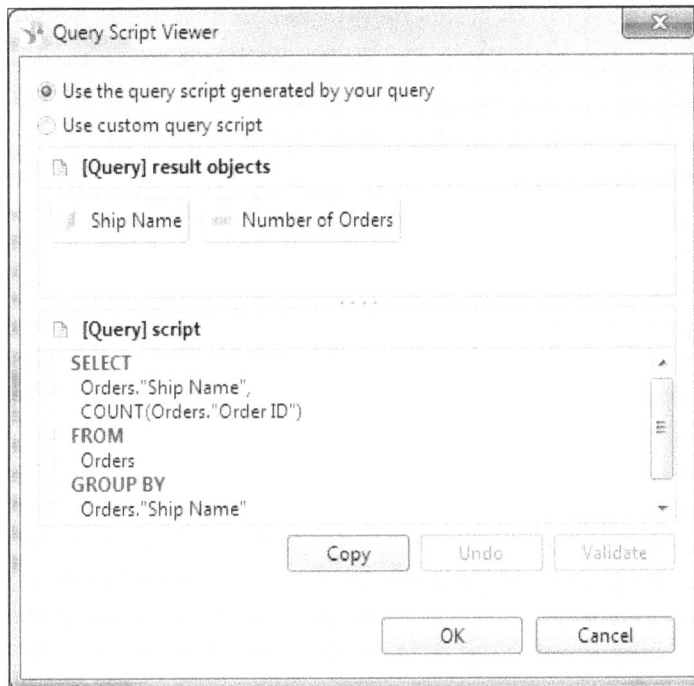

Now, let's remove **COUNT** from the measure definition; we will notice that 48 records are returned this time (this is the total number of records stored in the `Orders` table), as shown in the following screenshot:

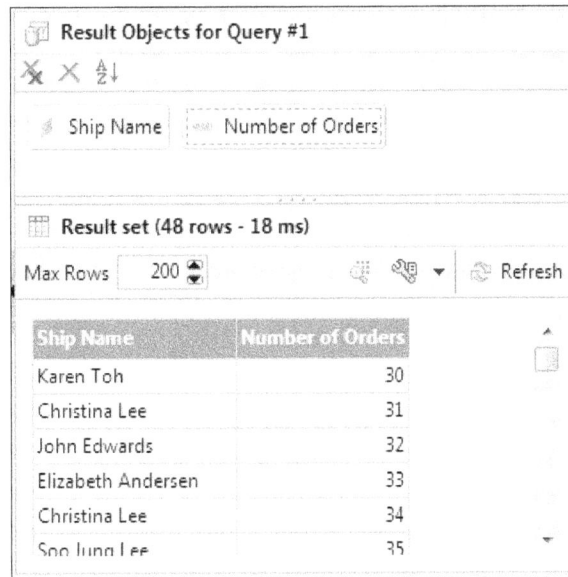

On the other hand, the projection function is used on the report level to aggregate data inside a micro cube to display the required results to the end user based on the selected dimensions and measures. Well, this might sound very difficult to understand, so let's look at an example.

Assume that we have a report query with the selected objects that are shown in the following screenshot:

The preceding data will be retrieved from database and stored in the micro cube behind the report. If we add all these objects to a table in our report, it will be exactly as displayed in the previous screen; it displays all retrieved data as it is without any kind of processing. However, what if we only selected Ship City and Number of Orders to be displayed in the report's table? Then extra processing is required to calculate Number of Orders per Ship City from the data retrieved by our query. The projection function will be used in this case to aggregate Number of Orders per Ship City, and because we have **SUM** as a projection function, it will add the number of orders to get the number per Ship City. So, for **Chicago**, the total number of orders will be 4 (**Company J**) plus 2 (**Company Y**), which equals 6 orders. Note that we used **COUNT** as a database aggregation function to calculate the number of orders, while we used **SUM** as the projection function to aggregate this measure on the report level.

In the following section, we will discuss filters, which is the last type of business object.

Filters

Predefined filters (known as **conditions**) will help end business users define the required filters to be used in their analyses and reports, without the need to know business criteria and roles. It is very useful to maintain all the agreed business criteria and roles inside our Universe to be used directly by end users. For example, say we have the following account statuses:

- **N**: Normal
- **D**: Dormant
- **I**: Inactive
- **C**: Closed

Assume that there is a business rule which states that active accounts are the accounts that are normal or dormant.

The best practice is to create a predefined filter (active accounts) that will filter only normal and dormant accounts as per the definition. This filter will be available in the business model, and the end user can easily select this filter in his or her report or analysis to narrow the report results to only active accounts.

As a best practice, we should define all our business rules during business requirements-gathering sessions. Then, we need a data analyst to translate them into a technical IT form (usually, an SQL condition). Then, we need to create the corresponding conditions (predefined filters) in the Business layer.

> Filters in the IDT are equivalent to conditions in the UDT.

How to create a filter

We can create a filter using the **Native** SQL or the **Business** definition. The **Native** option will allow us to write the SQL code manually to create our filter, while the **Business** option will open the **Edit Business Filter** window. The **Edit Business Filter** window is a GUI that will help us create filters using drag-and-drop options and without the need to know SQL coding.

To create a filter that will only return orders that will be shipped to Chicago, we should perform the following steps:

1. Navigate to the `Orders` folder.
2. Right-click on the `Orders` folder and navigate to **New | Filter**.
3. Type `Shipped to Chicago` in the **Name** field.
4. Make sure that **Native** is selected.
5. Type the following condition in the **WHERE** field:

   `Orders."Ship City"='Chicago'`

The filter should look like the following screenshot:

Now, let's try to create a business filter to filter Miami orders with the following steps:

1. Create a new filter under the `Orders` folder.
2. Type `Shipped to Miami` in the **Name** field.
3. Select the **Business** filter type.
4. Click the **Edit Filter** button.

5. Go to `Ship City` and select values from the list. Then select **Miami**, as shown in the following screenshot:

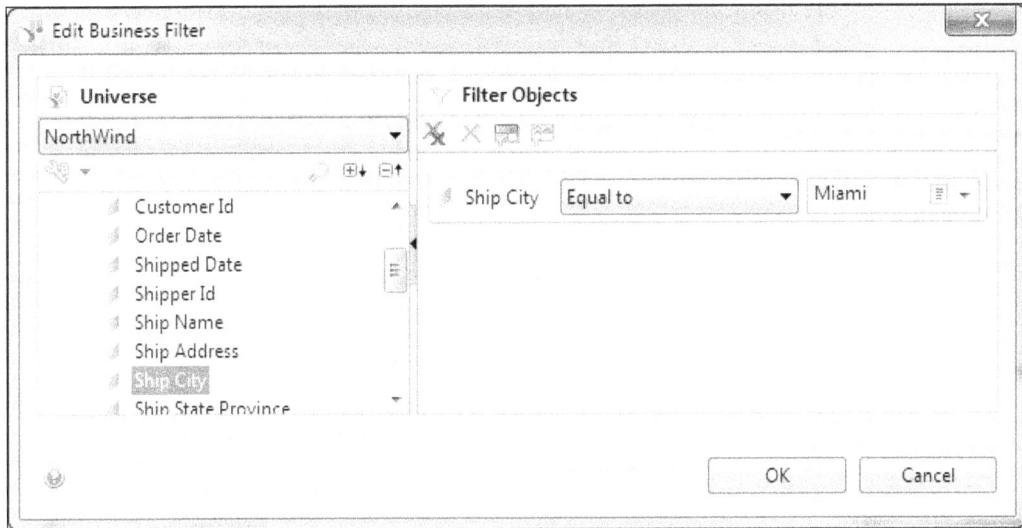

Filter properties

We can set the filter to be used as a mandatory filter in our Universe or folder by defining the filter scope from the filter's **Properties** window. The following options are available in this window:

- **Apply on Universe**: This filter will be applied on every query generated using this Universe.

- **Apply on Folder**: This filter will be applied if any object is used from this folder.

- **Apply on List of Values**: This filter will be applied on all the LOVs generated for each object inside this class (folder). Note that this option is available only after you select **Apply on Folder**.

We can see these options in the following screenshot:

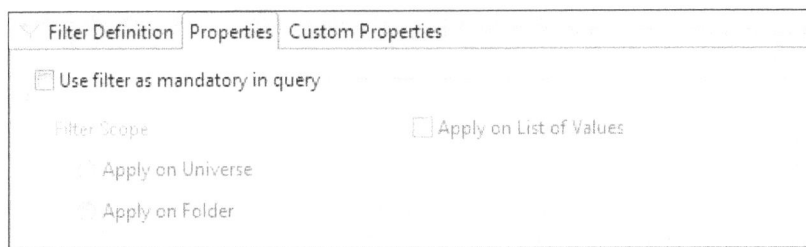

Summary

In this chapter, we started with the process of business requirement gathering and how this will affect our Business layer. Then, we had an overview of the main panels in the Business layer window and discussed the main function of each one. After that, we discussed in detail the main features and functions in the Business layer pane, such as how to sort an object in the Business layer and how to search for a specific object using the search panel. Then, we learned how to populate our Business layer with different types of objects such as dimensions, measures, attributes, and filters. We discussed the properties and functions inside each object in detail.

In the next chapter, we will talk about a very important topic, which is how to test your Universe by detecting issues and problems and then how to solve and fix them.

6
Testing Your Universe

In this chapter, we will talk about how to test your Universe before publishing it and making it available to be used by end business users. Testing is an important step in any product development life cycle.

Testing a Universe is a challenging task as it is a special product with a special output. The tests cases should not test the combination of objects but they should be business-oriented. Imagine that we have a Universe of 10 objects and we want to create test cases to test all the possible combinations. This will be 10! (factorial 10), which equals 3,628,800.

We can think about this subject in a different way. Instead of testing the Universe the hard way, let's try to think how to test it in a smart way. This can happen if we take a moment to think about the main building blocks of the Universe. The main idea of our approach is to make sure that Universe resources are implemented in the right way. This will help us to achieve a good percentage of the required testing to certify a Universe from the technical side. On the other hand, we still need to do business testing as well as **User Acceptance Testing (UAT)**.

Universe testing is an important subject although many designers skip this step. Skipping the Universe testing phase may lead to displaying wrong data to the end users. Wrong data will be the first step in losing confidence and reliability on the BI system in the organization and will engender a failed BI project.

In this chapter, we will learn the following topics:

- The Universe development life cycle
- Testing our Universe integrity using the **Check Integrity** wizard
- Using the **Queries** editor to create queries that test the functional part of the Business layer

The Universe development life cycle

The Universe development life cycle is very close to the project life cycle because it is a project or part of a project at the end. A typical BI project will require the following deliverables:

- A rich and user-friendly presentation layer that can be used by end business users to build their own reports and on-the-fly analysis
- A set of standard reports and analysis
- Training for end users on how to use the presentation layer and standard reports

Each deliverable will pass through the standard project life cycle starting with the initiation phase and ending with the close phase. Here, we will focus on the Universe development life cycle phases mentioned as follows:

- Initiation
- Planning and design
- Implementation and development
- **Quality assurance (QA)** and testing
- Closing

We will discuss each phase in the upcoming sections.

Initiation

In this phase, we will approach the business and complete the following actions:

- Gathering business requirements and defining the expected final deliverables. We need to specify how many Universes are required based on the requirements
- Agreeing on the definition for the required business objects and agreeing on any formulas or calculations that should be used to create custom objects
- Agreeing on business filters, business rules, and security profiles
- Defining user acceptance criteria that will be used to accept final deliverables
- Setting any time or budget constrains

> It is very important to know that UAT test cases and acceptance criteria should be defined in the initiation phase and even before starting project implementation.

Planning and design

In this phase, the project will actually start and we should perform the following actions:

- Estimating the required time, resources, and budget required to complete the project.

- Starting the system analysis and defining source systems then completing mapping specifications between source systems and Universe business objects.

- Designing the Data Foundation and Business layers. In the Data Foundation design document, we should specify every single detail such as tables, columns, joins, aliases, and contexts. While on the other hand, we should also specify business objects, filters, LOV, navigation paths, and so on in the Business layer design document.

Implementation and development

In this phase, we will start the actual development based on the completed design document in the planning phase. In this phase, we should complete the following actions:

- Creating a data connection
- Creating the Data Foundation layer
- Creating the Business layer

Quality assurance and testing

In this phase, we should start testing our Universe. There are two main types of testing:

- **System Integrity Test (SIT)**
- **User Acceptance Test (UAT)**

We will discuss each one in detail in the upcoming sections as this is our main topic here.

SIT

In this process, we will test the integrity of our Universe. This means that we will follow a list of actions (test cases) and give a score to our Universe based on the testing results to decide whether it is passed (can move to the next phase of testing) or failed (return to the developers for rework). In this phase, we will test the Universe from the technical side and we should spot obvious errors and mistakes. In SIT, we will have specific test cases for each Universe resources:

- Connection
- Data Foundation
- The Business layer

Find the following sample test cases for each Universe resource:

- Sample test cases for Data connection:
    - Test the data connection and make sure that the connection can be established

- Sample test cases for Data Foundation:
    - Check the Data Foundation structure and make sure all tables and columns exist in the database
    - Check the syntax for joins
    - Check SQL design traps (loops, fan, and chasm traps).

- Sample test cases for the Business layer:
    - Make sure that all business objects can be successfully parsed
    - Check LOV

We will use the **Check Integrity** wizard (explained later in this chapter) to check the integrity of our Universe. If the Universe is SIT-certified and has successfully passed the required test case, then we can move to the next phase of testing, which is UAT.

> SIT testing can be done on the same development environment.

UAT

In this phase, we will check the logical and functional part of the Universe. We will need business users to go and check the Universe and compare it against the initial defined acceptance criteria. If it is accepted, then the Universe will be certified and will be ready to be moved to the production environment to be used by end business users. Any required training should take place in this phase as well and we should make sure that business users can access the information and generate their own reports and analyses. In this phase, we should make sure that:

- Business rules are covered
- The objects return data expected by the business
- The formulas implemented return the results expected by the business
- The object's navigation is user friendly for business users

We will use the **Queries** tab under the Business layer left panel, which will be discussed in detail later in this chapter, to complete UAT testing for our Universe.

Finally, after the Universe passes the UAT testing phase, we can move to the last phase of the project, closing.

> The best practice is to perform UAT testing on a separate UAT testing environment (a separate server and separate installation).

Closing

In this phase, the Universe is moved to the production environment and should be ready to be used by end business users.

In the next section, we will learn how to use the **Check Integrity** wizard to perform SIT testing and how to use the **Queries** tool to perform UAT testing.

Using the Check Integrity wizard

The **Check Integrity** wizard is a tool that can help us discover many issues in our Universe. We can use this to check the entire Universe or to check a specific Universe resource such as Data Foundation, Business layer, or even a specific folder in the Business layer.

The **Check Integrity** wizard will perform an integrity check against a set of defined rules. We can perform the integrity check against all the defined rules or some of them. Some rules are related to Data Foundation objects such as tables and joins. Some of them are related to the Business layer such as business objects and list of values.

The **Check Integrity** wizard will help us discover errors such as:

- A business object mapped to an unknown database table or column
- A wrong database function or SAP BO function used in business object definition

> The integrity wizard will perform an integrity check only and will help us to spot integrity issues. We still need to perform another test to check the logic and design using **Query Builder**.
>
> The time consumed by the **Check Integrity** wizard will be proportionate with the number of objects to be tested.

Now, let's try to check the integrity of the NorthWind Universe and check what kind of errors will be highlighted with the help of the following steps:

1. Open the NorthWind Data Foundation layer and navigate to the Data Foundation tab from the left-hand side panel.

2. Right-click on NorthWind.dfx and select **Check Integrity...**, as shown in the following screenshot:

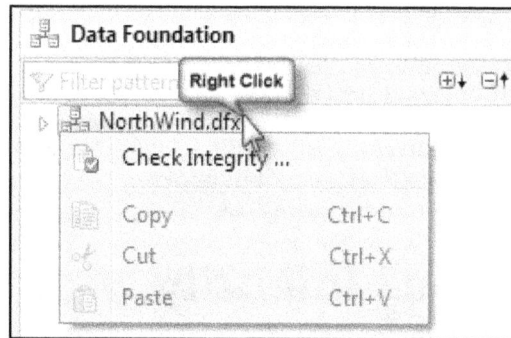

The **Check Integrity** window will open and then we should select all the available rules, or a set of them, to check our Data Foundation integrity against. In this example, select all the available rules as shown in the following screenshot:

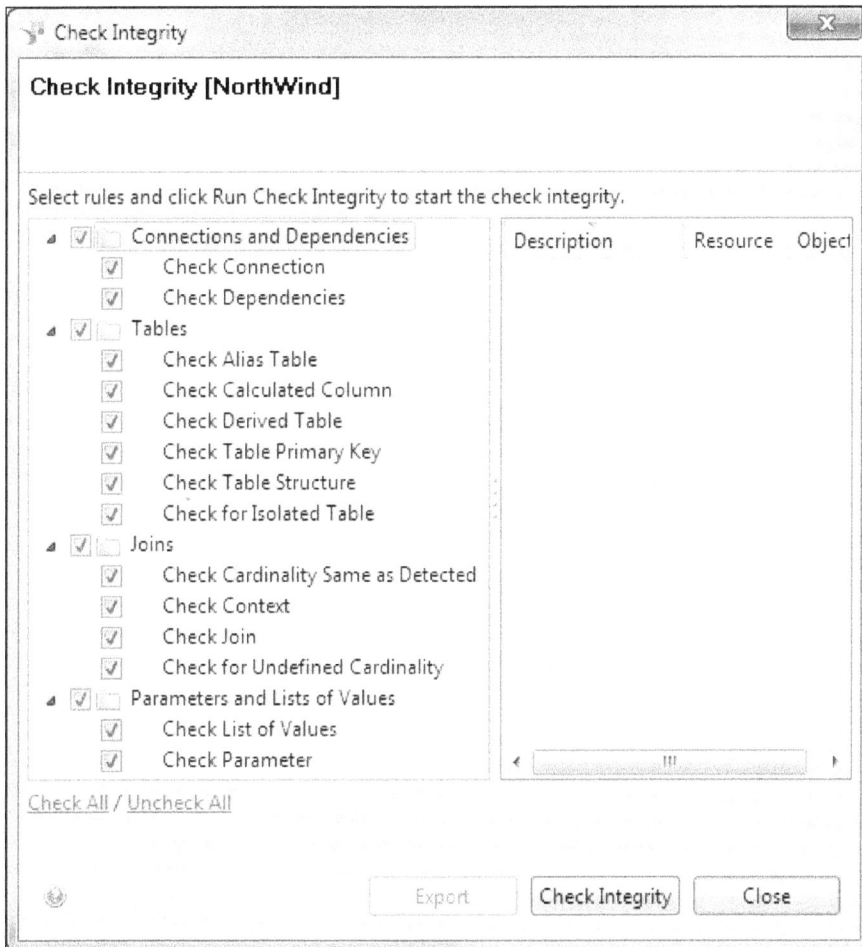

3. Click on the **Check Integrity** button to start the checking process. We will get the following window:

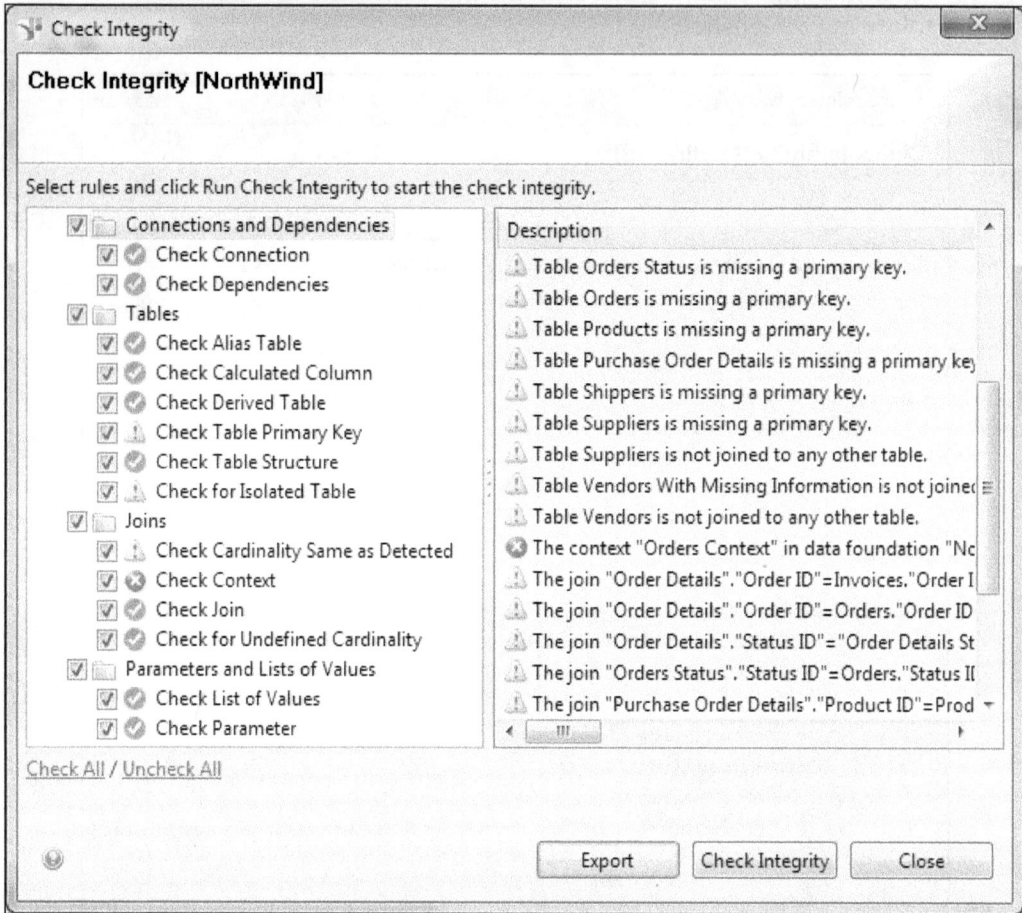

Check Integrity

Check Integrity [NorthWind]

Select rules and click Run Check Integrity to start the check integrity.

Rules	Description
☑ 🗀 Connections and Dependencies	⚠ Table Orders Status is missing a primary key.
☑ ✅ Check Connection	⚠ Table Orders is missing a primary key.
☑ ✅ Check Dependencies	⚠ Table Products is missing a primary key.
☑ 🗀 Tables	⚠ Table Purchase Order Details is missing a primary key
☑ ✅ Check Alias Table	⚠ Table Shippers is missing a primary key.
☑ ✅ Check Calculated Column	⚠ Table Suppliers is missing a primary key.
☑ ✅ Check Derived Table	⚠ Table Suppliers is not joined to any other table.
☑ ⚠ Check Table Primary Key	⚠ Table Vendors With Missing Information is not joined
☑ ✅ Check Table Structure	⚠ Table Vendors is not joined to any other table.
☑ ⚠ Check for Isolated Table	❌ The context "Orders Context" in data foundation "Nc
☑ 🗀 Joins	⚠ The join "Order Details"."Order ID"=Invoices."Order I
☑ ⚠ Check Cardinality Same as Detected	⚠ The join "Order Details"."Order ID"=Orders."Order ID
☑ ❌ Check Context	⚠ The join "Order Details"."Status ID"="Order Details St
☑ ✅ Check Join	⚠ The join "Orders Status"."Status ID"=Orders."Status I[
☑ ✅ Check for Undefined Cardinality	⚠ The join "Purchase Order Details"."Product ID"=Prod
☑ 🗀 Parameters and Lists of Values	
☑ ✅ Check List of Values	
☑ ✅ Check Parameter	

Check All / Uncheck All

[Export] [Check Integrity] [Close]

As we can see, the check results or alerts are categorized into the following:

- Passed (green tick)
- Warning (yellow exclamation point)
- Error (red cross sign)

We need to have a look at the warning alerts and fix the error alerts. We can use the right panel to find a brief description on each alert. We have one red alert related to the design loop that needs to be fixed. The error description is as follows:

```
"ERROR";"Check Context";"The context "Orders Context" in Data
Foundation "NorthWind" contains loops.";"Orders Context";
```

Loops are one of the SQL design traps that will cause wrong results to be displayed if not fixed. We will talk about other design traps and learn how to fix loops in *Chapter 7, The Data Foundation Layer – Advanced Topics*.

Before closing this window, we need to export the check results into a text file. Click on the **Export** button and select a name and path on your operating system to store that file. Then close this window.

> The file is saved in the semi colon (;) delimited .txt format. You can use MS Excel to convert it to a more readable Excel file.

Now, let's fix the raised error. Click on the **Show / Hide Check Integrity Problem** icon:

The following window will be displayed. Click on the **Errors** section and double-click on the error displayed to open it in the Data Foundation layer window:

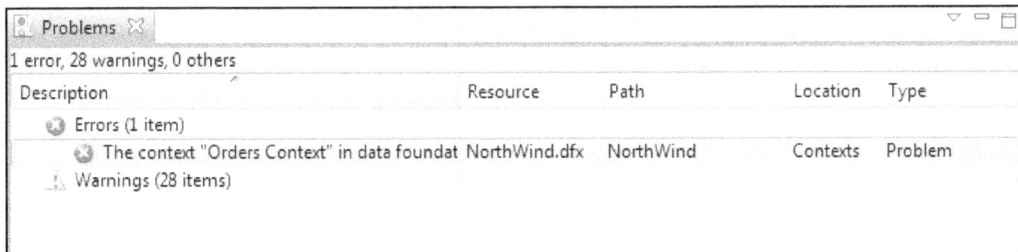

Problems					
1 error, 28 warnings, 0 others					
Description		Resource	Path	Location	Type
Errors (1 item)					
The context "Orders Context" in data foundat		NorthWind.dfx	NorthWind	Contexts	Problem
Warnings (28 items)					

We can also use the **Check Integrity** wizard to check the Business layer integrity in the same way that we used with Data Foundation.

> Business layer rules are different from Data Foundation rules.
>
> The **Check Integrity** wizard in the IDT is equivalent to **Check Integrity** under **Tools** in the UDT.

Finally, we need to make sure that we use the **Check Integrity** wizard every time before publishing the Universe into the repository.

Queries in the Business layer

In the previous section, we learned how to use the **Check Integrity** wizard to find integrity problems. The integrity issues can be automatically discovered and corrected by the IDT. On the other hand, the functional problems cannot be identified without human intervention. We will use the **Queries** tab in the Business layer left panel to generate test queries to test our Business and Data Foundation layers. We can build some queries and validate the results to make sure that our Business model is correct.

We can also build queries in the Business layer to analyze data and check the validity of the SQL query generated from this Business query. It is a useful tool to explore data and simulate what will happen in the Business object reports based on this Universe, without the need to create a customized report to perform functional tests.

> The **Queries** feature has many usages and we will use it heavily in *Chapter 7, The Data Foundation Layer – Advanced Topics*, to check design traps such as loops, chasm and fan traps.

To understand the difference between integrity and logic tests, let's examine the following example.

Open the NorthWind Data Foundation layer and check the join between Orders and Orders Details table to be:

    "ORDERS.ORDER_ID = ORDER_DETAILS.CUSTOMER_ID"

This is of course a no-sense join but let's see if the **Check Integrity** wizard will discover this. Click on the **Check Integrity** icon and select all rules under the **Joins** category and then click on **Check Integrity**, as shown in the following screenshot:

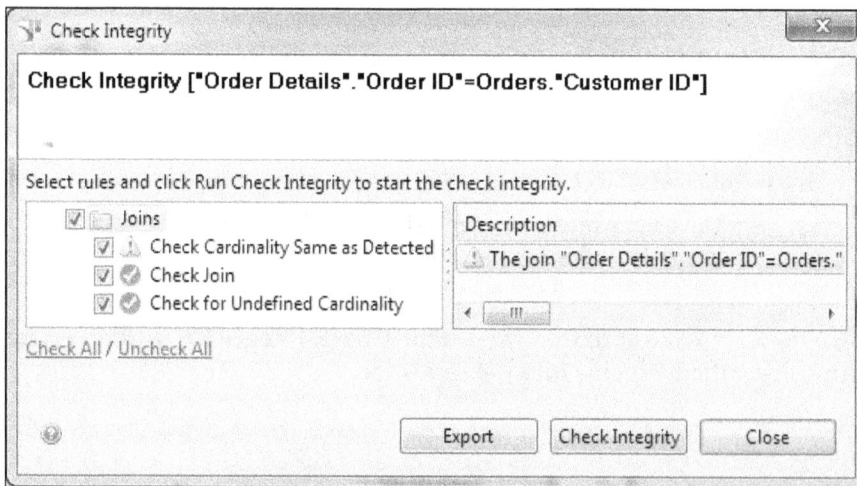

As you can see, only one warning alert is raised which is related to the join cardinality. The warning description is as follows:

```
"WARNING";"Check Cardinality Same as Detected";"The join "Order
Details"."Order ID"=Orders."Customer ID" in the Data Foundation
NorthWind has a different cardinality than the detected
cardinality.";""Order Details"."Order ID"=Orders."Customer ID"";
```

One easy way to discover this issue is to build a query from the **Queries** tab in the Business layer resource to test the join between those two tables with the following steps:

1. Save NorthWind Data Foundation; then open the NorthWind Business layer and navigate to the **Queries** tab from the left-hand side panel. Now, click on the **Insert Query** icon shown in the following screenshot:

    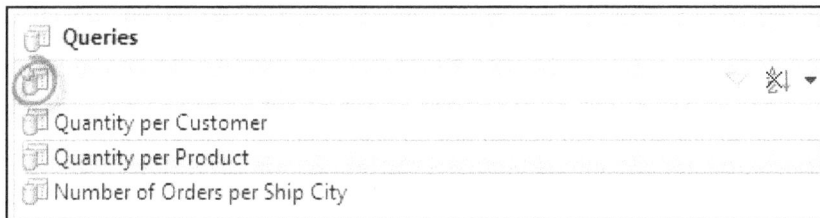

2. The **Query Panel** window will open. After that, we need to build the following queries:

    ◦   For result objects:

        ◦   Orders | Order Date

        ◦   Order Details | Quantity

    ◦   For query filters:

        ◦   Orders | Shipped to Chicago

We can now see the **Query Panel** window in the following screenshot:

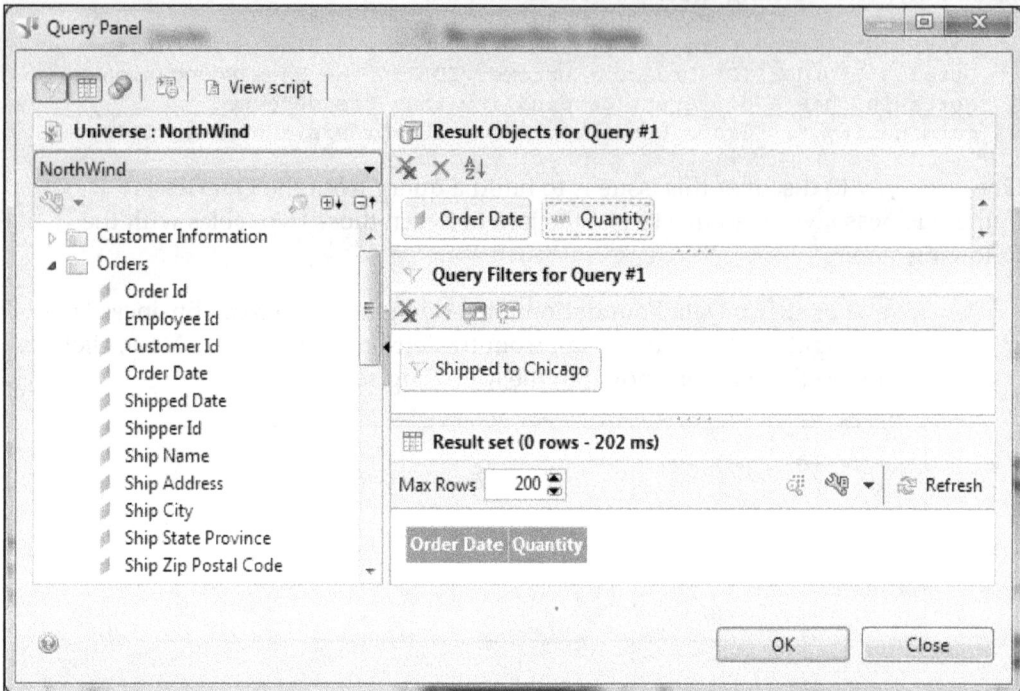

Make sure that you can see the **Data Preview** panel by clicking on the **Show / Hide Data Preview Panel** icon from the above toolbar.

3. Click on the **Refresh** button on the **Data Preview** panel to run the query and display sample results. (**Max Rows** is **200** by default)

    As you can see, no data have been retrieved. This can happen for many reasons such as:

    ◦   There are no matching records for our filter, that is, no orders will be shipped to Chicago

    ◦   There is a wrong join between database tables

    ◦   There is a data profile applied to the logged in user

4. Click on the **View Script** button to display our query SQL script. The following window will be displayed:

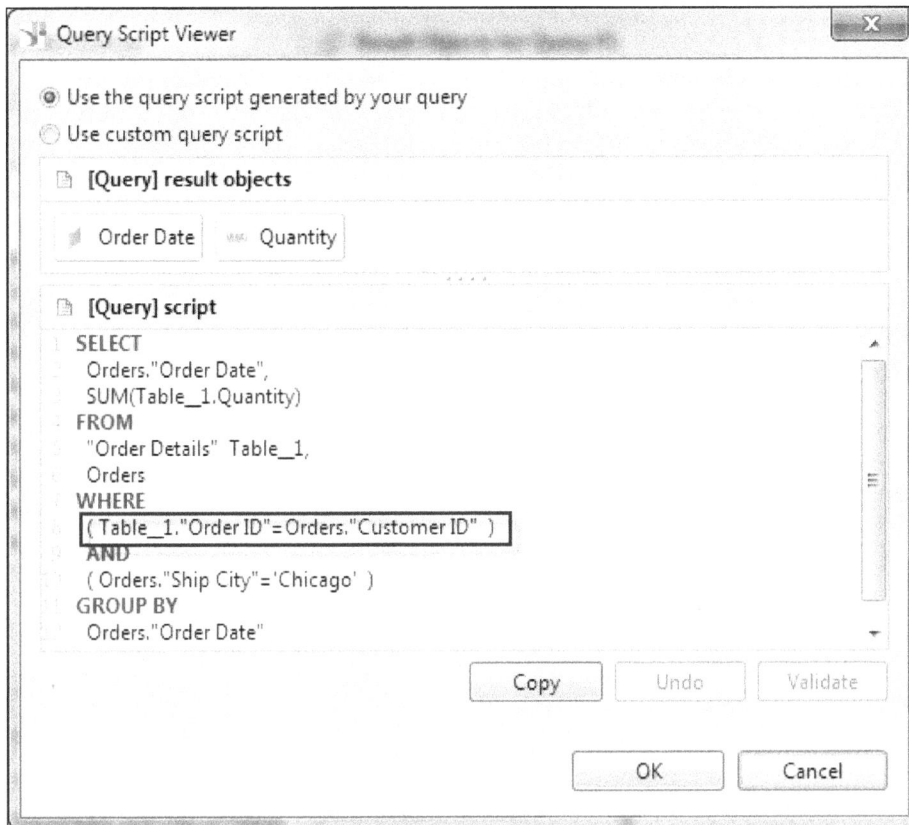

It is clear now that we have a wrong table join between the `Orders` and `Order details` tables after reviewing the SQL code. These kinds of errors can't be discovered automatically but you could use the **Queries** feature, build some queries, and check the results to validate your Business model.

Finally, the **Queries** editor is a powerful tool that can be used to build complex queries. We can use it to build:

- Simple (single table) queries
- Combined queries that include the following operators (`UNION`, `INTERSECT`, and `MINUS`)
- Queries with subqueries
- Ranked queries

> The **Queries** feature in the IDT is equivalent to **Query Panel** under **Tools** in the UDT.

Summary

In this chapter, we discussed the importance of testing our Universe before publishing it and making it available to end users. We went through different phases in the Universe development life cycle such as initiation, planning, implementation, testing, and closing. Then we discussed each phase briefly.

After that, we gave special attention to the testing phase as it is our main topic in this chapter. We also have discussed tools to accomplish two main test types: SIT, which can be performed by the **Check Integrity** wizard, and UAT, which can be performed by creating a business query in the Business layer from the **Queries** tab in the left panel.

In the next chapter, we will discuss advanced topics on Data Foundation. We will start with an introduction to data models (star schema, snow flake, and relational models). Then, we will discuss SQL design traps and how to fix each trap.

7
The Data Foundation Layer – Advanced Topics

We already learned how to create a Data Foundation resource in *Chapter 4, Creating the Data Foundation Layer*, and we already discussed the following topics in detail:

- How to insert database objects (database tables and views)
- Creating alias and derived tables
- Creating joins between Data Foundation objects
- Learning Data Foundation toolbars, menus, and features

In this chapter, we will talk about the advanced topics of Data Foundation that are related to the design. The Data Foundation design is a critical part of the success of our Universe, so we need to understand some important design concepts first before starting the design process. This will help us create a proper design for our Data Foundation, based on the collected business requirements.

After that, we will discuss some advanced techniques that can be used to solve some design issues (known as SQL design traps). We will also get to know how to configure and use Data Foundation parameters and properties to control the behavior of our Data Foundation layer.

Finally, we will discuss another important topic, which is **SQL design traps**. SQL design traps can affect the accuracy of figures generated by the queries generated using our Universe and should be fixed before publishing. We will talk about different types of SQL design traps and how to fix each one.

In this chapter, we will cover the following topics:

- Differentiating between OLTP and OLAP
- Differentiating between relational, star, and snowflake schemas
- Data Foundation design techniques (alias table, contexts, and shortcut joins)
- Finding, detecting, and fixing SQL design traps

Design concepts

In the design phase, we should consider the data model that we are going to use even before starting any development activities. This is part of the planning and design phases of the Universe development life cycle that we already discussed in detail in *Chapter 6, Testing Your Universe*. In the design phase, we should define the required database tables and the relationship (joins) between them. Then, the design becomes input for a Data Foundation developer who will be in charge of implementing it. A good design needs a good vision, and we should consider business requirements at this stage as well. It is not a right approach to create a new Data Foundation layer, start adding tables from scratch, and then start inserting new joins between them even if we have the right level of experience to do this. It is always important to take time to talk with the business, to understand their needs and the link between the entities (business rules). This will save time in the future and will make our lives easier when we want to find the impact of a specific change on our design model or Data Foundation. This concept should apply for almost everything in our lives.

In the upcoming sections, we will talk about two main design concepts that we should be aware of. We will discuss the following:

- Different types of information systems
- Different types of DWH models

Information systems

We can divide **Information Technology** (IT) systems into two main categories. The first category is designed to be an operational source system. This system should be able to handle a huge number of transactions in an efficient way, because it deals directly with the end user. Any delay in transaction processing will affect the end user directly and slow the required process. This system will be the source system, which is used as an input to our DWH. An ATM operation system in the banking industry is a good example of this category.

The second category, on the other hand, is designed to retrieve and display information in an efficient way. These systems are usually used for analysis and decision making, and are required to maintain historical information. In this section, we will discuss the main differences between them. We can see some examples for OLTP and OLAP systems in the following diagram:

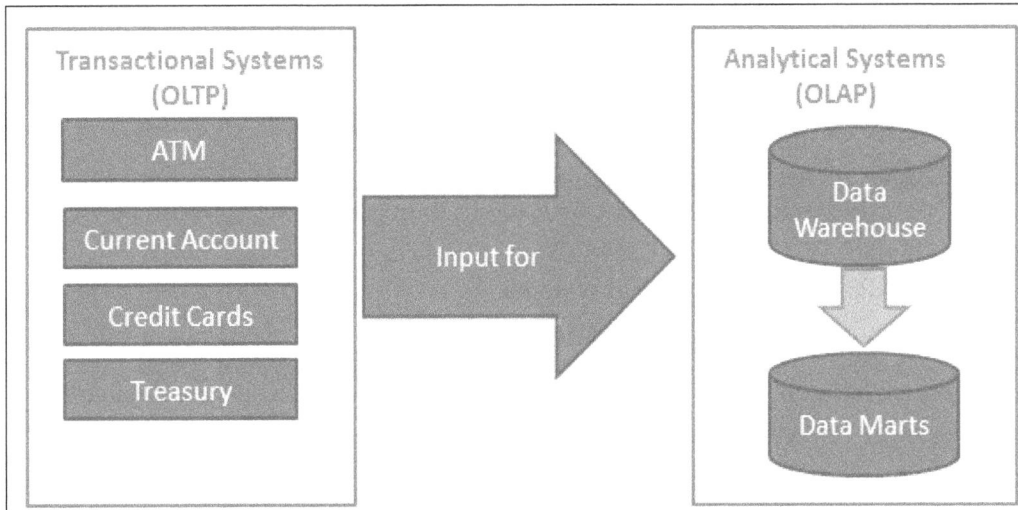

Online transactional processing

Online transactional processing (OLTP) refers to IT systems designed to process transactional operations. The aim of such a system is to manage transactional data with a lot of the INSERT, UPDATE, and DELETE SQL statements. These systems are optimized for writing but not for reading. Imagine that you are in front of an ATM machine withdrawing your money, and you find yourself waiting for 1 minute until you finally get your money because it takes time to process your transaction. This is why we need a system such as OLTP. OLTP systems will be the source input for data warehouse systems. We can find the following main characteristics in an OLTP system:

- OLTP uses a relational database type.
- An OLTP system doesn't require keeping historical information. Historical information is archived and backed up.
- OLTP is used for operational systems.
- OLTP targets end users.

Online analytical processing

Online analytical processing (OLAP), on the other hand, is an IT system designed to retrieve and display data as fast as possible. The main purpose of such a system is to optimize the reporting process by providing the right information at the right time. DWH is an OLAP system that is designed for reporting purposes only. OLAP-generated reports are used by executives and decision makers to analyze information and take actions. The main characteristics of an OLAP system are as follows:

- OLAP can use a multidimensional database type.
- An OLAP system requires keeping historical information. This information is very important for trend analysis. No backup is required, as it can be loaded again from source OLTP systems.
- OLAP is used for analytical systems.
- OLAP targets executives and decision makers.

There are three types of OLAP systems. These types differ based on the database schema type used. They are as follows:

- **ROLAP**: Relational online analytical processing
- **MOLAP**: Multidimensional online analytical processing
- **HOLAP**: Hybrid online analytical processing (a mix of relational and multidimensional databases are used)

In the following section, we will discuss database schema types in more detail.

The DWH schema types

In this section, we will talk about the difference between snowflake, star, and relational schemas.

The snowflake schema

A snowflake schema is a multidimensional model in which a fact table is in the middle and all other dimensional tables are around the fact table. The fact table should contain all measures and figures, as well as reference keys to dimensions. The dimension table can be linked to another dimension as well.

In the example in the following diagram, we can see that there are multiple levels of the `Product` and `Store` dimensions:

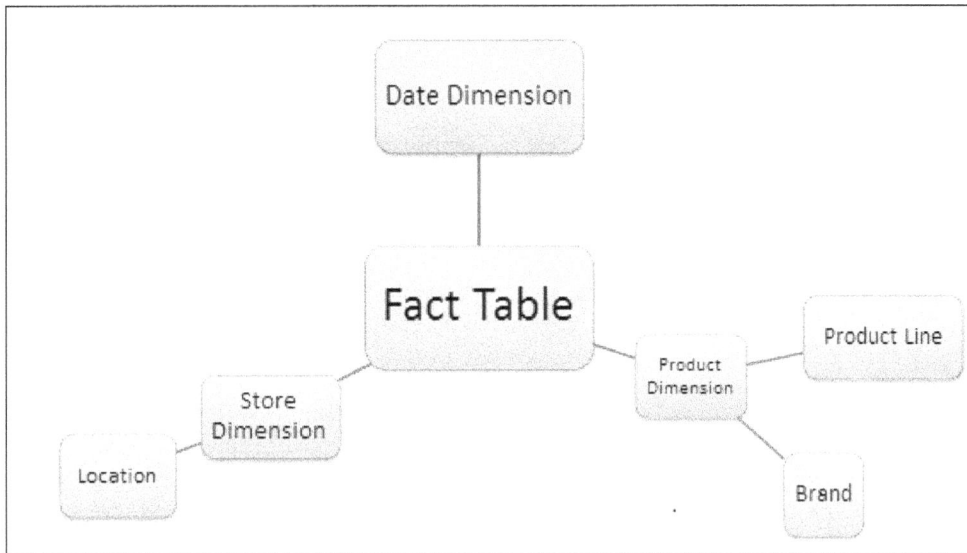

The star schema

A star schema is a special type of snowflake that takes place when the fact table comes in the middle, and there is only one level of dimension tables. This means that the relation is between the fact table and dimensional tables, and there is no relation between the dimension tables. The star schema is equivalent to the data mart, which means that we will aggregate the required data along with the required dimension. The following diagram shows an example of the star schema:

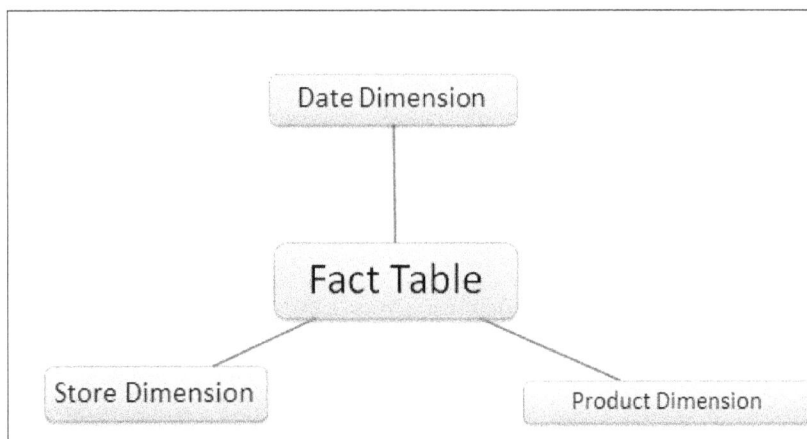

The relational model

In the relational model, relational database entities are used. We can also note that there are no fact or dimension entities in this model, and most entities are in the deformalized form. This model is most suitable for OLTP systems.

> For more information on design concepts and best practices, you can refer to *Ralph Kimball* design books at http://www.kimballgroup.com/.

Advanced design techniques of Data Foundation

In this section, we will talk about some features that will help us later in this chapter to solve SQL design traps. The main idea of the design techniques presented here is to control the SQL queries generated from our Universe. We will learn how to control the number of returned queries based on the selected objects.

Alias tables

An alias table, as discussed in *Chapter 4, Creating the Data Foundation Layer*, is a named copy of another database entity (table/view). We already learned how to create an alias table, and here we will learn how to use it to fix SQL design traps.

Context

Context is a join path definition between Data Foundation entities. The SQL engine will create and submit a separate query for each context. This will only take place if we have a report or query that contains business objects that refer to more than one context. We will learn how to create context to fix SQL design traps in the *SQL design traps* section.

> In the UDT, we can insert context by navigating to **Insert | Context**.

The shortcut join

A shortcut join is a join that will be decided at the runtime. We have, for example, three tables (Order Details, Products, and Purchase Order Details), and we join them as shown in the following figure:

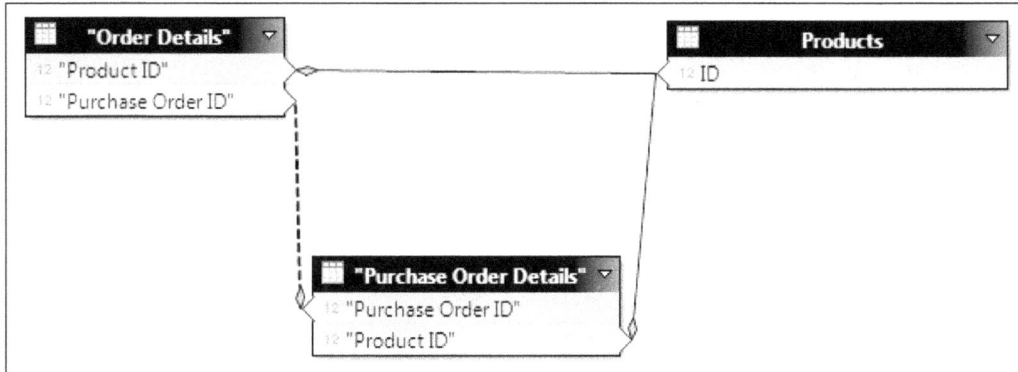

We have the following properties for shortcut joins:

- The shortcut join is presented as a dotted line to differentiate it from the normal join (join **3** in the preceding figure)

- Join will be included in the generated SQL query only if we need it to complete the link between the selected tables

To understand this, let's have an example:

- Let's consider a scenario where join **3** exists (the normal join). In this scenario, we will face the SQL design trap (loop), and we will get wrong results if we have a query based on the three tables mentioned earlier. We will discuss loops in detail in the *SQL design traps* section.

- Let's consider a scenario where join **3** does not exist (the normal join). In this scenario, we don't have a direct join between the Order Details and Purchase Order Details tables. If we have a query based only on these two tables, we will be forced to go to the Products table, as there is no direct path between the Order Details and Purchase Order Details tables.

- Let's consider a scenario where join **3** is a shortcut join. In this scenario, we will convert join **3** from a normal join to a shortcut join. In this case, this join will be only submitted if we make a query to retrieve data from the Order Details and Purchase Order Details tables (the case is explained in the second scenario). This is why we call it a shortcut join, because it will take the short path instead of the long one (Order Details, Products, and Purchase Order Details). On the other hand, this join will be treated as a nonexistent join if we have a query based on all three tables mentioned earlier (Scenario 1). Hence, we broke the loop.

These three scenarios are shown in the following screenshot:

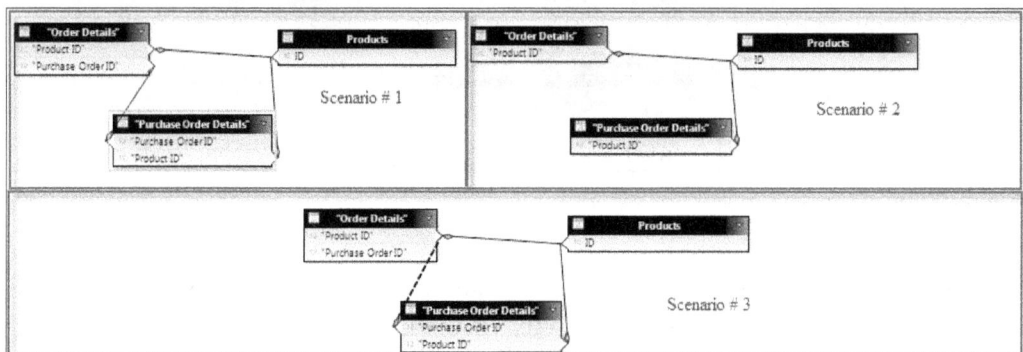

In the following section, we will talk about Data Foundation parameters.

Advanced Data Foundation properties

We have some advanced Data Foundation layer properties that can be used to control many aspects related to this layer.

To open Data Foundation layer properties, perform the following steps:

1. Open the NorthWind Data Foundation.
2. Navigate to the **Data Foundation** tab from the left panel, as shown in the following screenshot:

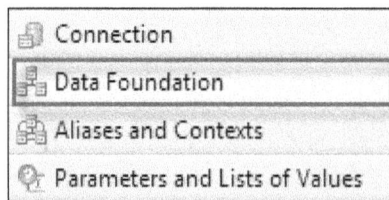

3. Then, click on the `NorthWind.dfx` Data Foundation layer from the upper panel, as shown in the following screenshot:

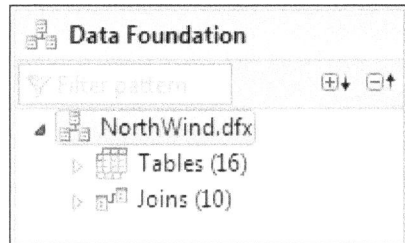

The following window will be displayed:

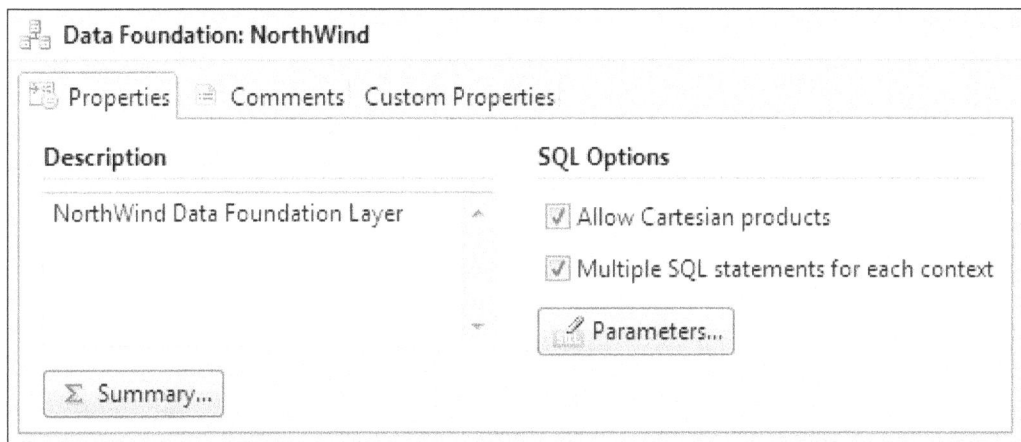

We can use this window to configure and edit the following properties.

Description

Here, we can write a description for our Data Foundation layer. Information about the database and purpose of this Data Foundation layer can be added here.

> A description is something used as a general statement to describe the associated object, while comments are details and can be used to hold information that Universe designers might be interested in checking out and knowing about.

SQL Options

From this properties group, we can enable/disable the following options:

- **Allow Cartesian products**: This option will allow a query to run even if the Cartesian product is detected. The Cartesian product can occur if you try to join two unjoined tables.

- **Multiple SQL statements for each context**: We already discussed this option in detail and how to use it to solve design traps in this chapter.

Summary

We can get a brief summary and statistics about our Data Foundation layer.

> The **Data Foundation Summary** option in the IDT is equivalent to **Summary** in the UDT (navigate to **File | Parameters | Summary**).
>
> There is a separate **Summary** page for the Data Foundation and Business layer in the IDT, while in the UDT, they were combined in one **Summary** page.

We can see the **Data Foundation Summary** window for NorthWind.dfx in the following screenshot:

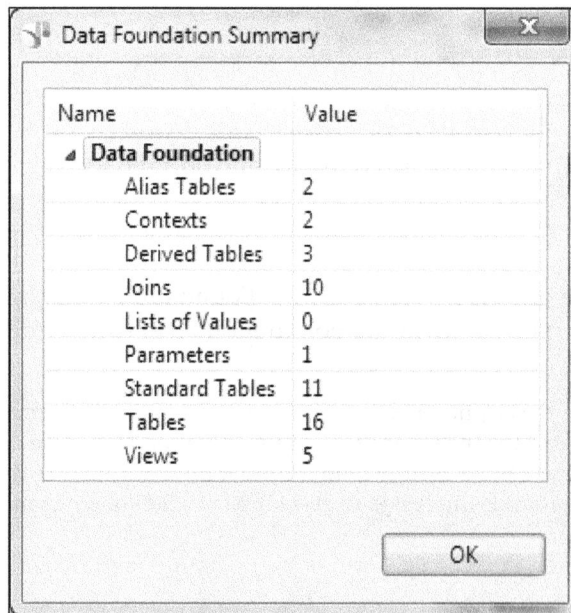

Name	Value
▲ **Data Foundation**	
Alias Tables	2
Contexts	2
Derived Tables	3
Joins	10
Lists of Values	0
Parameters	1
Standard Tables	11
Tables	16
Views	5

Parameters

We can access the Data Foundation parameters by clicking on this icon. We have many parameters, and it is beyond the scope of our book to talk about all these parameters. However, you can see the complete definition for each parameter at the official SAP BO IDT user guide under SAP BO product guide's URL at `http://help.sap.com/bobip41/`.

> Data Foundation parameters in the IDT is equivalent to **Parameter** in the UDT (navigate to **File** | **Parameters** | **Parameter**).
>
> There is a separate **Parameters** tab for Data Foundation and Business layer in the IDT, while in the UDT, they were combined in one **Parameters** window.

We can see the Data Foundation parameter window in the following screenshot:

Name	Value
ANSI92	No
AUTO_UPDATE_QUERY	No
BEGIN_SQL	
BLOB_COMPARISON	No
BOUNDARY_WEIGHT_TABLE	-1
COMPARE_CONTEXTS_WITH_JOINS	Yes
END_SQL	

Note that these parameters are very important, and as a best practice we suggest that you always set **ANSI92** to **Yes** for the query joins to be written with the INNER JOIN and OUTER JOIN keywords to:

- Be SQL-92 ANSI compliant
- Be easier to read
- Keep the code consistent
- Have performance benefits

We can also use BEGIN_SQL and END_SQL to add the SQL script before or after the generated SQL query.

For example, we can set the END_SQL parameter using the (@variable('BOUSER'), @variable('UNVNAME'), and @variable('DOCNAME')) values in order to send the username, Universe name, and report name with each submitted query. This will help the database administrator track locked or long-running queries.

> These are the runtime functions that can be used on the runtime:
> - You can use the @variable('BOUSER') function to get the current BO user
> - You can use the @variable('UNVNAME') function to get the Universe name used to generate the submitted query
> - You can use the @variable('DOCNAME') function to get the report name used to generate the query

SQL design traps

Sometimes, we might find that our query returns the wrong number of records or displays wrong figures. A logical step that we need to follow in that case is to analyze our SQL statement and make sure that there are no missing or no extra joins. The syntax analysis of the query is correct, and it returns a result. The main problem here is that we had the wrong number of records or wrong results, which are different from what we expected. This can happen if you have been trapped by one of the SQL design traps that we will discuss in this section.

Design traps appear when the queries return correct results but the cardinalities between the entities are not well defined. The join might seem to be logical at first glance, but after a deeper analysis we can find that it is not logical to join these tables together. Normally, we need at least three tables and two joins to have a trap. In this chapter, we will discuss three types of traps, but before that let's consider the following tables that we will refer to in this section's examples:

- CUSTOMERS: This table contains the CUSTOMER_ID as well as the customer's information for each customer
- CREDIT_CARDS: This table contains:
    - Credit card number (primary key)
    - Customer ID
    - Linked current account
    - Credit card type
    - Credit card limit

- CURRENT_ACCOUNTS: This tables contains:
    - ° Current account number (primary key)
    - ° Customer ID
    - ° Number of credit cards

> Design traps normally occur in relational models and rarely occur in star schema models.

The fan trap

A fan trap takes place when you join three tables with two (one to many) joins. The joins' sequence should be like one to many between the first two tables and then one to many between the other two tables. To remember this, let's assume that we have three tables (A, B, and C). The fan trap can happen when you join them as A -< B -< C.

Let's take an example; every customer might have multiple current accounts in a bank. The customer can issue many credit cards using the bank's current account. The relationship that we already described can be formulated as one customer mapping to many accounts and one account mapping to many credit cards. This is explained in the following figure:

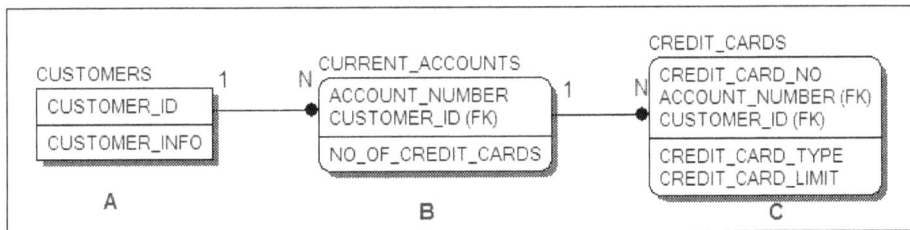

I'm sure that you already started to ask yourself what is wrong with such a relation. This relation sounds clear and logical, but it is not easy to define the number of rows returned by a query on these entities. In fact, the fan trap requires more conditions to occur, which are as follows:

- The query should display at least one dimension from table A.
- The SQL query should contain at least one field (dimension or measure) from table C (right table).
- The query also should display an aggregated measure based on table C from table B (middle table). Here, NO_OF_CREDIT_CARDS in the current accounts table (table B) is an aggregated measure, which is calculated based on the CREDIT_CARDS table.

The next query is based on the described example, and we can see that all three conditions already took place here:

- The CUSTOMER_ID dimension is a dimension selected from table A (first condition)

- The CREDIT_CARD_TYPE dimension is a dimension from table C (second condition)

- NO_OF_CREDIT_CARDS is an aggregated measure based on table C; it is stored in table B (third condition)

The following is the SQL query for the described example:

```
SELECT A.CUSTOMER_ID, C.CREDIT_CARD_TYPE, SUM
(B.NO_OF_CREDIT_CARDS)
FROM CUSTOMERS A, CURRENT_ACCOUNTS B, CREDIT_CARDS C
WHERE A.CUSTOMER_ID =B.CUSTOMER_ID
AND B.ACCOUNT_NUMBER =C.ACCOUNT_NUMBER
GROUP BY A.CUSTOMER_ID, C.CREDIT_CARD_TYPE
```

Now, let's translate this into numbers. Assume that the following data is stored in our tables:

CUSTOMERS

CUSTOMER_ID	CUSTOMER_NAME
1	ESSMAT

CURRENT_ACCOUNTS

ACCOUNT_NO	CUSTOMER_ID	NO_CREDIT_CARDS
10000000198	1	2

CREDIT_CARDS

CREDIT_CARD_NO	ACCOUNT_NO	CUSTOMER_ID	CREDIT_CARD TYPE	CREDIT_CARD_LIMIT
45807594625413	10000000198	1	Visa	$ 15,000.00
54897564123569	10000000198	1	Master	$ 20,000.00

The output result of our query will be as follows:

CUSTOMER_ID	CREDIT_CARD_TYPE	NO_OF_CREDIT_CARDS
1	**Visa**	2
1	**Master**	2

As you can see, we simulated the fan trap, and our query will return wrong numbers. From our query result, we see that the customers have two Visa cards and two Master cards, which is wrong. We can see also that it is very easy to overcome the fan trap by adjusting our objects in the Business layer.

> The fan trap will occur if we displayed CREDIT_CARD_ LIMIT instead of CREDIT_CARD_TYPE in our query as well. The fan trap appears because of the NO_OF_CREDIT_CARDS columns, which is from the middle table (table B) that is based on the third table (table C). At the same time, our query will select from all three tables; this will result in the use of the two (one to many) defined joins.

Before we start discussing how to fix fan traps, let's first try to identify the fan trap case from the NorthWind Universe that we will work on.

First, open the NorthWind Data Foundation layer and check the relation between the following three tables:

- Customer
- Orders
- Order Details

As you can see in the following figure, the relation between these tables is one to many between the Customers and Orders tables, as one customer can have many orders. The relation is also one to many between the Orders and Order Details tables, as one order can have many records in the Order Details table. This means that the first part of the fan trap, which is relation cardinality between tables in Data Foundation, already took place.

The second part of the fan trap will depend on the query (Business layer). This means that it is possible that all queries against these three tables will not return a wrong number of records. Only queries that satisfy the three conditions defined earlier in this section will cause the fan trap and return the wrong number of records.

The relation between these three tables is shown in the following figure:

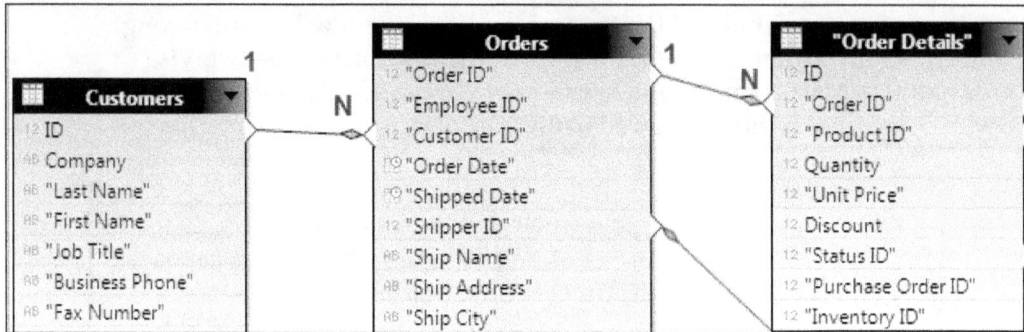

Now, let's build a query to simulate the fan trap with the following steps:

1. Go to the `NorthWind` Business layer.

2. Select **Queries** from the left panel in the `NorthWind` **Business Layer** window.

3. Create a new query based on the information displayed in the following table:

Result objects	Customers.Id
	Customers.First Name
	Customers.Last Name
	Orders.Order Id
	Orders.Shipping Fee
	Order Details.Id
	Products.Product Name
	Order Details.Quantity
Query filters	Customers.Id = 3

The query results should be like the following screenshot:

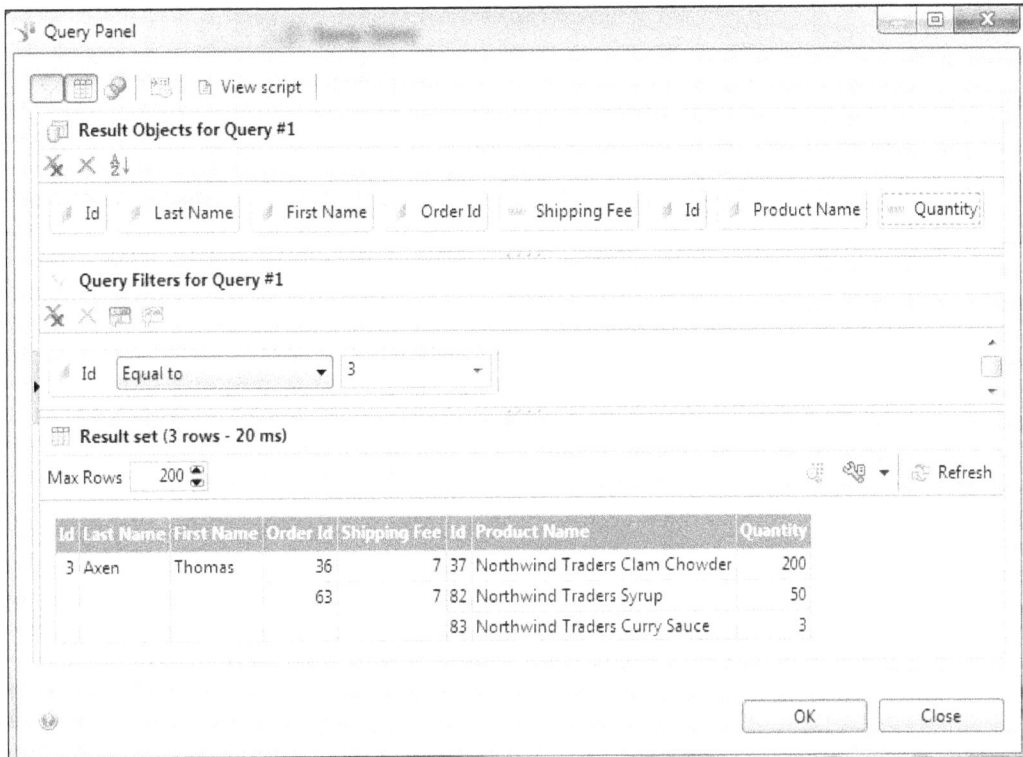

As you can see, **Thomas** placed two orders. The first one (Order ID: 36) is 200 clam chowders. The second one (Order ID: 63) is 50 syrups and 3 sauces. The shipping fees for the first as well as for the second order is $7.

Now, let's try to remove `Order Details: Id` and `Products: Product Name` and see what will happen. The result is displayed in the following screenshot:

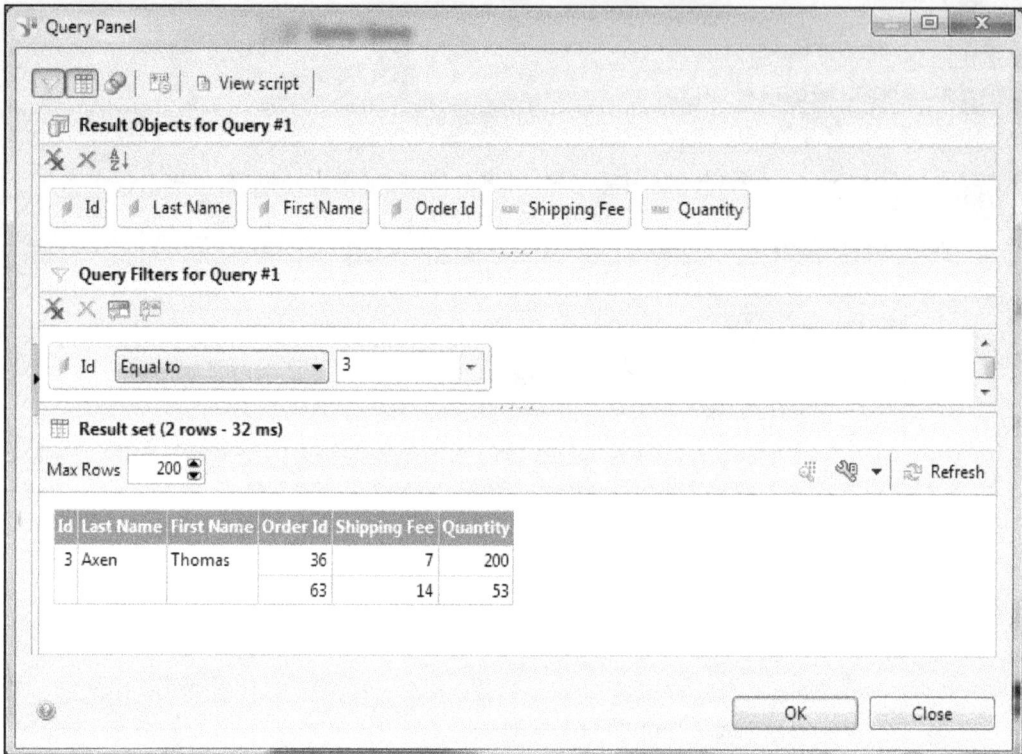

As you can see, the shipping fees for the first order is $7 as expected, but for the second orders it shows $14. This is because the first order has only one order detail record, while for the second order there are two order details records. This is because the second order is a set of two different products. Before we move forward, let's check the SQL query behind this example by clicking on **View Script**. The SQL query is shown in the following screenshot:

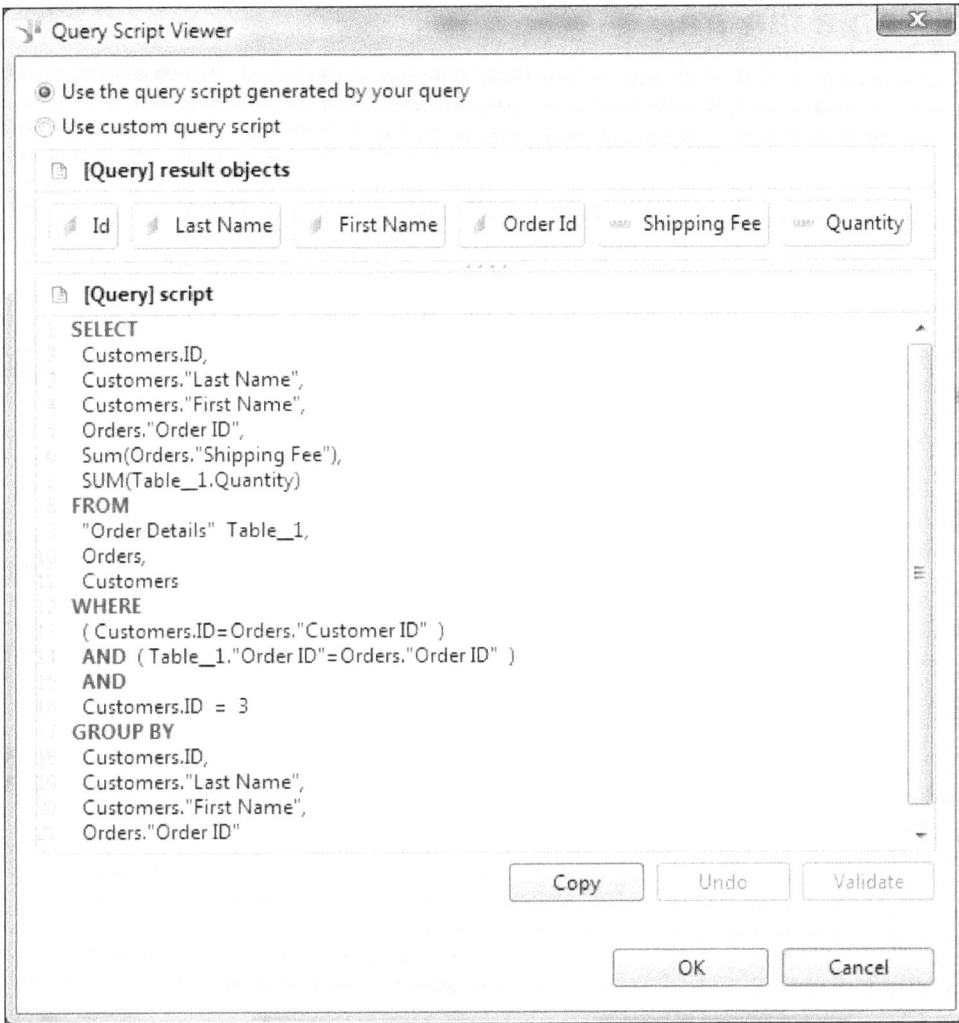

```
Query Script Viewer                                              X

  Use the query script generated by your query
  Use custom query script

  [Query] result objects

    Id      Last Name     First Name     Order Id     Shipping Fee     Quantity

  [Query] script

    SELECT
      Customers.ID,
      Customers."Last Name",
      Customers."First Name",
      Orders."Order ID",
      Sum(Orders."Shipping Fee"),
      SUM(Table_1.Quantity)
    FROM
      "Order Details"  Table_1,
      Orders,
      Customers
    WHERE
      ( Customers.ID=Orders."Customer ID" )
      AND ( Table_1."Order ID"=Orders."Order ID" )
      AND
      Customers.ID = 3
    GROUP BY
      Customers.ID,
      Customers."Last Name",
      Customers."First Name",
      Orders."Order ID"

                          Copy        Undo        Validate

                                     OK          Cancel
```

As you can see, it is only one query. Finally, save the query, because we will run it again after we apply the fix.

In the following section, we will find how to fix the previous aggregation issue.

Solving a fan trap

The fan trap is not harmful like other design traps. Actually, we can live with many fan traps in our Universe if we handle them in our business model or even if we simply enable a feature in our Universe preferences.

The solution is to enable **Multiple SQL statements for each measure**. This option is available under the Business layer properties. To access it, we need to perform the following steps:

1. Open `NorthWind` Business layer from the **Local Projects** window.

2. Select the **Business Layer** tab from the left panel in the `NorthWind` **Business Layer** window.

3. Select the `NorthWind` Business layer.

4. Make sure that the Business layer properties are displayed, and then select the **Query Options** tab.

5. Check the **Multiple SQL statements for each measure** checkbox, as shown in the following screenshot:

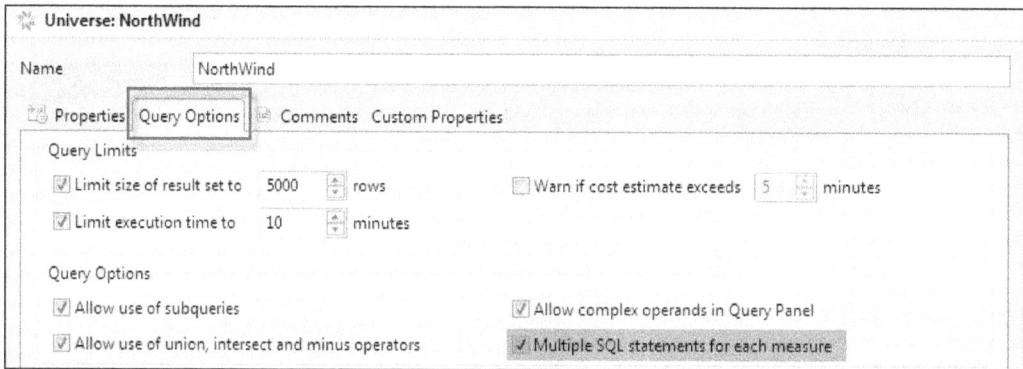

After you open the `NorthWind` Business layer, you can control what you want to see on the right panel. By default, it will display the Data Foundation layer and Business layer together. You can expand any one of them at any time so that you can see only the Data Foundation layer or only the Business layer properties on the right panel, as shown in the following screenshot:

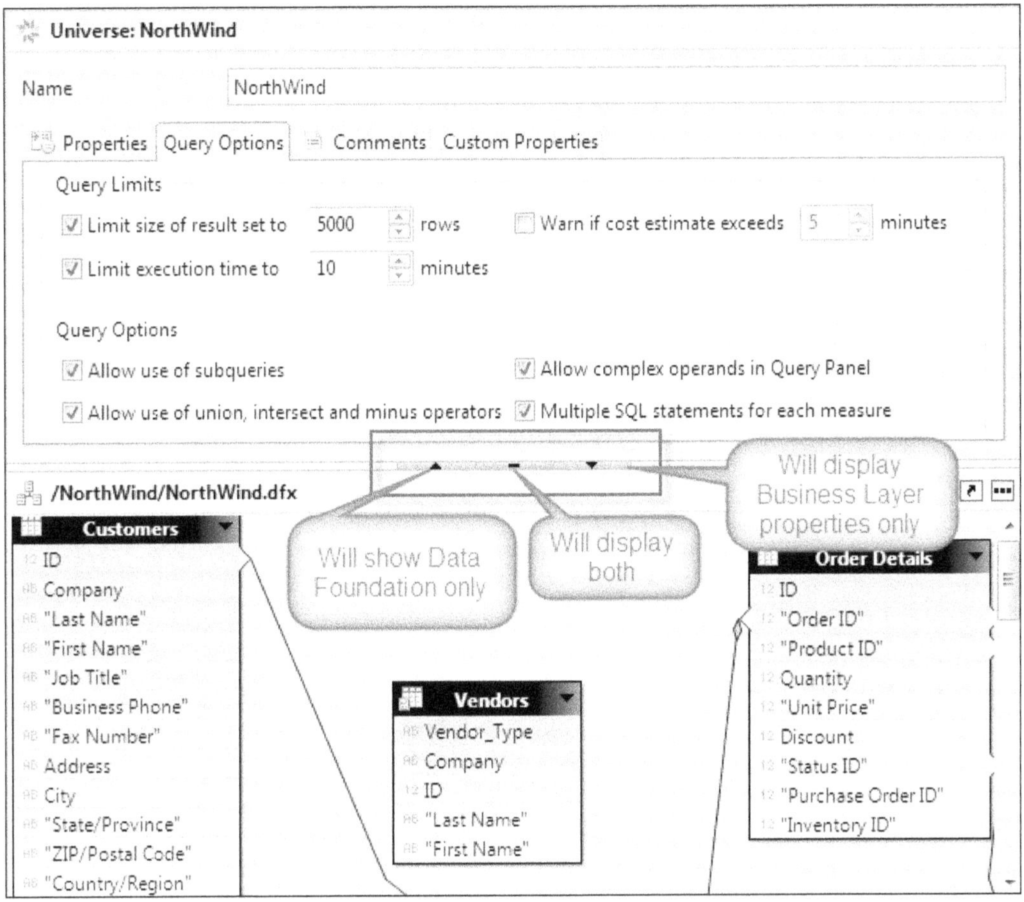

Now, let's go back to the NorthWind Business layer and see how this will solve our fan trap. Open the query that we saved earlier and click on **Execute Query**. You should see the following output:

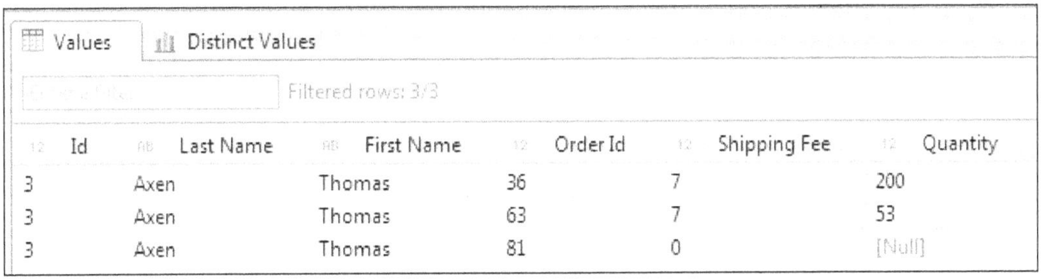

Id	Last Name	First Name	Order Id	Shipping Fee	Quantity
3	Axen	Thomas	36	7	200
3	Axen	Thomas	63	7	53
3	Axen	Thomas	81	0	[Null]

As you can see, the issue is fixed, and now our query returns the correct values. The shipping fees are not summed; as a result, there are two lines with the **7** value. To find out why, click on **Edit Query** and then on **View Script**. We can see the SQL script generated by our query in the following screenshot:

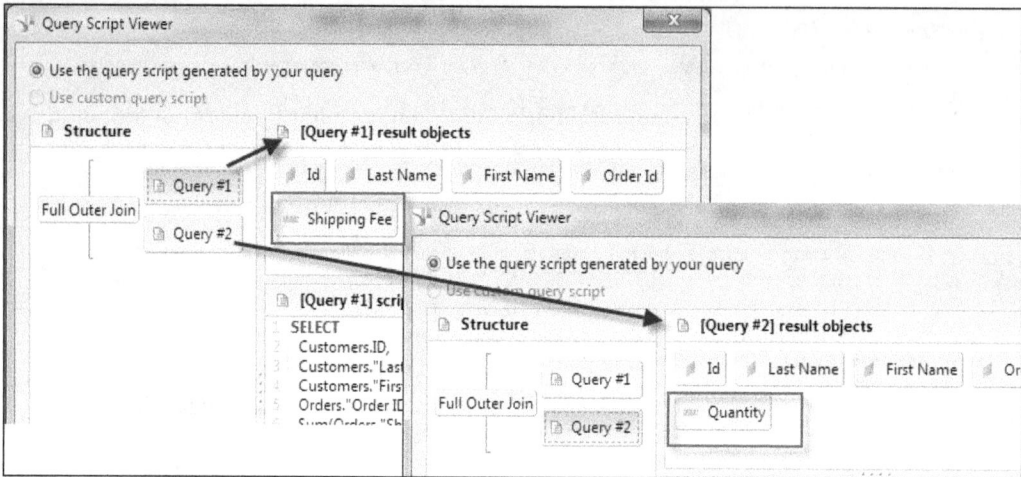

The Universe engine will generate separate queries for each set of measures in our query. This is the main purpose of checking the **Multiple SQL statements for each measure** option in Universe properties. This will allow the Universe query engine to discover if there is a possible fan trap based on the defined cardinality between tables. Then, it will generate a separate SQL statement for each set of measures.

> A set of measures are measures which come from the same table. For example, if we added discount to our query, it will be part of **Query #2** along with Quantity, because they both come from the same Order Details table.

The chasm trap

A chasm trap can take place when two (many to one) joins converge to one table. The joins' sequence should be many to one between the first two tables and then one to many between the other two tables. To remember this, let's assume that we have three tables (A, B, and C). The chasm trap can happen when you join them as A >- B -< C.

Let's take an example; every customer might have multiple current accounts. The customer might also have many credit cards. The relationship that we already described can be formulated as one customer mapping to many accounts and one customer mapping to many credit cards. This example is explained in the following figure:

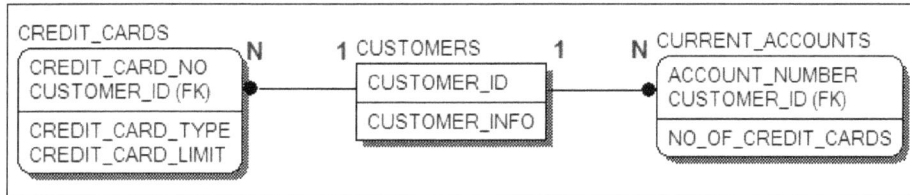

In the following query, we will try to display each CUSTOMER_ID along with the number of credit cards and number of accounts owned by him:

```
SELECT A.CUSTOMER_ID, COUNT (C.CREDIT_CARD_NO), COUNT
(B.ACCOUNT_NUMBER)
FROM CUSTOMERS A, CURRENT_ACCOUNTS B, CREDIT_CARDS C
WHERE A.CUSTOMER_ID =B.CUSTOMER_ID
AND A.CUSTOMER_ID = C.CUSTOMER_ID
GROUP BY A.CUSTOMER_ID
```

Now, let's translate this into numbers. Assume that the following data is stored in our tables:

The output result of our query will be as follows:

CUSTOMER_ID	NO_OF_ACCOUNTS	NO_OF_CARDS
1	4	4

As you can see, the main problem in the chasm trap is that there is no clear relationship between the left and right tables (CREDIT_CARDS and CURRENT_ACCOUNTS tables in our case). We can easily tell which account belongs to which customer. We can also tell which credit card belongs to which customer, but we can't tell which account is related to which credit card as there is no direct join or relationship between these two tables.

Before we start discussing how to fix chasm traps, let's first try to identify the chasm trap case from NorthWind Universe that we will work on with the following steps:

1. First open the NorthWind Data Foundation layer.

2. Insert the Purchase Order Details table.

3. Create a new join between the Purchase Order Details and Products tables using Purchase Order Details.Product ID = Products.ID.

4. Detect the join cardinality.

Now, create a new Data Foundation view and name it Chasm Trap View from the following three tables:

- Products

- Order Details

- Purchase Order Details

The **Chasm Trap** Data Foundation view should look like the following screenshot:

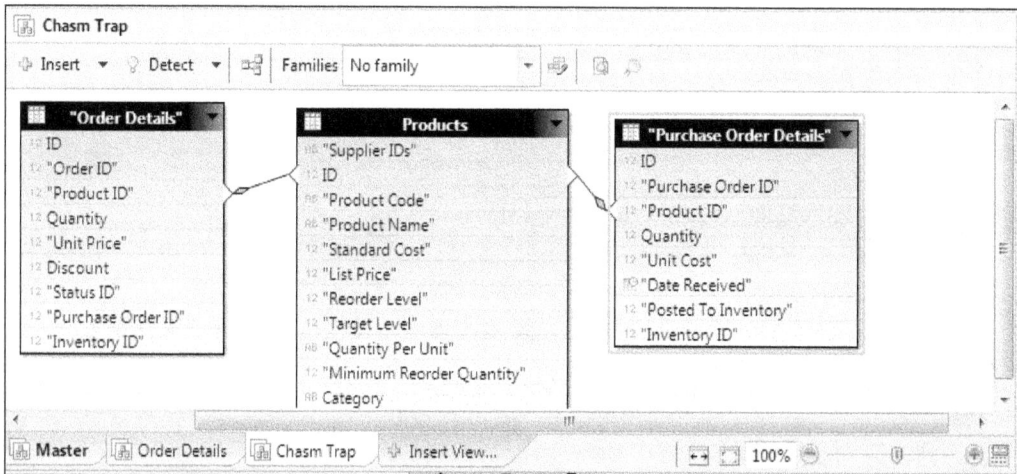

As you can see, the relation between these tables is one to many between the `Products` and `Order Details` tables, as one product can be part of many orders, and this implies that there are many records in the `Order Details` table. The relation is also one to many between the `Products` and `Purchase Order Details` tables, as one product can be part of many purchase orders, and this implies that there are many records in the `Purchase Order Details` table as well. To simplify this, the same product can be sold to many customers through many orders. The same product can also be purchased many from many suppliers when the product inventory is low in quantity.

The question now is if you can identify, with the current defined relationship, the purchase order used to get the current product sold by a specific order. The answer is no because there is no direct relationship between the `Order Details` and `Purchase Order Details` tables. This kind of question could not be solved as we do not have the required data to answer this business requirement. The results will be wrong, and the key figures returned will make no sense.

Go to the `NorthWind` Business layer and perform the following steps:

1. Select **Queries** from the left panel in the `NorthWind` **Business Layer** window.
2. Create a new query based on the information displayed in the following table:

Result objects	`Products.Id`
	`Products.Product Name`
	`Order Details.Id`
	`Order Details.Quantity`
Query filters	`Products.Id = 1`

This query will show us how much was sold of the **Chai** product and by which order. The query results should looks like the following screenshot:

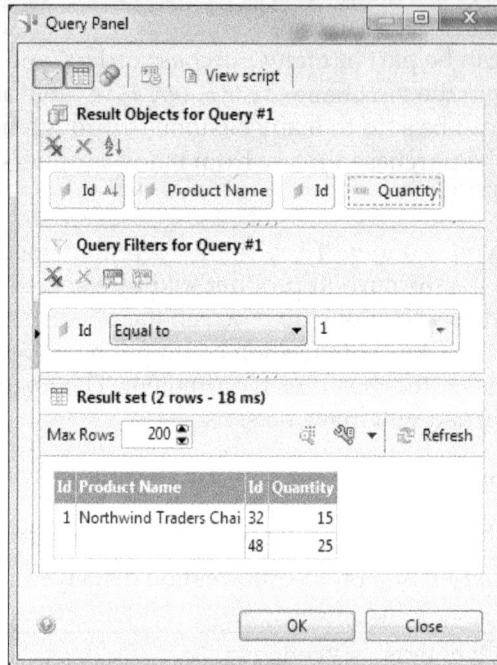

As you can see, **Chai** was sold in two orders. The quantity of the first one (Order ID: 32) is 15, and the quantity of the second one (Order ID: 48) is 25. The total number of items sold by **Chai** is 40.

Now, let's try to query the same **Chai** product but from the inventory point of view. We will try to find how many purchase orders contain the **Chai** product and how many items there are in each purchase order.

Go to the `NorthWind` Business layer and perform the following steps:

1. Select **Queries** from the left panel in the `NorthWind` **Business Layer** window.

2. Create a new query based on the information displayed in the following table:

Result Objects	Products.Id
	Products.Product Name
	Purchase Order Details.Id
	Purchase Order Details.Quantity
Query filters	Products.Id = 1

This query will show us how many items were purchased from the **Chai** product and by which purchase orders. The query results should look like the following screenshot:

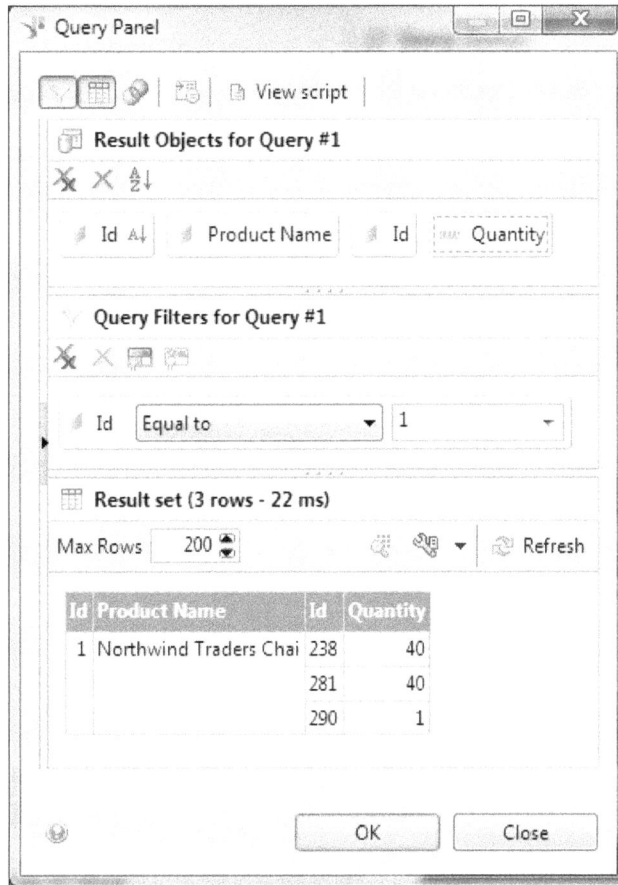

The query results show **Chai** products ordered in three purchase orders (Purchase Order IDs: 238, 281, and 290). The total received **Chai** quantity is 81.

Now, let's query the quantity from both tables:

Result objects	Products.Id
	Products.Product Name
	Order Details.Quantity
	Purchase Order Details.Quantity
Query filters	Products.Id = 1

The query result should be as follows:

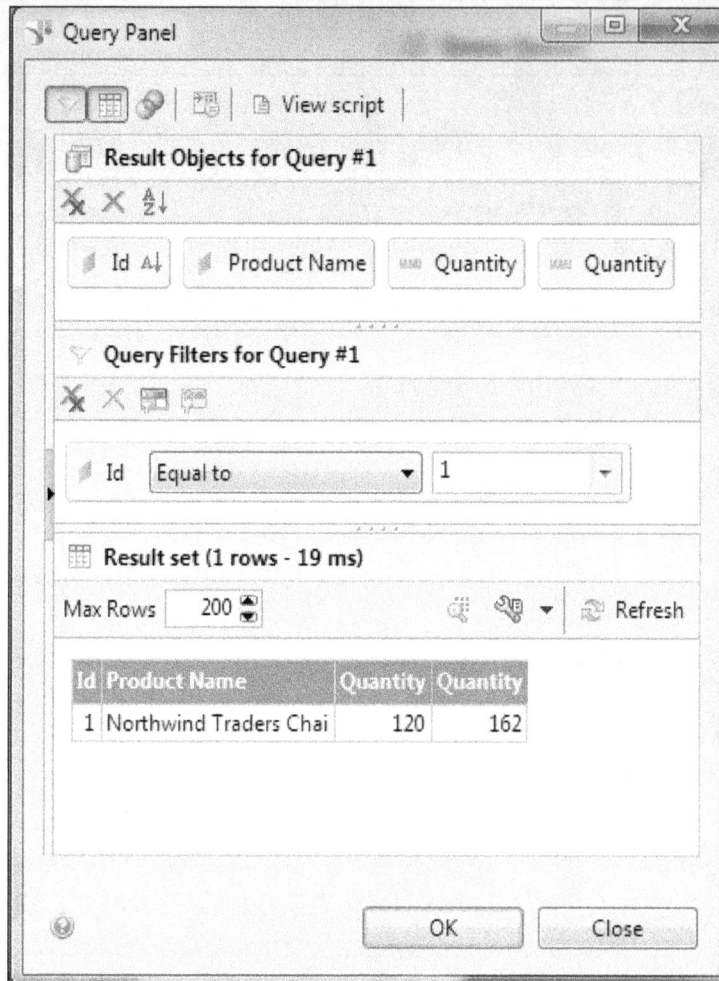

As we can see, the query generated should return the number of **Chai** items sold (40 items. which is the first query) and the number of **Chai** items purchased (81 items, which is the second query). The query result is not as we expected (120 sold and 162 purchased). This is because we have two records generated from the first query (Order Details) and three records generated from the second query (Purchase Order details). Thus, the sold quantity is multiplied by 3 (*120 = 40 * 3*) and the purchased quantity is multiplied by 2 (*162 = 81 * 2*). Save the query because we will use it after we apply the fix together.

Solving the chasm trap using context

We need to understand context and how it works before we start using it. Context is a defined join path that tells the SQL engine to generate a separate SQL query for each context. It is a logical grouping, and in the NorthWind Universe we have two clear contexts, which are Orders and Inventory, as we discussed in *Chapter 2, Aligning BI Solutions with Business Demands*. To define a context, we need to select joins related to the context's purpose.

To create a context, we need to perform the following steps:

1. Open the NorthWind Data Foundation layer.
2. Navigate to **Aliases and Contexts** from the left panel.
3. Click on the **Detect Contexts** icon, as shown in the following screenshot:

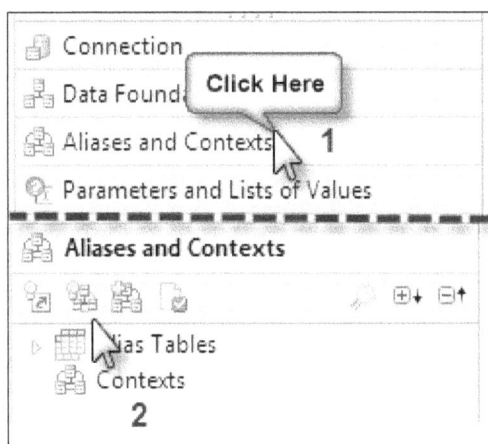

4. Then, select both the suggested contexts. Note that joins that will be included in the context are marked by the green plus sign, while excluded joins are marked with the gray negative sign.

> We can use color families introduced in *Chapter 4, Creating the Data Foundation Layer*, to visually distinguish between contexts.

We can see the **Contexts Detected** window in the following screenshot:

Now, let's go back to our query and run it again. The result is shown in the following screenshot:

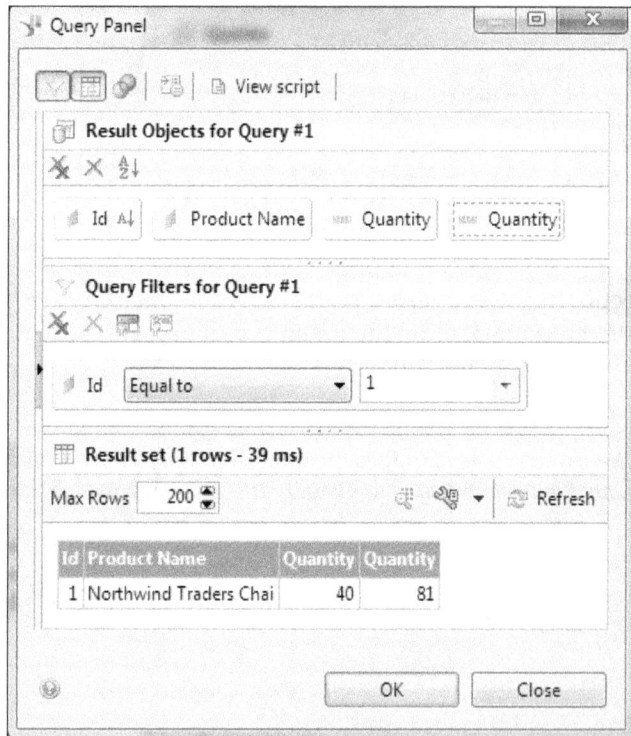

Congratulations! The chasm trap is fixed by the created contexts.

We can also create manual context and add/exclude joins ourselves, but we need to make sure that we define the right join paths, or we might face troubles later on. We might face issues and spend hours to investigate, only to find that it was because of the wrongly defined context.

Solving the chasm trap using an alias table

Context is the most suitable way to solve the chasm trap, but in a complex situation we might find some difficulties in defining the right context. Here, we might use an alias table to fix the chasm trap. In this method, we will create an alias table from the middle table to break the relation between the left and right tables. To make it simple, let's go back to our main example. We have three tables (A, B, and C), and the chasm trap occurs because the relationship between these three tables is A >- B -< C. The solution is to create an alias table from table B, say B*. The relationship should be A >- B and B* -< C) now. As you can see, there is no connection between A and C now, and we can adjust our report query. This can be implemented using a combined (Union) query or the merge dimension feature. From the design perspective, this solution will fix the chasm trap, and we don't have to worry about wrong results or number of records again.

> The main idea of this solution is to split the chasm trap into two independent parts.
>
> When there are several contexts, the user needs to choose the context that will be used. This is a major problem of this functionality because most of the time business people do not know which one they need to choose, so they do not want this functionality in the Universe.

We can find the alias table fix for the `NorthWind` chasm trap example in the following figure:

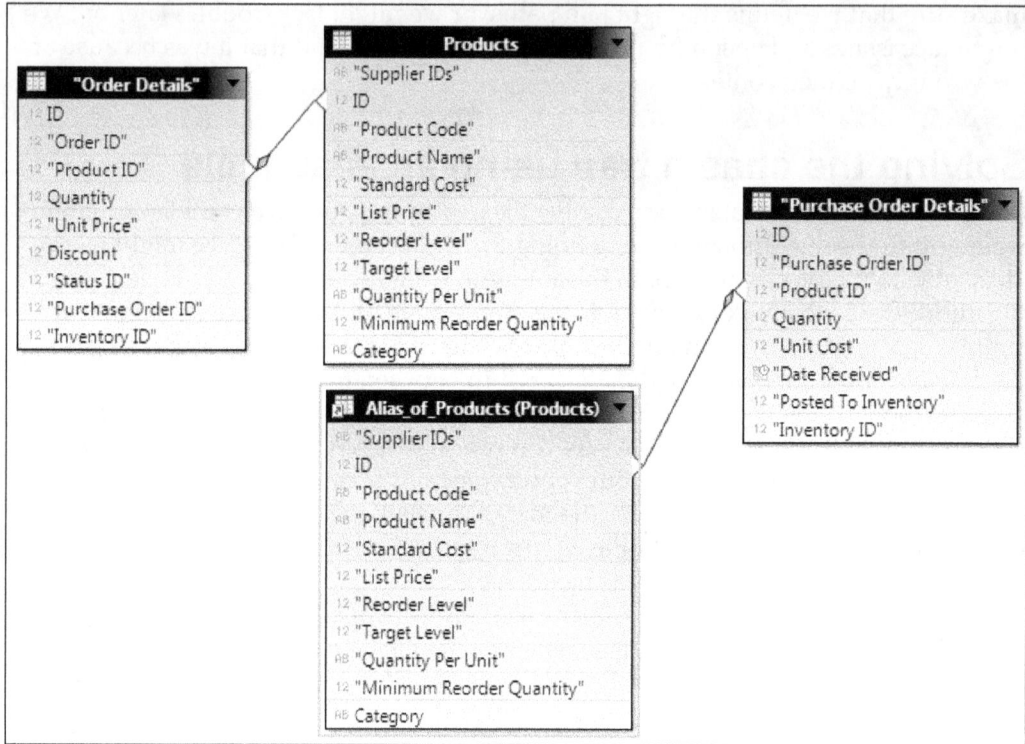

Loop

A loop can take place when you join at least three tables together. This will result in fewer records that are expected when you query those three tables on the same time. For example, if we have three tables (A, B, and C), the relationship between these three tables should be A >- B, B >- C, and C >- A, as we can see in the following diagram. Loops could be represented as circles, and this is the main reason to call this a loop trap simply because there is no start and no end to this relationship, and we will not be able to tell how these tables are linked together using one scenario.

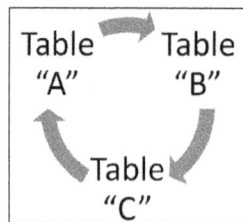

Loops are the easiest design issue to be discovered and solved. Before we start, we need to create a loop in `NorthWind` Data Foundation with the following steps:

1. Delete the two contexts that we created in the previous section.

2. Create a new join between the `Order Details` and `Purchase Order Details` tables by `Order Details`. `Purchase Order ID` = `Purchase Order Details`.`Purchase Order ID`.

Now, we have a loop between the following three tables:

- `Order Details`

- `Products`

- `Purchase Order Details`

To visualize the created loop, perform the following steps:

1. Open `NorthWind` Data Foundation.

2. Navigate to **Aliases and Contexts** from the Data Foundation left panel.

3. Go to the **Loops** area and click on the **Visualize Loops** icon, as shown in the following screenshot:

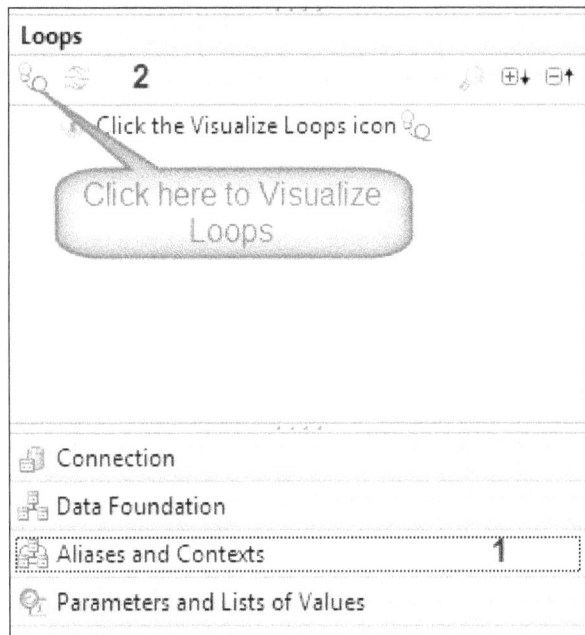

Now, a list of existing loops will be displayed. We should see only one loop because there is only the one we just created. We can select a loop to visualize it on the Data Foundation area, as shown in the following screenshot:

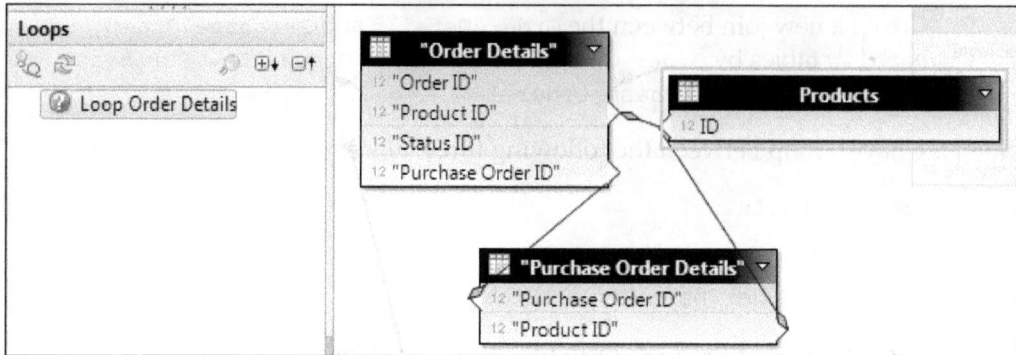

Before we start fixing this loop, let's see how it will affect our last query's results, with the following steps:

1. Go to the NorthWind Business layer.
2. Go to **Queries**.
3. Open and execute the last saved query.
4. Notice the following error message:

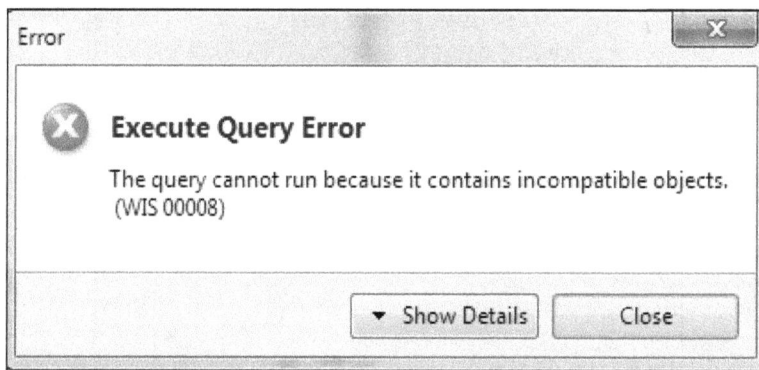

Now, let's try to fix this loop and check the query again.

Fixing the loop using the shortcut join

The shortcut join is one of the options that we can set while creating a new join. If this option is checked, then this will tell the SQL engine to ignore this join when the loop takes place. This will occur when we create a query that selects from tables (A, B, and C), assuming that there is a loop between these tables. This join will be considered by the Universe SQL engine only if we try to select from the two tables involved in this join.

Let's try to implement this with the following steps:

1. Switch to the NorthWind Data Foundation window.

2. Double-click on the join between the Order Details and Purchase Order Details tables.

3. Check the **Shortcut join** option and click on **OK**, as shown in the following screenshot:

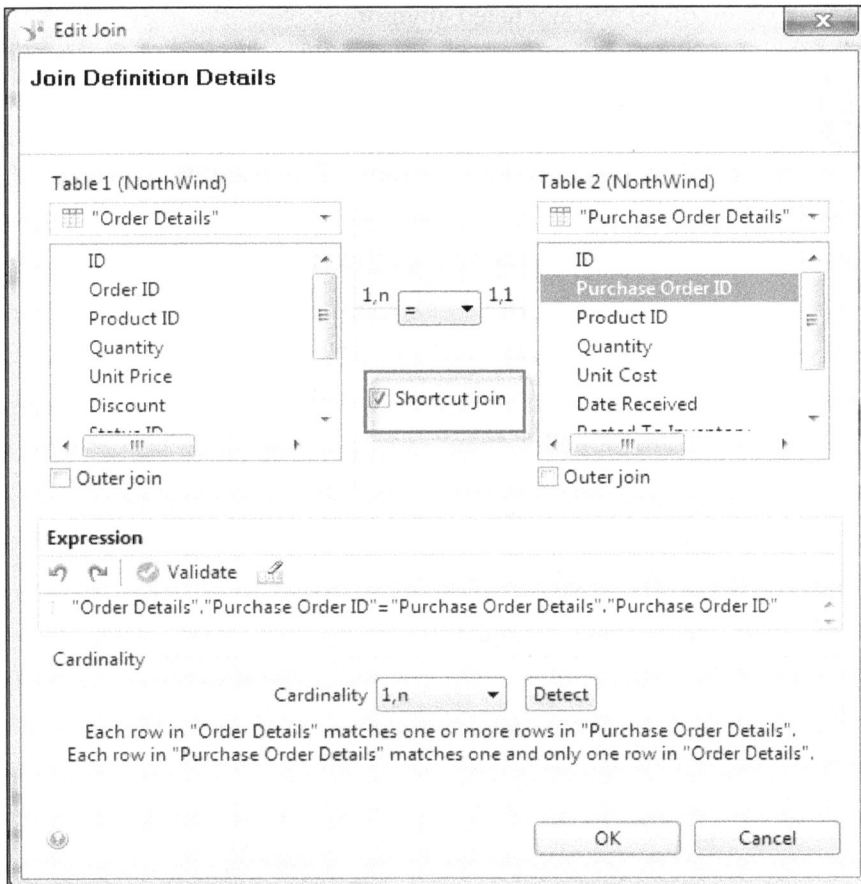

In the following figure, we can see that this join is displayed as a dotted line to indicate that this is a shortcut join:

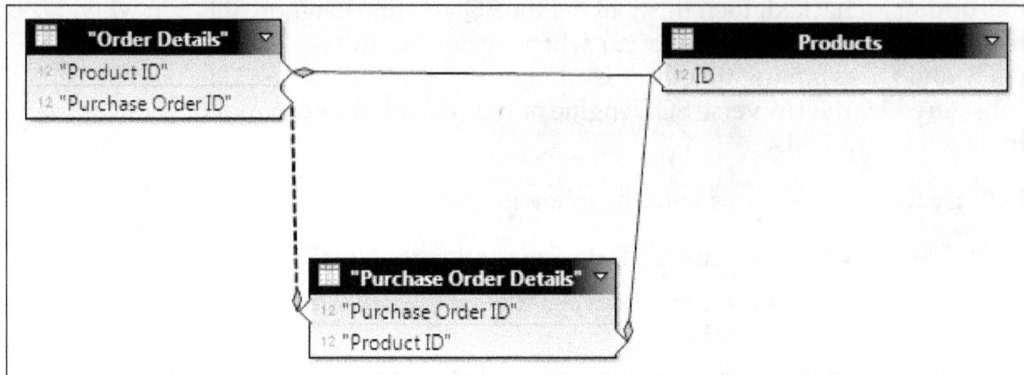

Now, navigate to the **Loops** area and click on the **Detect Loops** icon again. Make sure that the loop is solved and not listed anymore.

Let's go back and execute the last saved query in the NorthWind Business layer. We can notice that we didn't get an error message and the query can be executed, but we got the wrong results. This is because we removed the contexts that we created earlier to solve the chasm trap between these tables. The result is shown in the following screenshot:

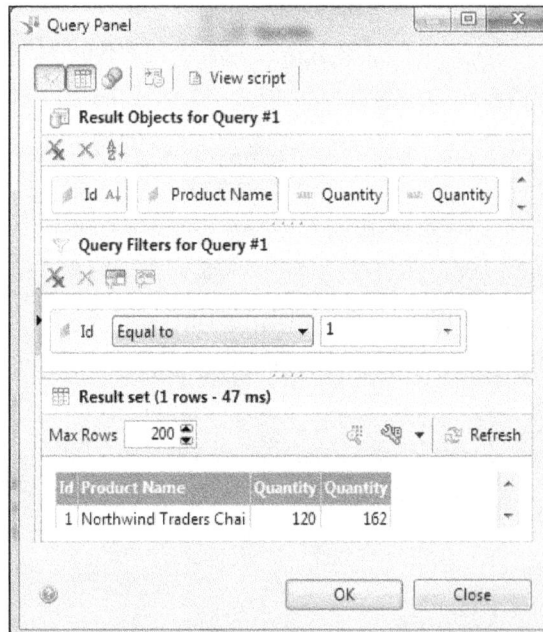

In the next topic, we will see how contexts could solve the loop issue themselves. This is the reason why they need to be deleted before trying to detect loops in the previous use case.

> We usually select the weak join to be the shortcut join. The weak join means the join used least number of times by the Universe/business users.
>
> Try **View Script** used by the query mentioned in the preceding screenshot. Note that the shortcut join is ignored in this case because we selected objects from all three tables. Now, try to remove the product ID and product name. Click on **View Script** again and notice that the shortcut join is used only when we select data from the Order Details and Purchase Order Details tables.

Fixing the loop using context

As we already learned what context is and how to use it, we can now imagine how context will fix the loop. First, let's revert the shortcut join to a normal join. Then, go to the **Loops** area and click on the **Detect Loops** icon. Make sure that you can see our loop listed again.

Before we create context, let's try to understand how this will solve a loop. As we discussed earlier, context is a logical grouping for related joins that will make sure that a separate query is issued for each context. The idea here is that we want to implement this to break the loop. This can be achieved if we categorize loop joins into two categories (contexts).

The main idea of solving a loop by context is to exclude the same join that we nominated to be the shortcut join from both orders context as well as purchase orders context.

Now, navigate to the **Aliases and Contexts** window and click on the **Detect Context** option. We should get the following error message:

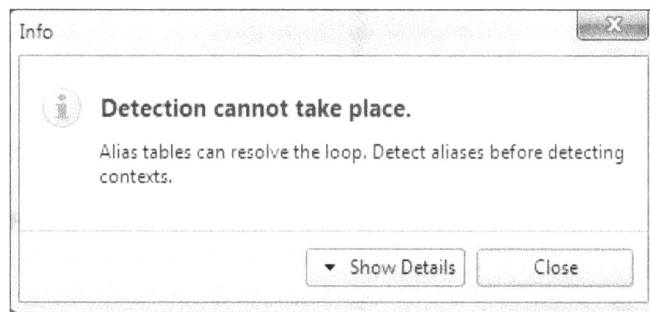

This message gives us a hint that using aliases to resolve loops is preferred rather than using context. We will come back to this topic later, but for now we need to insert two contexts manually as follows:

- **Orders Context**: This will include the following joins:
    - ° `Order Details` to `Orders`
    - ° `Order Details` to `Invoices`
    - ° `Order Details` to `Products`
    - ° `Order Details` to `Order Details Status`

The following figure shows the **Orders Context**:

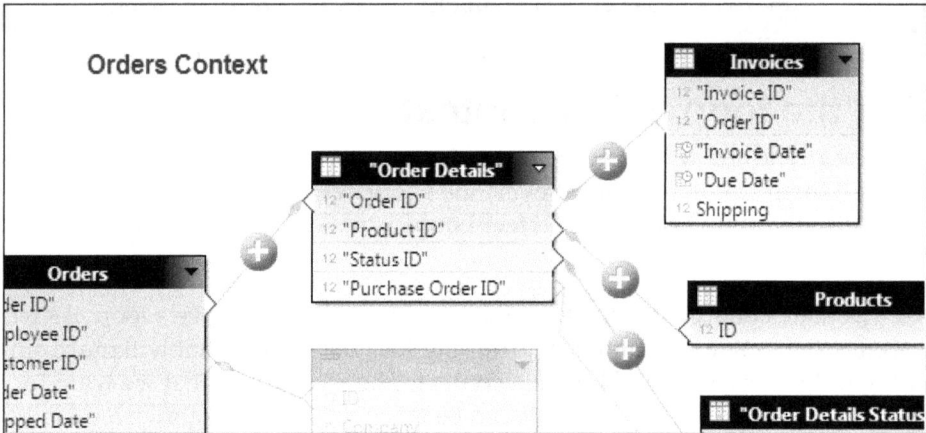

- **Purchase Orders Context**: This will include the following join:
    - ° `Products` to `Purchase Order Details`

The following figure shows the **Purchase Orders Context**:

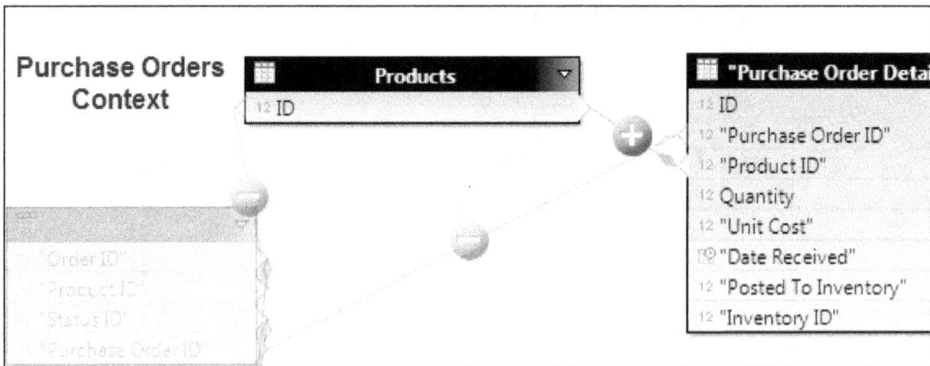

Now, navigate to the **Loops** area again and click on the **Detect Loops** icon. Note that the loop is detected, but it also mentions that the loop is fixed by context, as shown in the following screenshot:

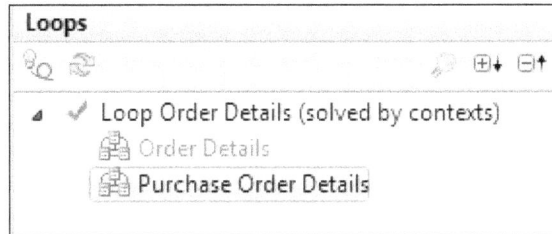

After that, we need to go back to our query and check the results. This time we will get the correct expected results because we solved the chasm trap and loop using the same context.

> We need to make sure that the cardinality is defined for all joins in the Data Foundation layer if we want to use the **Detect Context** feature to automatically detect contexts.

Fixing the loop using an alias table

This is the last method that we can use to fix loops. The idea of fixing the loop using an alias table is almost the same as what we were trying in the earlier two methods. We will use an alias table to break the loop. To do this, perform the following steps:

1. Go to NorthWind Data Foundation and delete the two created contexts.

2. Navigate to the **Aliases and Contexts** window and click the **Detect Aliases** icon. The following window will be displayed to indicate that we need to create an alias table for the Products table to solve the loop:

3. Check the suggested solution, as displayed in the following window, and then, click on **OK** to confirm:

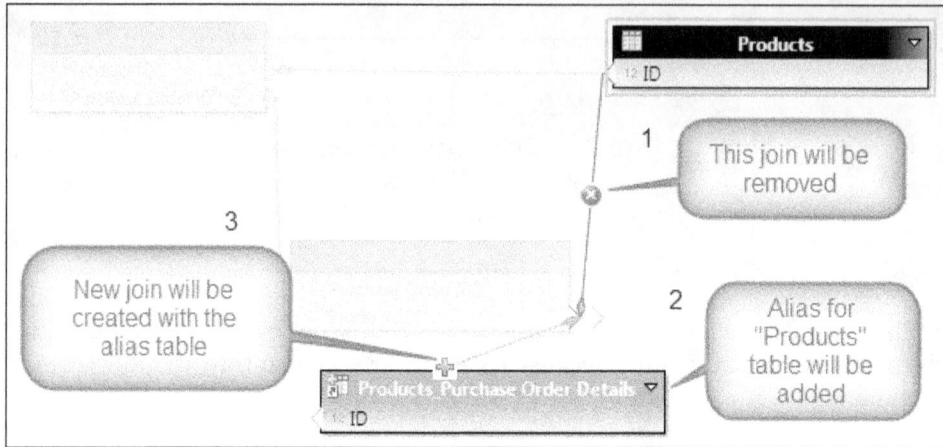

The final solution should be as displayed in the following figure:

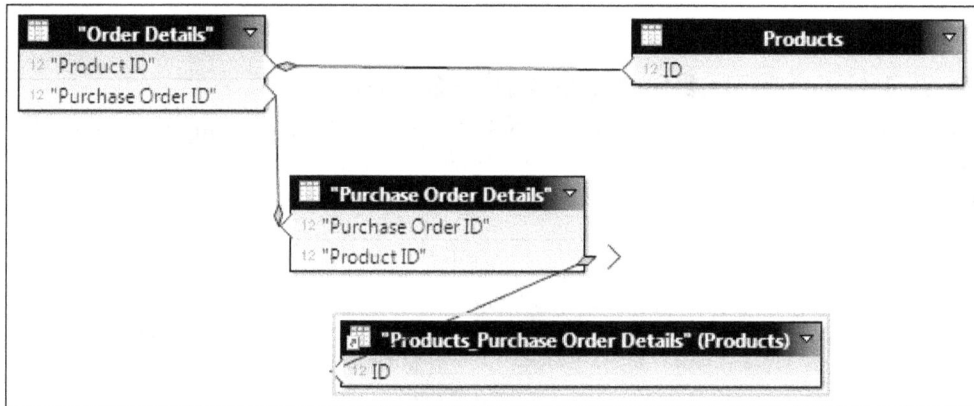

Summary

In this chapter, we had an introduction to information systems such as OLTP and OLAP. Then, we discussed the difference between snowflake, star schema, and relational database design models. After that, we talked about design traps and how they will affect our SQL query. Then, we went through many design traps such as fan, chasm, and loops. Later on, we got to know how to fix each trap using advanced Data Foundation features such as contexts, aliases, and shortcut joins. In the next chapter, we will talk about advanced Business layer features that we haven't introduced yet.

8
The Business Layer – Advanced Topics

In the previous chapter, we discussed many principles and the best practices related to designing the Data Foundation layer. In this chapter, we will discuss some advanced topics related to the Business layer. We already covered the basic concepts of the Business layer in *Chapter 5*, *Creating the Business Layer*. Here, we will cover the remaining topics that we haven't covered yet, such as **list of values** (**LOVs**) and navigation paths. We will also get to know some important advanced features such as aggregate awareness and index awareness. Finally, we will learn how to use the Translation Management Tool to translate our Business layer, and then we will discuss the properties of the Business layer.

In this chapter, we will cover the following topics:

- Creating and using an LOV
- Creating and using navigation paths, which are also known as **hierarchies**
- Using the index awareness feature to make use of indexed columns to enhance queries' response time
- Using the aggregate awareness function to select the summarized table at runtime, based on the selected objects in the report query
- Some functions available in the IDT to BO developers
- Using the Translation Management Tool to translate our Universe
- Learning how to use the advanced properties of the Business layer

List of values

A list of values is used when the end user is prompted to select a value for a specific dimension such as region, for example. Usually, LOVs are assigned with a dimension because they are used in filters. The LOV will generate a query to display the distinct values for the associated dimension.

> We should create LOVs for dimensions with less than 100 distinct values in order to make sure that they are user friendly and easy to navigate.
>
> It is not recommended that you create an LOV for any business object based on the fact table. We should use the dimension table instead. For example, if you have the country code, which is stored in the Customers fact table as a foreign key and in the Country dimension as a primary key, we should then build an LOV on top of the country code stored in the Country dimension table.
>
> It is not recommended that you build an LOV for attributes or measures because it will generate a nonsense LOV, for example, a list of PO box numbers is nonsense while it is better to build LOV on the City dimension in this case. It also does not make sense to build an LOV on the Order Quantity measure, and we should rather use a quantity bucket based on defined ranges of quantities, for example, 0-10 orders will group all orders with quantity between 0 and 10, 11-100 orders will group all orders with quantity between 11 and 100, and so on.

Some LOVs can be assigned to more than one dimension. For example, we can use city LOV with the following dimensions:

- Customer City
- Shipped From City
- Shipped To City

There are different types of values:

- **List of values based on a dimension object**: We can use this type to create a simple LOV based on the Business layer objects that already exist.
- **Static list of values**: We can use this type if we have a slowly changing dimension. A slowly changing dimension is a dimension that will not change frequently, for example, Stat. (surely, we will not need to add a new Stat dimension or modify the name of the existing one).
- **List of values based on custom SQL**: Here, we can create a complex LOV using the SQL editor to write the SQL query that will be used to generate this LOV.

Let's discuss each of these in more detail.

List of values based on a dimension object

In this type of LOV, we will build our LOV list using the query editor. We can add one or more dimensions as well as filters. The LOV can be assigned to a dimension once it is created. The generated output of LOV will be displayed when the end user is prompted to select a value for this dimension. We can use this type of LOV if we want to generate a simple LOV based on the Business layer objects that are already created.

There are two methods to display this type of LOV explained in the following sections.

List of values based on the query panel

To create a LOV using the query panel, we need to perform the following steps:

1. Open the NorthWind Business layer.

2. Go to the **Parameters and Lists of Values** section, as shown in the following screenshot:

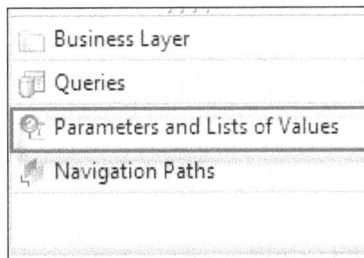

    Business Layer
    Queries
    Parameters and Lists of Values
    Navigation Paths

3. Click on the create new LOV icon and select **List of values based on business layer objects**, as shown in the following screenshot:

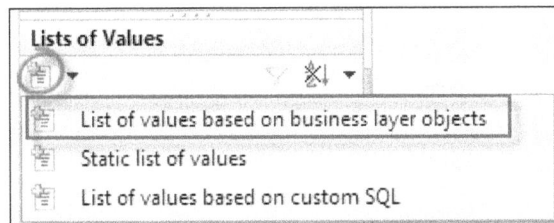

    Lists of Values

    List of values based on business layer objects
    Static list of values
    List of values based on custom SQL

4. After that, enter City in the LOV's **Name** field.

5. Then, select **List of values based on the Query Panel** in the **Definition** tab.

6. Select the `City`, `State Province`, and `Country Region` dimensions from `Demographic Info` under `Customer Information`, as shown in the following screenshot:

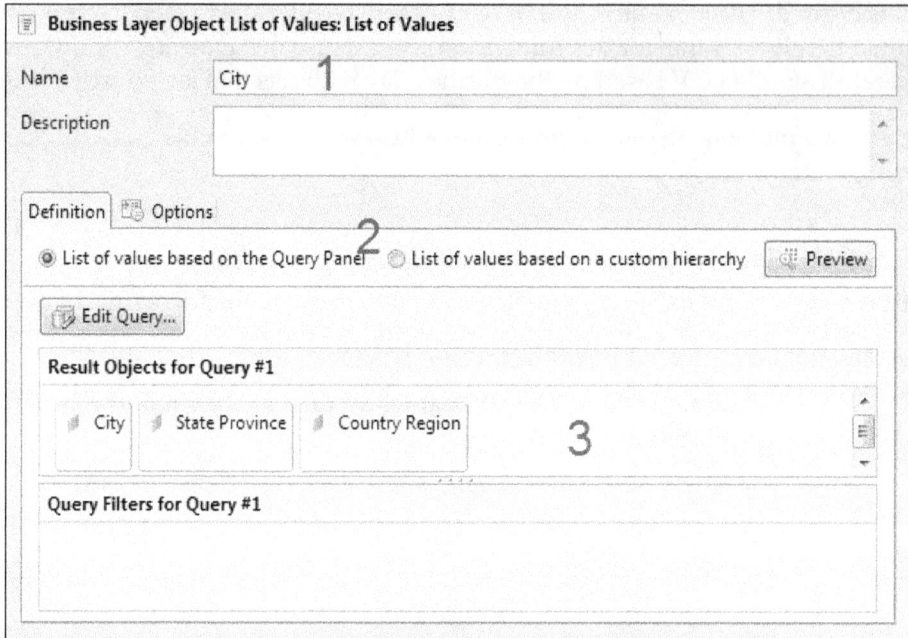

7. Click on the **Preview** icon to display and verify the LOV. The following screenshot displays the result:

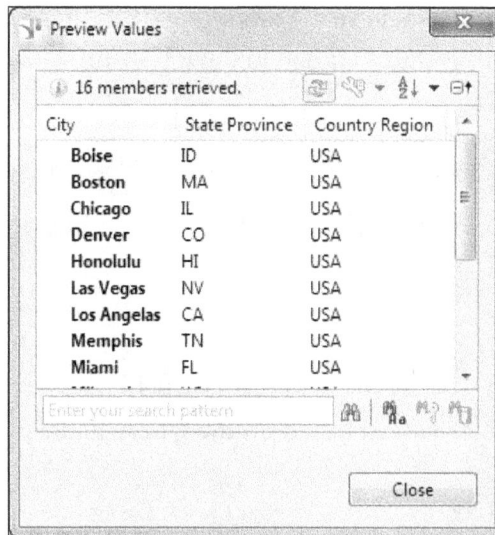

> Only the first dimension will be passed to the associated prompt if you select more than one. The remaining dimensions are displayed to give more information about the selected value.

List of values based on a custom hierarchy

This type of LOV is the same as the previous one. The only difference is that in this type, the LOV will be displayed as a hierarchy instead of in the tabular or raw data format. To create an LOV based on a custom hierarchy, we need to perform the following steps:

1. Open the City LOV, and then select **List of values based on a custom hierarchy** in the **Definition** tab.

2. Add the customer's demographic information in the order Country Region, State Province, and City, as shown in the following screenshot:

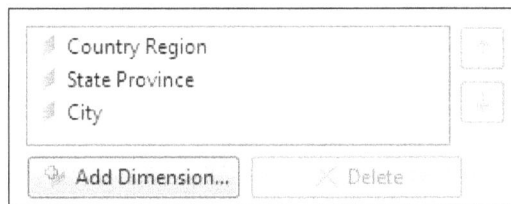

3. Click on **Preview** to display the LOV. The following screenshot displays the result:

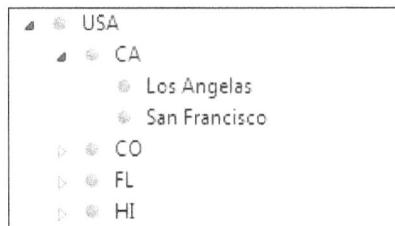

As we can see, the LOV is displayed as a hierarchy. The Country Region dimension is displayed at the first level, but only **USA** is displayed at this level because we have only one value under this level. Then we can see State Province under each country at the second level, and finally, we can see the list of cities under each state.

You can also see that we can expand/collapse any value under any level to show/hide the values under it.

Static list of values

In this type, we can create a static LOV based on some static values stored in CSV files. We can use this type of LOV if the data integrated does not have to be refreshed frequently — slow-changing data.

We need to perform the following steps in order to create a static LOV:

1. Create CSV file with the following steps:

    1. Create a new CSV `Country Region.csv` file using a text editor.
    2. Insert the `USA`, `Germany`, `China`, and `France` values into the CSV file.
    3. The CSV file should look like the following screenshot:

2. Create an LOV with the following steps:

    1. Click on the create new LOV icon.
    2. Select **Static list of values**, as shown in the following screenshot:

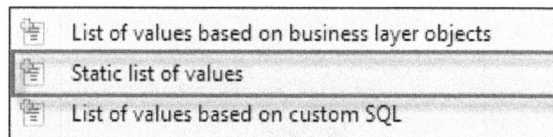

    3. Enter `Country Region` in the LOV name.

3. Import the CSV file with the following steps:

    1. Click on the **Import** icon.
    2. Click on the **Browse...** icon and navigate to the `Country Region.csv` file.
    3. Select **Character** and use **;** as **Data Separator**.
    4. Select **None** for **Text Delimiter**.
    5. Leave **Date Format** as the default.

6. Uncheck **First row contains column names** as we don't have a column header here.

7. Check **Replace existing data with new data** to make sure that you refresh the LOV and use the values stored in the file.

The **Import List of Values** window is shown in the following screenshot:

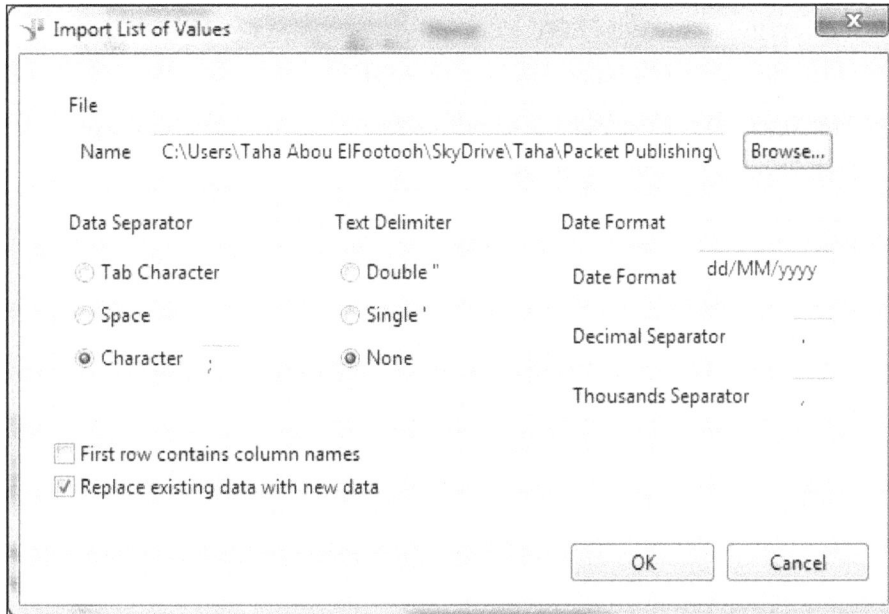

8. Click on **OK**. The following window will be displayed:

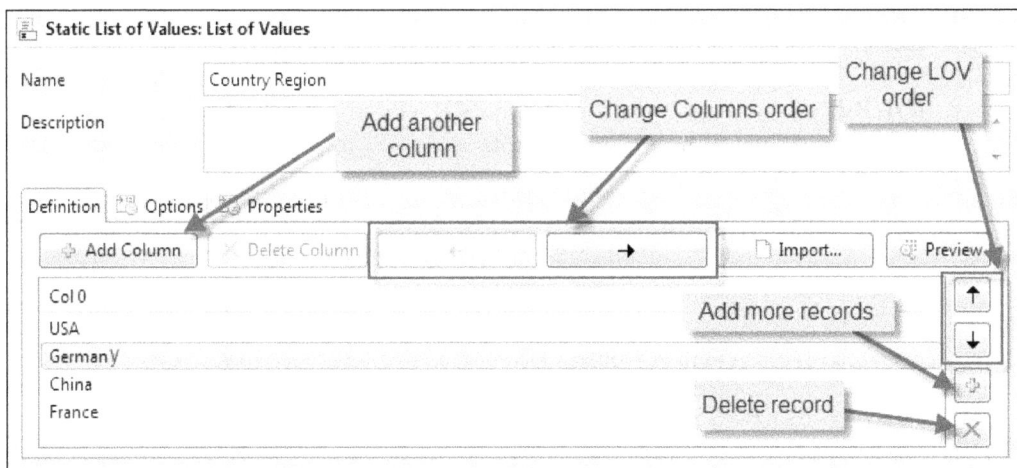

We can see that the data is successfully imported. Next, we will talk about the list of values based on custom SQL, which is the last type of LOV.

List of values based on custom SQL

In the **List of values based on custom SQL** type, we will define the custom SQL statement to generate the required LOV with the following steps:

1. Click on the create new LOV icon.

2. Select **List of values based on custom SQL**.

3. Type `Customer ID LOV` in the LOV name.

4. Click on the **Edit SQL** button.

5. Select the following columns from the `Customers` table:

    ◦   `ID`

    ◦   `First Name`

    ◦   `Last Name`

The following screenshot shows **Selected Columns**:

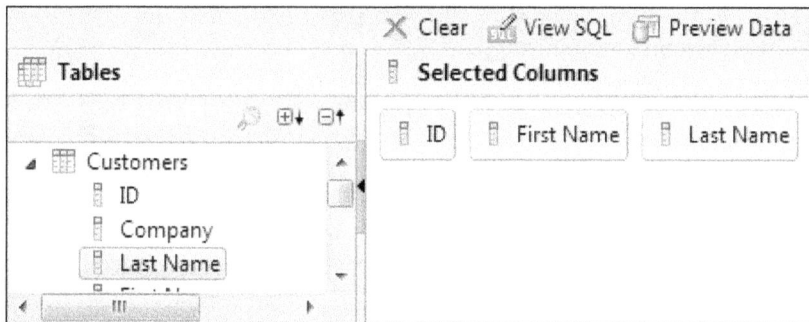

SQL Builder will generate the proper SQL statement based on your selection, as shown in the following screenshot:

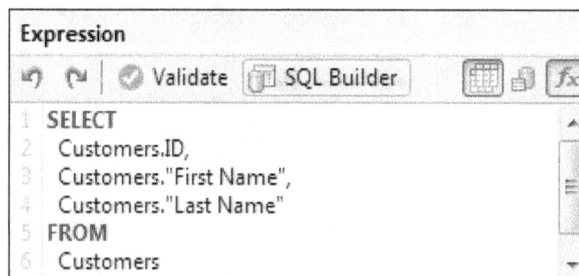

6. Click on **Preview** to display the values in this LOV. The following screenshot displays this LOV:

In the following section, we will talk about navigation paths, which are also known as hierarchies.

> The difference between LOVs based on custom SQL type and LOVs based on dimension objects is that you can use a specific SQL query that will be used only for the LOV definition. For example, you could write a custom SQL sentence to display the customer's full name instead of creating a temporary or dummy object to hold the concatenation between the first and last names.

Navigation paths

We can use navigation paths in BO-reporting tools to navigate from upper levels of a hierarchy to the lower levels (drill down) or from lower to upper levels (drill up). For example, a typical **branch** hierarchy could contain country, state/province, city, and branch names. A navigation path is defined by a set of dimensions with a specific order. The order is very important and should be as expected by the end user, because the navigation path will flow from the higher dimension in the hierarchy to the lower dimensions.

> Navigation paths can use dimensions only in their definition. Attribute objects are not allowed.

Navigation paths can be based on the dimensions order inside folders (the default navigation path) or customized by the BO developer/designer. The designer will create a navigation path based on the selected dimensions, which not need be in the same folder. The designer will also define the order of the selected dimension. This order will define the flow of this navigation path (hierarchy levels).

The default navigation path

The default navigation path type of the navigation path is defined by the order of dimensions inside folders. We might need to change the order of dimensions inside each folder to get the desired flow of the navigation path.

For example, let's have a look at the default navigation paths inside the NorthWind Business layer.

First, let's have a look at the current dimension order inside the Demographic Info folder with the following steps:

1. Open the NorthWind Business layer.

2. Navigate to Customer Information.

3. Then, navigate to **Demographic Info**. As we can see in the following screenshot, the dimension is not in the correct logical order:

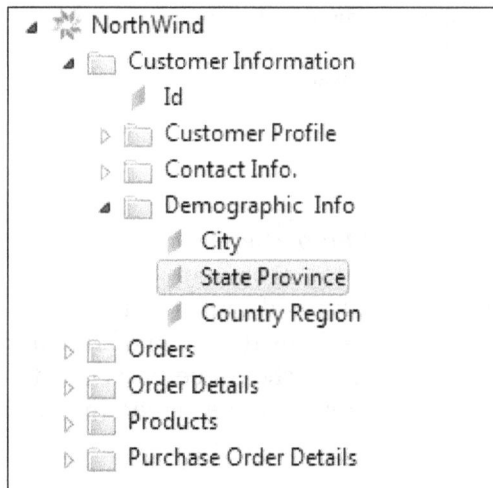

4. Then, navigate to **Navigation paths** from the left panel, as shown in the following screenshot:

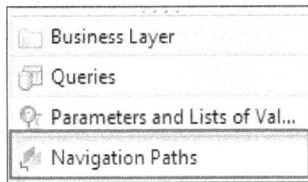

5. Select **Demographic Info** as the **Default** navigation path, as shown in the following screenshot:

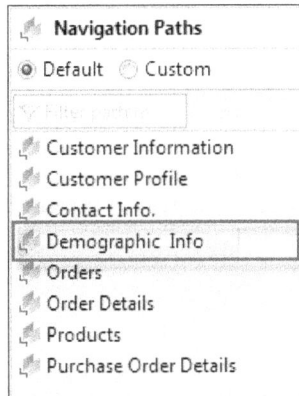

Note that the dimensions inside the **Demographic Info** default navigation path are in the same order as we saw in `Demographic Info` under the `Customer Information` Business layer folder, as displayed in the following screenshot:

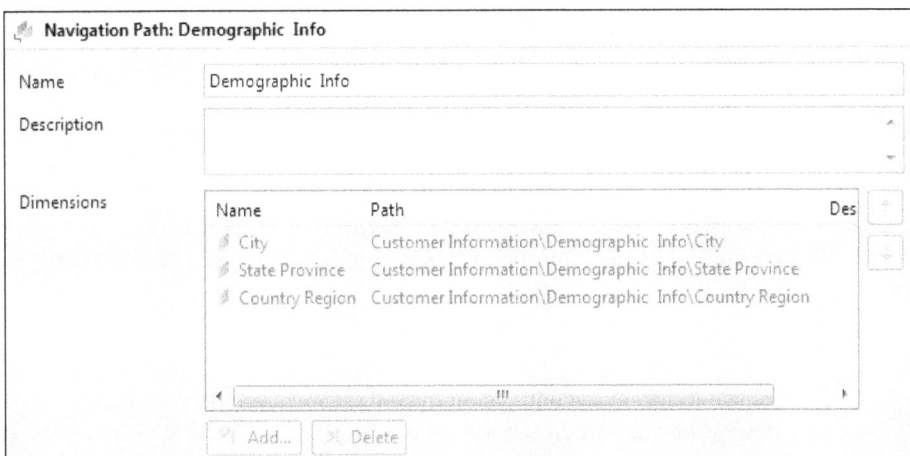

6. To fix this, navigate to the **Business Layer** tab from the left panel. Then navigate to `Customer Information | Demographic Info`. After that, reorder the dimensions as `Country Region`, `State Province`, and `City`, as shown in the following screenshot:

Now, we have the expected dimension order inside the **Demographic Info** navigation path, as shown in the following screenshot:

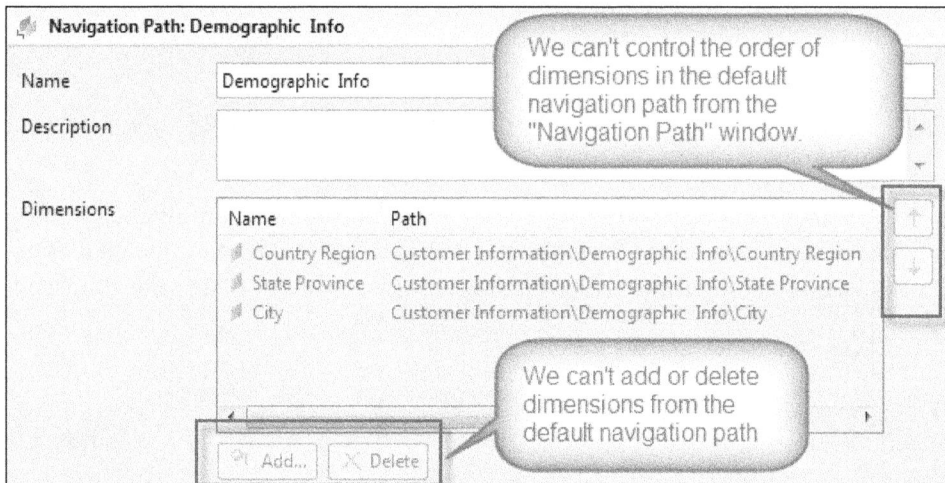

As we can see in the preceding screenshot, the options are disabled. We can't add or delete any dimension inside the default navigation path. Also, we can't control their order from the navigation path window.

> The best practice is to always create the dimensions in the correct logical order, as we will get an undesired navigation flow in the default navigation path if we have a nonlogical order.

The custom navigation path

The custom navigation path is a flexible hierarchy that can be customized in the Universe designer. The designer is not restricted by a set of a dimensions defined inside a folder. In this type, we can select dimensions from different folders and control the order of the dimension inside the custom navigation path, regardless of their actual order inside the Business layer folders.

Let's try to create a custom navigation path with the following steps:

1. Open the NorthWind Business layer and go to the **Navigation Paths** tab on the left panel.

2. Select **Custom**.

3. Then, click on the **Insert Navigation Path** icon, as shown in the following screenshot:

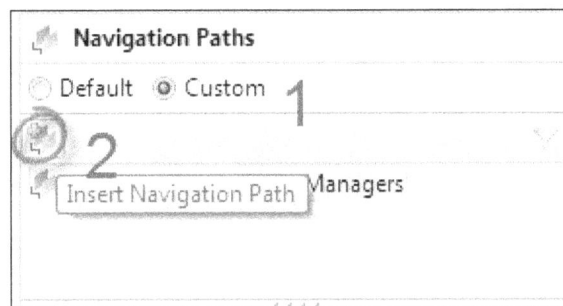

4. After that, enter Demographic Account Managers Hierarchy in the custom navigation path name.

5. Add the following dimensions:

    ° City

    ° Country

    ° Account Manager Name

    ° State Province

6. Change the order of the dimensions to Country, State Province, City, and Account Manager Name using the arrows on the right-hand side.

> You can use the *Shift* key to select more than one dimension at a time while adding dimensions to the custom navigation path.

We can see the navigation path definition for `Demographic Account Managers Hierarchy` in the following screenshot:

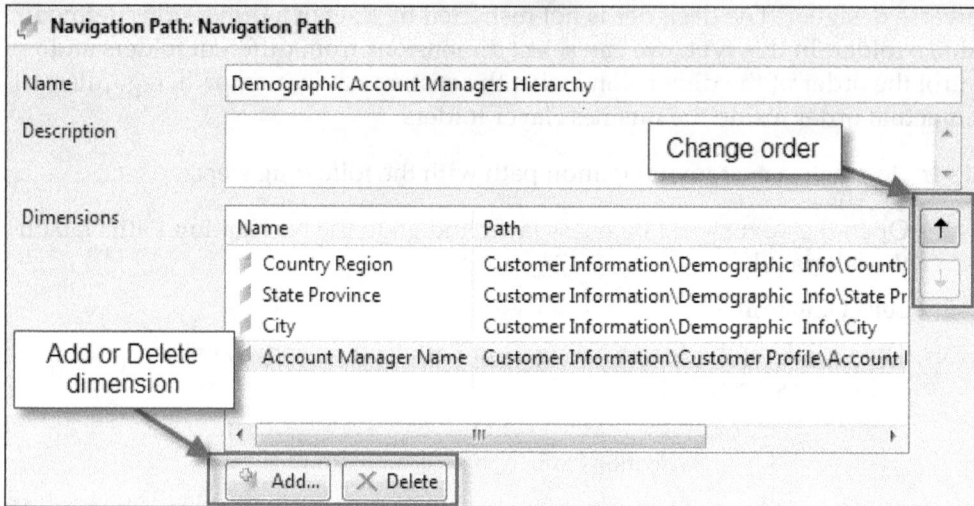

We can see how to drill up and down using the `Demographic Account Managers Hierarchy` navigation path in the BO Webi report in the following screenshot:

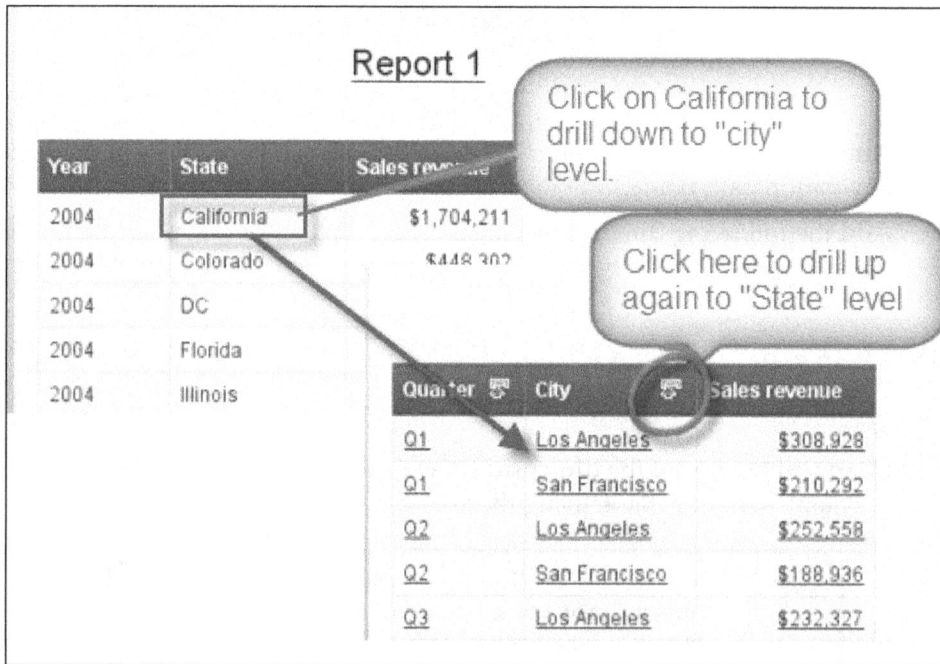

Index awareness

Index awareness is a feature that will help the IDT use key columns while generating SQL queries to speed up data retrieval. The main idea of this feature is to use the available database index. A query based on an indexed database column will retrieve data faster than a normal column. To make it easier, let's take an example first and perform the following steps:

1. Open the `NorthWind` Business layer and then navigate to the **Business Layer** tab from the left panel.

2. Create a new `Status Name` dimension under the `Orders` folder.

3. Go to the **Queries** tab from the left panel and create the following query:

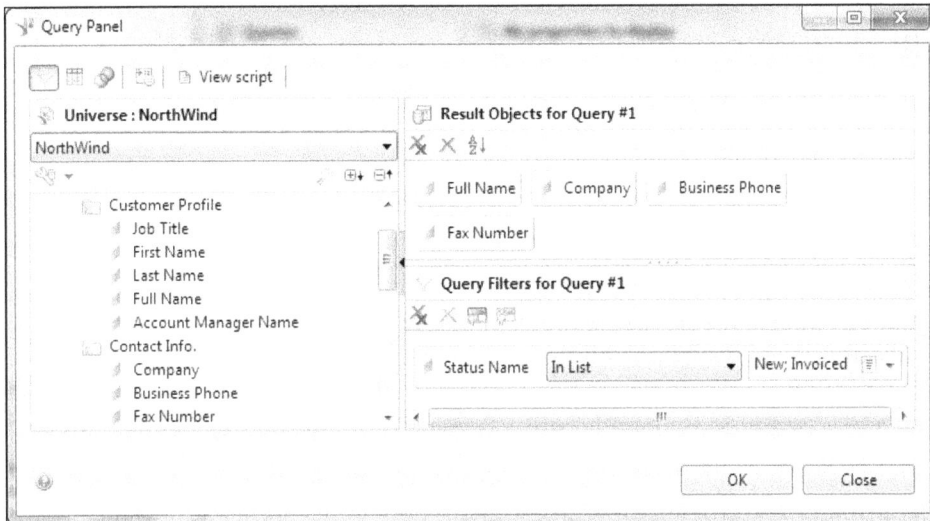

4. Then click on **View Script** to display the following SQL code generated by this query:

```
SELECT
{fn concat(Customers."First Name",{fn concat(' ',Customers."Last Name")})},
Customers.Company,
Customers."Business Phone",
Customers."Fax Number"
FROM
Orders,
Customers,
"Orders Status" Table__3
WHERE
( Customers.ID=Orders."Customer ID" )
AND ( Table__3."Status ID"=Orders."Status ID" )
AND
Table__3."Status Name" IN ('New','Invoiced' )
```

We can see the relation between the `Orders`, `Customers`, and `Orders Status` tables in the following figure:

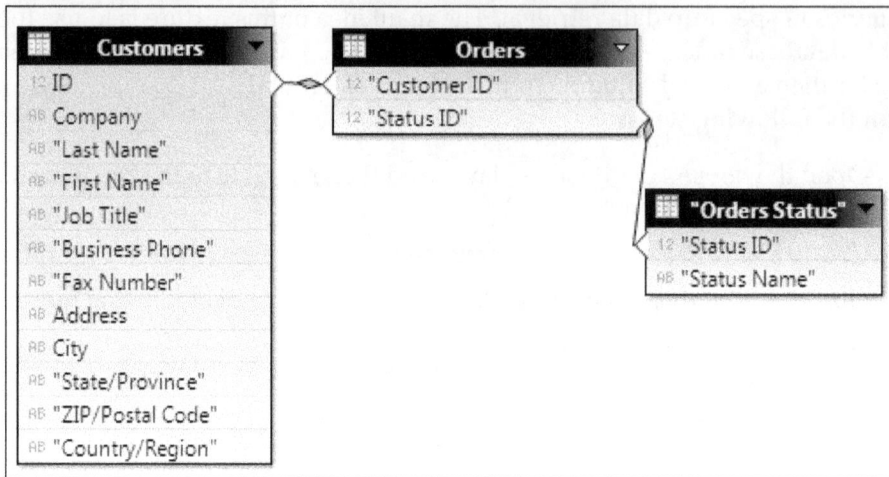

As we can see, we have a filter on the status name to display the customer's information with new and invoiced orders only.

Now, let's have a closer look at our example. We have three tables in the FROM clause of our query. We have one dimension and two facts table. As we can see, the original query displays data from the `Customers` table only. However, as we need to filter their order status to display customers with the `New` and `Invoiced` orders, the `Orders` and `Orders Status` tables are automatically included by the IDT engine.

In the next section, we will discuss how to enhance the performance of this query by adding primary and foreign keys' index awareness to the status dimension.

> Index awareness should be considered for the dimensions used in the `where` clause query to filter the query output based on one or many selected values.
>
> Index awareness can be configured for dimensions' business objects only, not for attributes or measures.

Primary keys

Defining a primary key for the Status Name dimension will inform the IDT to use Status ID from the Orders Status table in the where clause instead of the Status Name column. This should enhance the query performance, because Status ID is a primary key in the Orders Status table. Usually, we build database indexes on the primary key column to enhance the query performance.

> We already discussed the concepts of primary and foreign keys in the *Joining tables* section of *Chapter 4, Creating the Data Foundation Layer*.

So, let's define the primary key and find out how this will affect our query, with the following steps:

1. Open the NorthWind Business layer and navigate to the **Business Layer** tab on the left panel.

2. Navigate to the Orders folder and click on the Orders Status dimension to edit its definition.

3. Click on the **Keys** tab, as shown in the following screenshot:

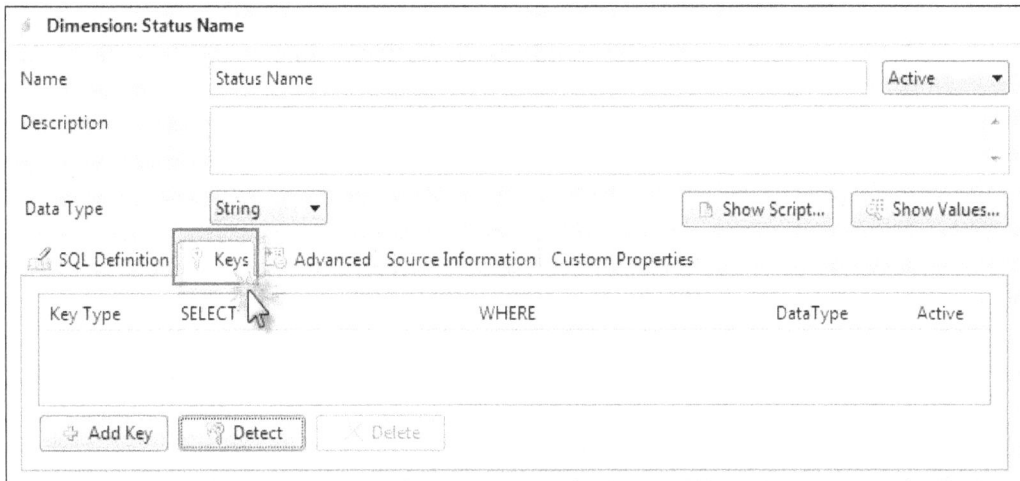

4. Then click on the **Add Key** button. The default type for the key first created is the primary key. If we add any new key after the primary key, it will be the foreign key type by default.

5. Click on the **Select** definition for the created primary key.

6. Select the `Orders Status` table and double-click on `Status ID`, as shown in the following screenshot:

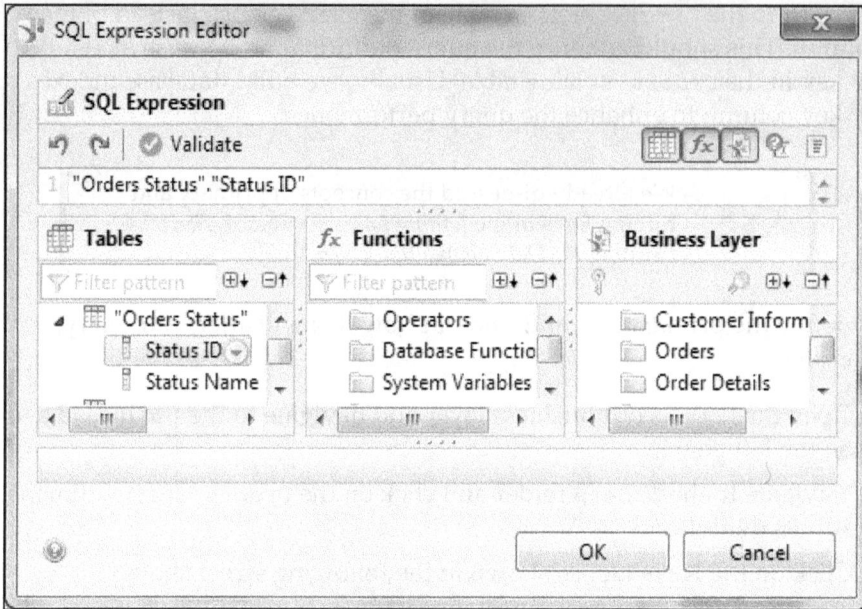

7. Click on **OK** and make sure that **Primary Key** is created, as we can see in the following screenshot:

8. Now save your Business layer, and let's go back and check the script for the query that we created earlier.

   The script should look like the following screenshot:

```
SELECT
 {fn concat(Customers."First Name",{fn concat(' ',Customers."Last Name")})},
 Customers.Company,
 Customers."Business Phone",
 Customers."Fax Number"
FROM
 Orders,
 Customers,
 "Orders Status"  Table_3
WHERE
 ( Customers.ID=Orders."Customer ID"  )
 AND  ( Table_3."Status ID"=Orders."Status ID"  )
 AND
 Table_3."Status ID"  IN  ( 0,1  )
```

As we can see, the `Status Name` filter changed from `"Status Name" IN ('New', 'Invoiced')` to `"Status ID" IN (0,1)`. The IDT query engine will detect that we are using a non-index column in the `where` clause, and as we defined a primary key for this non-index column, it will automatically replace our query filter behind the scene and force it to use the primary key indexed column defined with this dimension.

The main advantage of this is that the end users can still filter by status name, because it contains the values that are relevant for them (new, closed, invoiced, and so on), while they will get the best performance as if they were using the primary key in their query (`Status ID`), without the need to remember and enter the status IDs (0,1,2, and so on).

> Each dimension can have only one primary key. A primary key should be a column from the same table.

Foreign keys

To understand a foreign key, let's have a look again at the previous query. As we can see, all the required information to be displayed is extracted from the `Customers` table, and we added two extra tables and joins to filter the new and invoiced `Status Name` orders. In order to enhance the performance, we need to reduce the number of unreferenced tables and joins. So let's try to do it together with the following steps:

1. Navigate again to the `Status Name` dimension and open the **Key** tab.

2. Then add a new foreign key, and after that click on the **Select** definition.

3. Select the `Orders` table and then double-click on `Status ID`. The following **SQL Expression Editor** window will open:

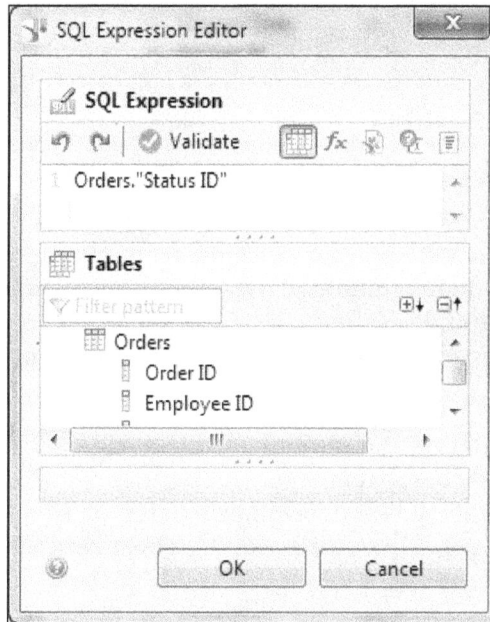

The **Key** tab for the `Status Name` dimension should look like the following screenshot:

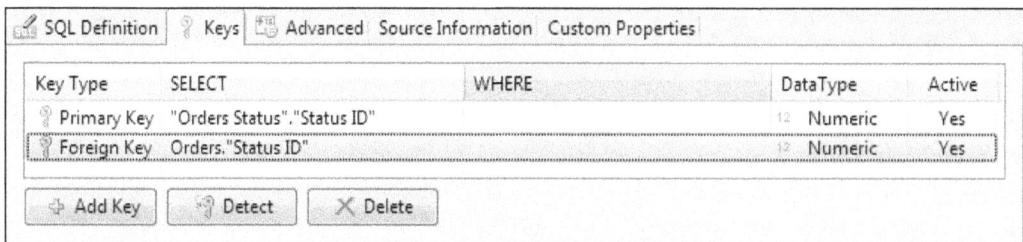

Key Type	SELECT	WHERE	DataType	Active
Primary Key	"Orders Status"."Status ID"		Numeric	Yes
Foreign Key	Orders."Status ID"		Numeric	Yes

Add Key   Detect   Delete

4. Now navigate again to our query and check how it will be changed:

```
SELECT
 {fn concat(Customers."First Name",{fn concat(' ',Customers."Last Name")})},
 Customers.Company,
 Customers."Business Phone",
 Customers."Fax Number"
FROM
 Orders,
 Customers
WHERE
 ( Customers.ID=Orders."Customer ID" )
 AND
 Orders."Status ID" IN (0,1 )
```

As we can see, the `Orders Status` table has been removed from our query, and we are referencing the `Orders Status` table directly. Indeed, removing a join will enhance the performance of the affected query, especially for large tables.

> You can define many foreign keys for a dimension.

Aggregate awareness

The aggregate awareness feature is used to increase performance by leading the report query to select objects from the aggregated table instead of the detailed table at runtime. There are three main steps to set up the aggregate awareness feature:

1. Insert the aggregated tables into our Data Foundation layer.

2. Use the `@Aggregate_Aware()` function with common objects.

3. Detect and set the incompatible objects.

As we don't have any aggregated tables in `NorthWind`, we will create an aggregated derived table to simulate a data mart table.

Inserting aggregated tables

The first step is to insert the data mart aggregated table into our Data Foundation layer. As we don't have one, we should create the aggregated derived table to simulate the case. In this example, we will create the `Yearly Order Details` derived table to aggregate the order quantity using `Order Year`, `Order Quarter`, and `Order Month`. These dimensions will be based on `Order Date` from the `Orders` table. To create the aggregated derived table, perform the following steps:

1. Open the `NorthWind.dfx` file from the **Local Projects** window.

2. Create a new derived table as follows:

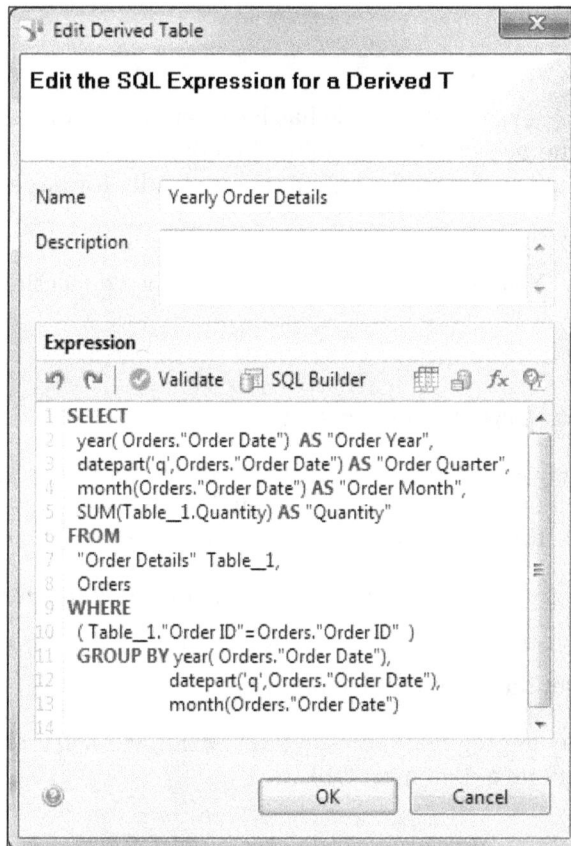

3. Select the required three tables, then right-click and navigate to **Insert | View from Selection....** After that, enter `Aggregate Awareness` in the **Name** field. Note that this step in not necessary, but we perform it just to focus on the three tables that we will use in this example. The view should be as displayed in the following screenshot:

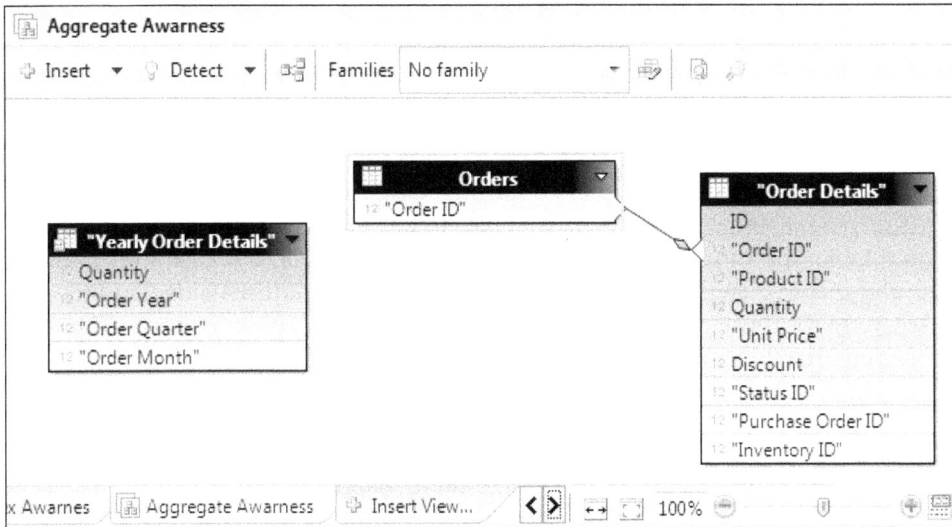

4. Go to NorthWind.blx and add columns under Yearly Order Details (the newly created derived table) to the Order folder; do not add the Quantity measure as it is already exists. We will see how to make these aggregate aware in the next section. The final Business layer should look like the following screenshot:

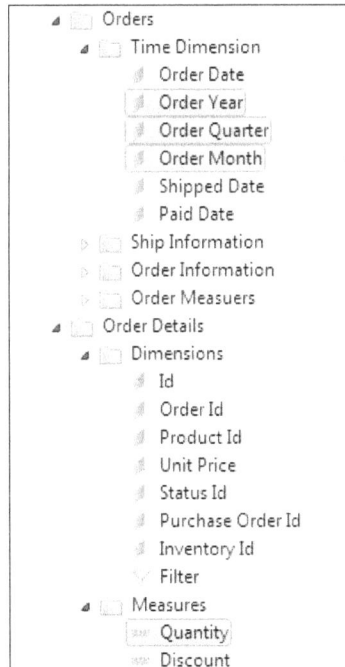

Now, our Data Foundation is ready by inserting the aggregated table, and we can move to the next step.

Defining the aggregated objects

The second step is to modify all the common business objects between the detailed tables (the `Orders` and `Order Details` tables in our example) and the aggregated data mart table (the `Yearly Order Details` derived table in our case). We need to use the `@Aggregate_Aware` function inside all the common dimensions and measures between, to make those common objects aggregate aware. This function will tell the query engine that it can retrieve these objects from many places based on the defined object orders, which will be the parameters of the `@Aggregate_Aware` function.

For example, we need to modify the **SELECT** clause for the `Quantity` measure in `Measures` under `Order Details` to `@Aggregate_Aware("Yearly Order Details".Quantity, "Order Details".Quantity)`.

We can see the measure path for the `Quantity` measure in the following screenshot:

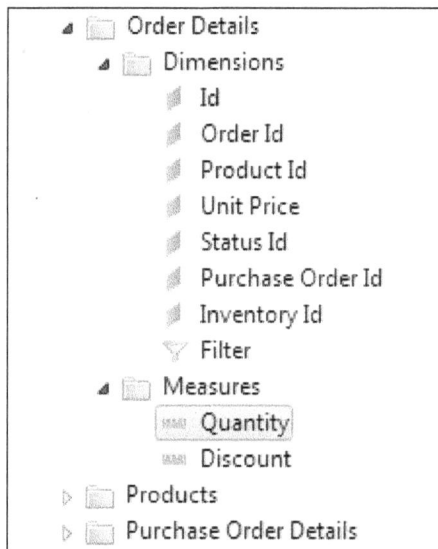

We can see the new definition of the `Quantity` measure in the following screenshot:

Measure: Quantity		
Name	Quantity	Active ▼
Description		
Data Type	Numeric ▼	Projection Function: Sum ▼

SQL Definition   Advanced   Source Information   Custom Properties

SELECT	@Aggregate_Aware("Yearly Order Details".Quantity,"Order Details".Quantity)	SQL Assistant...
WHERE		SQL Assistant...
Extra Tables		...

The `@Aggregate_Aware("Yearly Order Details".Quantity, "Order Details".Quantity)` function will tell the SQL engine that it is possible to retrieve `Quantity` from the `Yearly Order Details` table only if all the query objects are compatible with this table. If not, it will check the second table and so on. We will discuss how to set the incompatible objects in the next section. Note that we can have many parameters for the `@Aggregate_Aware` function. Each parameter will represent a possible source table for the selected business object. In an ideal situation, all parameter tables should be aggregated tables, while only one of them will be the detailed original table. The order of the function parameters (tables) is very important, as the SQL engine will try to find the most suitable source table for the selected object based on the order (from right to left).

> **Rule of thumb**
>
> We should put the most aggregated table in the first parameter of the `@Aggregate_Aware` function. The most aggregated table is the one with least number of dimensions and measures (smallest table). Then, we should put the second most aggregated table as the second parameter and so on.

Before moving to the next section, we need to make the following objects aggregate aware as well:

- Order Year: @Aggregate_Aware("Yearly Order Details"."Order Year", year(Orders."Order Date"))

- Order Quarter: @Aggregate_Aware("Yearly Order Details"."Order Quarter", datepart('q',Orders."Order Date"))

- Order Month: @Aggregate_Aware("Yearly Order Details"."Order Month", month(Orders."Order Date"))

Note that each dimension can be retrieved from the aggregated table or calculated from the Order Date column in the Orders table.

> Here, we used the specific functions of MS Access SQL to calculate year, quarter, and month.

In the following section, we will see how to set the incompatible objects for each table, which is the last step to make our Universe aggregate aware.

Detecting the aggregation navigation

Now, we need to define the aggregation navigation by detecting the incompatible objects for each table defined in the Data Foundation layer. This will let the SQL query engine know which parameter of each @Aggregate_Aware function should be used, based on the other selected objects. The SQL engine will generate a query with the best possible performance by trying to use the aggregated table whenever possible. Again, we need to carefully select the order of parameter tables of the @Aggregate_Aware function in order to achieve this.

> The best way to do this is to think of it in the reverse order. Instead of defining the incompatible objects for each table, define the compatible one. In our example, the compatible objects with Yearly Order Details are Order Year, Order Quarter, Order Month, and Quantity, because these objects are based on columns from this table. This means that all the other objects are incompatible.

Let's find out how to do this with the following steps:

1. Click on the **Actions** menu.

2. Select **Set Aggregate Navigation...**, as shown in the following screenshot:

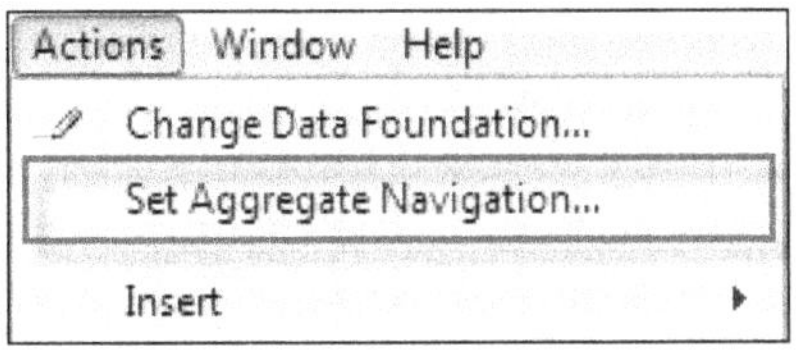

3. Then click on the **Detect Incompatibility** button, as shown in the following screenshot. We can set it manually as well, but here we will go with the easy way.

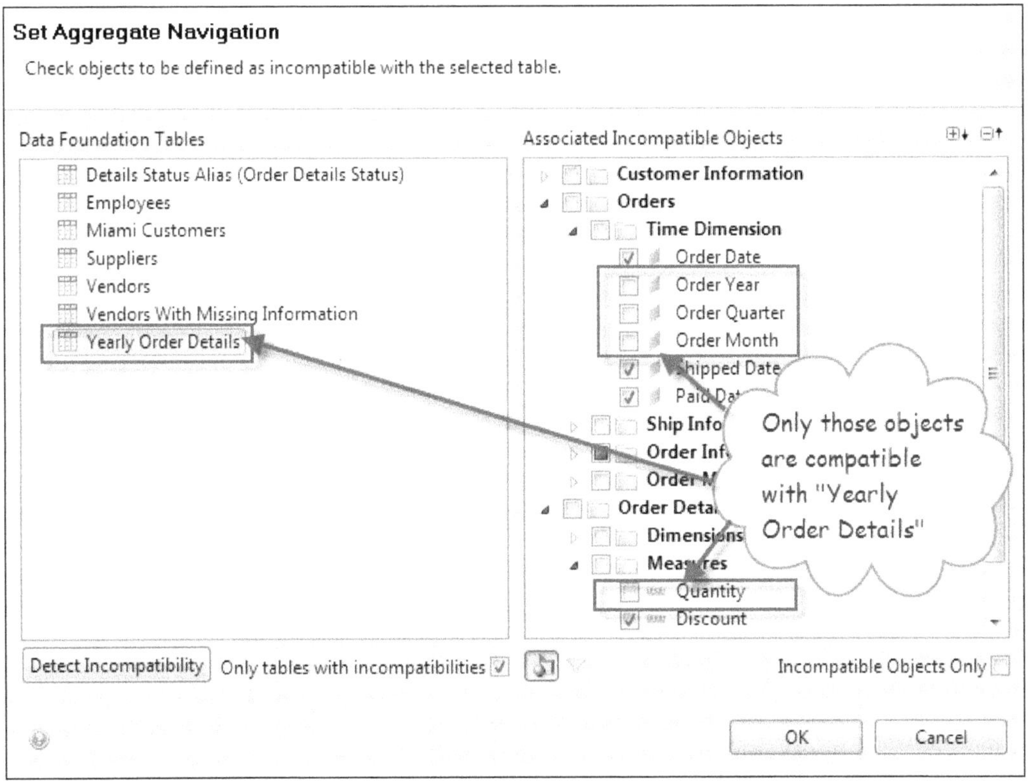

As we can see in the previous screenshot, when we select the `Yearly Order Details` table from the left panel under **Data Foundation Tables**, we will be able to see that all the objects are checked as noncompatible objects in the right panel under **Associated Incompatible Objects**, except the objects that are already mentioned (`Order Year`, `Order Quarter`, `Order Month`, and `Quantity`).

You might notice that not all tables are listed on the left panel under **Data Foundation Tables**. This is because we already checked the **Only tables with incompatibilities** option at the bottom. We might also check the **Incompatible Objects Only** option in order to display only the incompatible objects in the right panel.

Finally, let's examine the effect of the aggregate awareness on the SQL that will be generated by the query, with the following steps:

1. Go to `NorthWind.blx` and navigate to the **Queries** tab.

2. Create the query shown in the following screenshot:

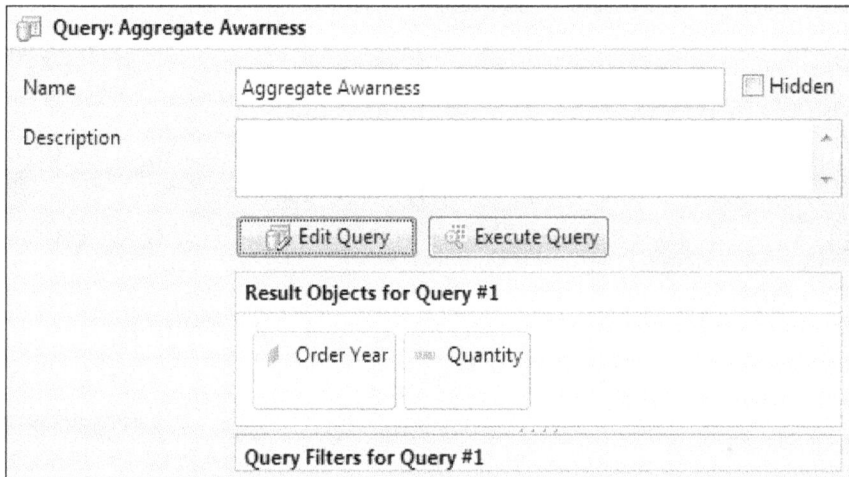

As we can see, the SQL engine can retrieve the required information from two places: from the `Yearly Order Details` aggregated table or from the two detailed tables (`Orders` and `Order Details`). To achieve the best performance, the SQL engine should be able to detect if it is possible to retrieve all query objects from the `Yearly Order Details` aggregated table. To check how this will affect the generated SQL query, edit the query and click on the **View Script** button. The following query will be displayed:

```
SELECT
  Table_8."Order Year",
  Table_8.Quantity
FROM
  (
  SELECT
  year( Orders."Order Date")  AS "Order Year",
  datepart('q',Orders."Order Date") AS "Order Quarter",
  month(Orders."Order Date") AS "Order Month",
  SUM(Table_1.Quantity) AS "Quantity"
FROM
  "Order Details"  Table_1,
  Orders
WHERE
  ( Table_1."Order ID"=Orders."Order ID"  )
  GROUP BY year( Orders."Order Date"),
           datepart('q',Orders."Order Date"),
           month(Orders."Order Date")

  ) Table_8
```

Aggregated Derived table

As we can see, the SQL engine used the aggregate aware feature to decide to go with the aggregated derived table that we created to simulate the data mart.

Now, let's add the `Discount` measure to our query and see what will happen. This measure is displayed in the following screenshot:

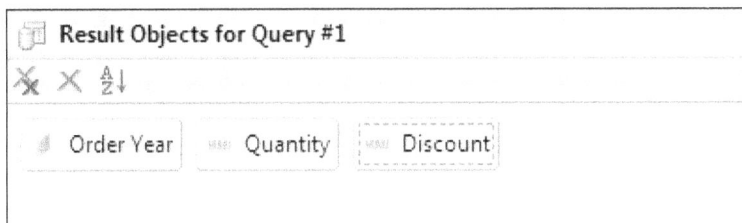

Result Objects for Query #1

Order Year   Quantity   Discount

To add the `Discount` measure, edit the query and click on **View Script** to see the generated SQL statement shown in the following screenshot:

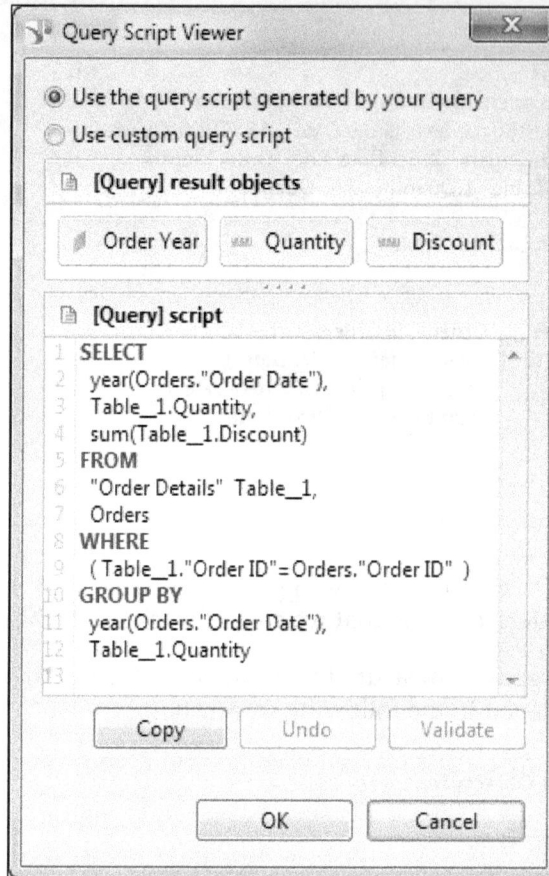

As we can see, as the `Discount` object can be only retrieved from the `Order Details` table and is incompatible with the `Yearly Order Details` aggregated table, the SQL engine goes to the second parameter of the aggregate aware function for the `Order Year` and `Quantity` objects. As a result, the entire query is based on the detailed tables, not on the aggregated one.

In the following section, we will talk about business object-specific functions.

Common business objects' specific functions

We can use two types of functions to create a complex business object. The first type is specific functions of the database SQL. This type will be available only in Universes based on single-source Data Foundation. We will be able to access database functions based on the used database driver in the data connection. For example, we can use TO_CHAR() to cast a date into a string based on the used format, while in Teradata, we can use the CAST function to do the same.

The second type is specific functions of business objects. This type can be used with multisource Universes. There are some common functions that we can access regardless of the database type, and this is our target in this section. The **Functions** window is shown in the following screenshot:

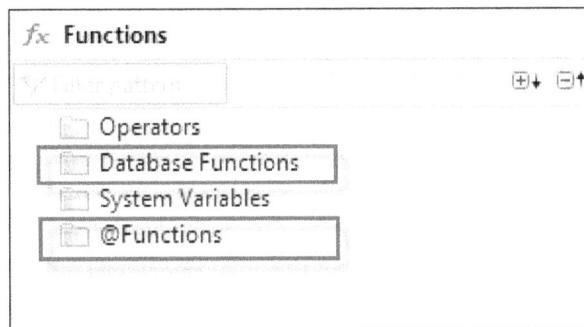

As we can see in the preceding screenshot, we have four main folders under **Functions** of **SQL Expression Editor**:

- **Operators**: This folder contains common database operators such as +, -, *, and so on.

- **Database Functions**: This folder contains valid database functions based on the used database driver which is defined in the connection.

- **System Variables**: This folder contains system variable names such as BOUSER, DOCNAME, UNVNAME, and so on. We can retrieve the value of these variables using the @Variable() BO function. For example, @Variable('BOUSER') will retrieve the value of the current logged-in user.

- **@Functions**: This folder contains the functions that we will discuss in detail in this section. The list of **@Functions** is shown in the following screenshot:

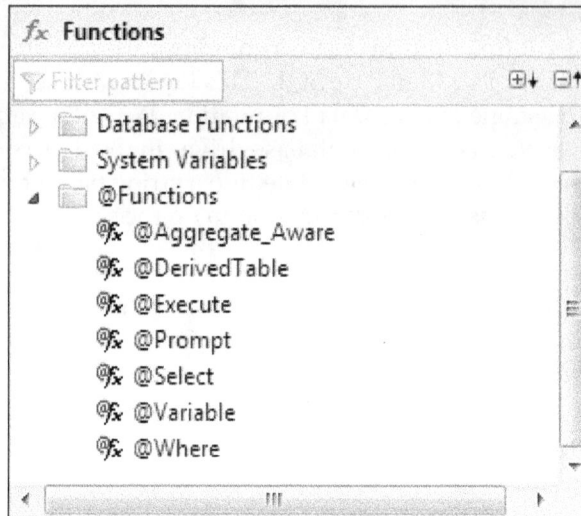

@Aggregate_Aware()

We use the `@Aggregate_Aware()` function inside business object definitions to make them aggregate aware. This SQL engine will decide the fastest aggregated table to retrieve this object based on the parameter order, as we described early in this chapter.

We can see the syntax of this function in the following screenshot:

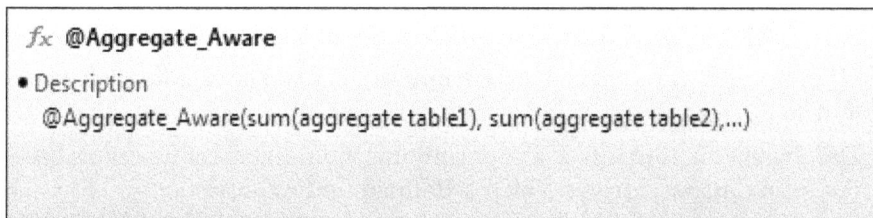

@DerivedTable()

The `@DerivedTable()` function can be used to refer to derived tables, as we discussed in *Chapter 4, Creating the Data Foundation Layer*.

We can see the syntax of this function in the following screenshot:

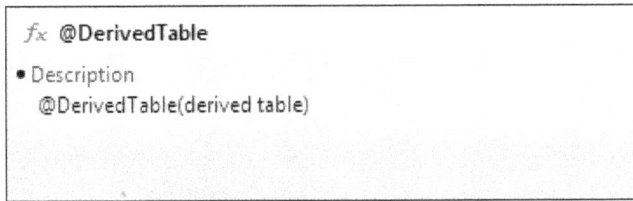

The following is an example of a nested derived table:

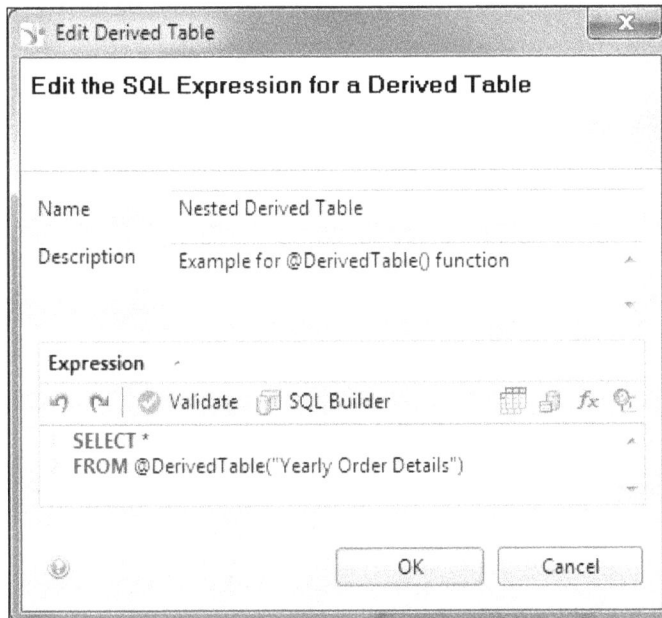

@Prompt()

The @Prompt() function is used to prompt the end user for parameter values. We have more advanced options in the @Prompt() function, such as to define the prompt data type and associated LOV, and whether it is mandatory or optional.

We can see the syntax of this function in the following screenshot:

> *fx* **@Prompt**
>
> • Description
>
>   Standalone Prompt: @Prompt('message','type',
> {'value1','value2',...}|'folder\business layer object'|'list of
> values',Mono|Multi[:Any|Leaf],free|constrained|primary_key,persist
> ent|not_persistent,{'default value1','default value2',...})
>
>   Parameter Prompt: @Prompt(parameter)

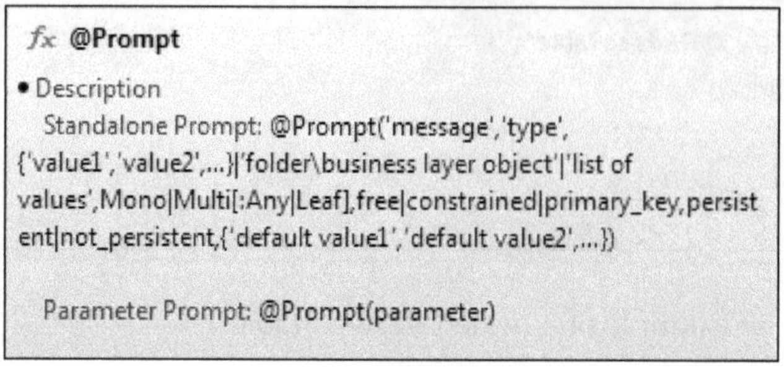

@Select()

The `@Select()` function will replace its occurrence with the `select` definition for the passed business object.

We can see the syntax of this function in the following screenshot:

> *fx* **@Select**
>
> • Description
>   @Select(folder\business layer object)

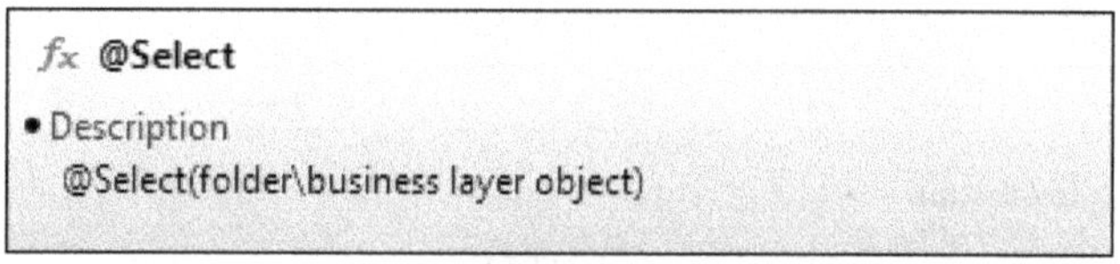

@Variable()

The `@Variable()` function is the simple version of the prompt, as it will ask the end user to enter the value for this variable.

We can see the syntax of this function in the following screenshot:

> *fx* **@Variable**
>
> • Description
>   @Variable('variable')

@Where()

The `@Where()` function will replace its occurrence with the `where` definition for the passed business object.

We can see the syntax of this function in the following screenshot:

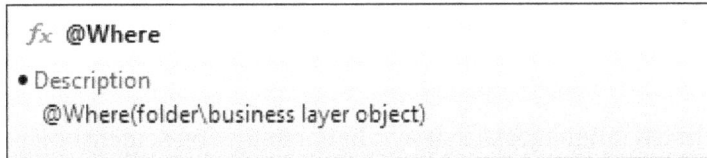

fx **@Where**

- Description
  @Where(folder\business layer object)

Multilingual Universes

We can create a Universe one time and use the Translation Management Tool to add translation with different locales to your SAP BO objects. We can use the Translation Management Tool to translate reports, dashboards, and many SAP BO resources as well. The Translation Management Tool can be used to translate the .unv Universe's old version as well as the .unx new version.

The Translation Management Tool is an interface that can help us import BO resources and add as many locales as we need (up to 130 locales). Then we can start manual translation for object names, titles, and description. This will help us because once we create a Universe, we will be able to separate the translation activates from the development ones.

In this section, we will just take a small example to help us understand the main use of the Translation Management Tool with the following steps:

1. Open **Translation Management Tool**, as shown in the following screenshot:

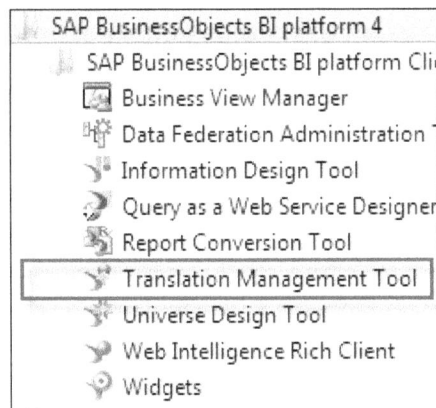

SAP BusinessObjects BI platform 4
   SAP BusinessObjects BI platform Cli
     Business View Manager
     Data Federation Administration
     Information Design Tool
     Query as a Web Service Designer
     Report Conversion Tool
     Translation Management Tool
     Universe Design Tool
     Web Intelligence Rich Client
     Widgets

2. Import one of the Universes that we have in our repository. Then, add the following two locales:

   ° **French (France)**
   ° **Arabic (Saudi Arabia)**

The selected languages are shown in the following screenshot:

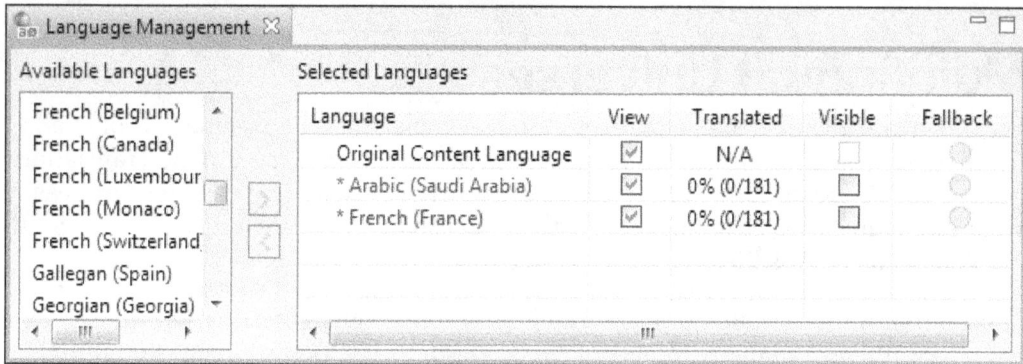

3. Select the objects that you want to translate, such as the following:

   ° Universe name and description
   ° Dimensions, attributes, and measures
   ° Business objects' associated formats

We will get the following window:

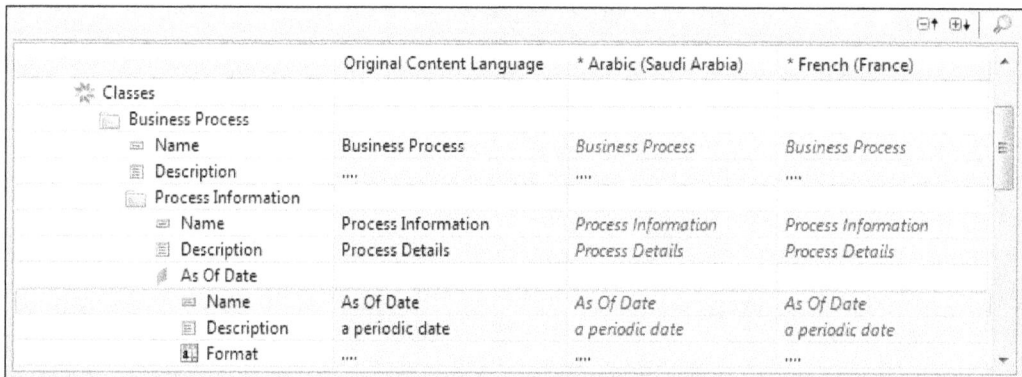

4. Then, you can write the translation in the text editor:

This is just a small introduction to the tool and how to use it to translate our Universes to make them multilingual.

Advanced Business layer properties

We have some advanced Business layer properties that can be used to control many aspects related to this layer.

To open Business layer properties, perform the following steps:

1. Open the NorthWind Business layer.

2. Navigate to the **Business Layer** tab from the left panel, as shown in the following screenshot:

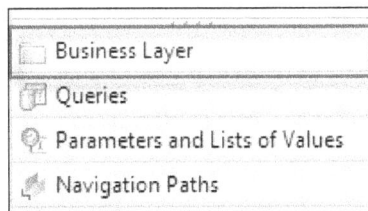

3. Click on **NorthWind Business Layer** to display its properties. The **Properties** section is shown in the following screenshot:

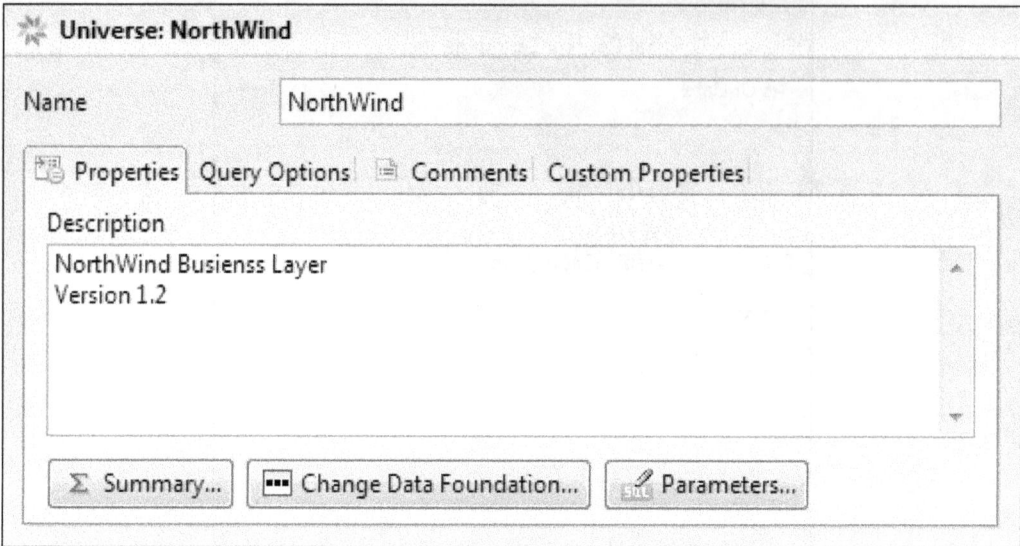

Universe: NorthWind

Name | NorthWind

Properties   Query Options   Comments   Custom Properties

Description

NorthWind Busienss Layer
Version 1.2

Σ Summary...   Change Data Foundation...   Parameters...

From this window, we can access Business layer properties.

> The Data Foundation and Business layer properties were grouped in the earlier Universe designer version under Universe parameters.

Description

The **Description** field aims to describe the Universe purpose here. The Universe description is shared and displayed to the business users when they want to import a Universe.

> It is recommended that you write a description for all objects. Don't leave them blank; just add a few words that help describe the associated object.
>
> It is also recommended that you add the Universe version because it will help you be sure this is the right Universe version when you test it.

Summary

We can click on the **Summary...** button to get summary information about the objects inside our Business layer as well as the associated Data Foundation.

Let's click on the **Summary...** button to display the following window:

Name	Value
Business Layer	
Attributes	3
Business Layer Items	74
Business Layer Objects	63
Business Layer Views	1
Dimensions	55
Filters	3
Folders	13
Lists of Values	4
Measures	5
Navigation Paths	1
Parameters	0
Queries	5
Data Foundation	
Alias Tables	2
Contexts	2
Derived Tables	3
Joins	10

Change Data Foundation

We can change the Data Foundation associated with our Business layer at any time. However, we need to make sure that all the tables refreshed by the currently implemented objects inside our Business layer will be there; otherwise, the object will not parse, and we will need to define the object's `select` part again in order to parse it correctly.

Let's click on the **Change Data Foundation...** button to display a list of available Data Foundation files inside our project and select a new one. Currently, we will see only one Data Foundation resource displayed, because we have only one Data Foundation resource created in our project.

It is recommended that you check the integrity of your Universe
if you change the Data Foundation reference to make sure that
everything is OK and to help you discover if there are any errors
or warnings that need your action.

We can see the **Select a Data Foundation** window in the following screenshot:

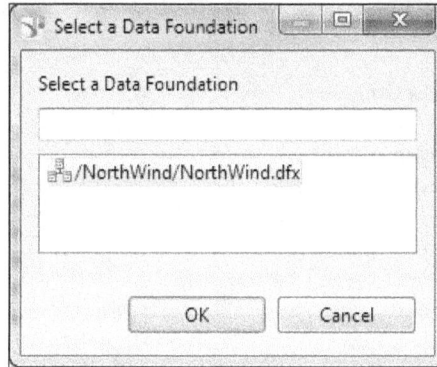

Parameters

We can use the **Parameters** window to access and modify the query's script
parameters, as displayed in the following screenshot:

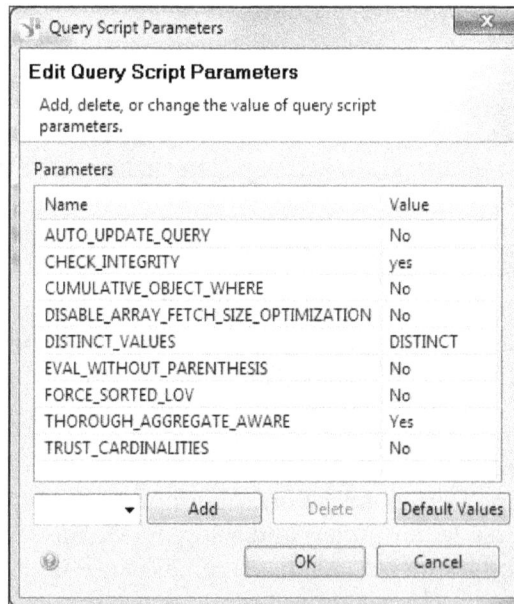

Summary

In this chapter, we learned that we need to create an LOV when the user is prompted to select one or more values for a specific dimension or attribute. Then we learned how to create different types of LOVs such as LOVs based on dimensions, static LOVs, and LOVs based on custom SQL.

In the second part, we discussed navigation paths, formally known as hierarchies. We used navigation paths to define the drill path object either based on the hierarchical order of dimensions inside a folder (default navigation path) or based on a customized order specified by the Universe designer.

After that, we learned how to use the index awareness feature by defining primary and foreign keys to make the IDT aware of the indexed column and to use it to fine tune the performance of SQL statements generated from reports and queries. Then we also learned how to use the aggregate awareness function to enhance the performance of our queries, using the summarized tables whenever possible. Then we had an overview of common business objects' specific functions. After that, we learned how to use the Translation Management Tool to translate our Business layer. Finally, we introduced advanced properties of the Business layer.

In the next chapter, we will learn how to secure our Universe.

Data Security and Profiles

In this chapter, we will talk about how to secure your Universe. As we discussed in *Chapter 2*, *Aligning BI Solutions with Business Demands*, BI makes the right data available for the right people at the right time. However, it is not just a question of making the data available; we also need to secure it and consider who should see what.

In this chapter, we will learn the following topics:

- Getting to know how to open the Security Editor and the difference between Universes/profiles and users/groups views
- Creating a Data Security Profile using the IDT Security Editor
- Creating a Business Security Profile using the IDT Security Editor
- Assigning security profiles to users or groups
- Creating a security matrix to map security profiles to associated users and groups

Understanding the security model

Before we start talking about how to create security profiles or how to assign them, let's first try to understand what security profiles are and let's have an overview on the SAP BO IDT security model.

There are two main security models that can be adopted:

- The first one is to allow everyone to see everything by default; you just apply restrictions or security rules to a set of specific users to restrict their access
- The second model is to deny everyone access by default; you start giving access to a specific set of users on data that they are allowed to access

The first security model is the adopted one in the SAP BO Universe. This means that by default any user who has access to the Universe will be able to see all objects available in this Universe as well as data that can be generated from a query based on this Universe. To apply security mechanism, we will create a set of security rules or restrictions known as **profiles** and then we will assign them to a specific list of users to restrict their access. This may sound risky because confidential data may be exposed by unexpected end users if you forget to apply the security rules on one of those targeted end users.

Security profiles are a set of rules or restrictions related to data, connections, objects, or SQL limitations. We have two types of security profiles:

- **Data Security Profiles**: They are designed to secure Data Foundation resources inside our Universe. Their aim is to restrict access to database data.

- **Business Security Profiles**: They are used to secure Business layer resources in our Universe. Their aim is to restrict access to business rules.

Security profiles are stored with the Universe on the repository. So, the first step to create a security profile is to log in to the repository. Then, we have to select a Universe; after that, we can start creating our security profile.

Security profiles can be assigned to one user or multiple users but also to one or multiple groups. One security profile can have many restriction rules from the same type. This means, for example, if we create a Data Security Profile, we can define a set of data security rules related to data, connection, and SQL limitation inside this profile; but, of course, we can't mix business and data restriction together and we will also need to create a separate profile to store business rules and data rules. We will use the Security Editor to create security profiles and assign them to the corresponding users.

> Security Editor in the IDT is equivalent to **Manage Security** under **Tools** in the UDT.

Generally, we have five main steps to apply a security to our Universe:

1. Log in to a repository.
2. Select a Universe.
3. Create security profiles.
4. Assign a security profile to users or groups.
5. Test restriction rules inside security profiles.

Working with the Security Editor

The first step to create a security profile is to open the Security Editor. In this section, we will try to be more familiar with the Security Editor, then we will focus on Data and Business Security Profiles with the following step:

1. Click on the Security Editor icon to open the Security Editor, as shown in the following screenshot:

This will open following window:

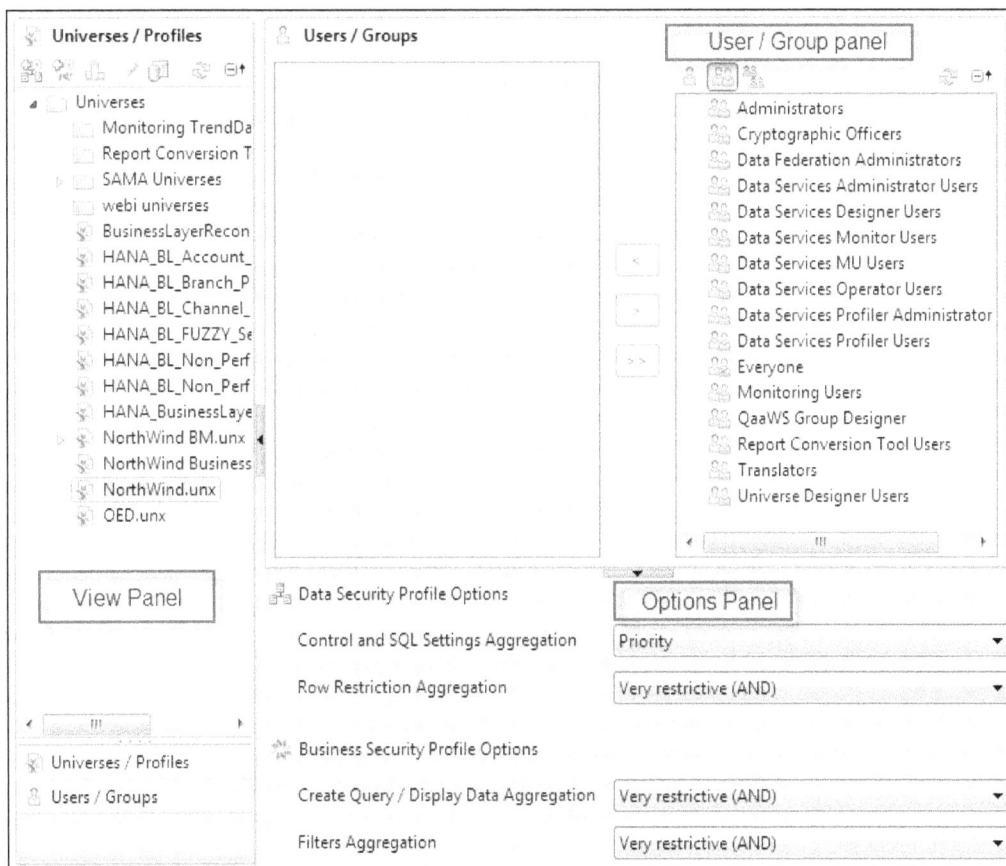

As we can see, the **Security Editor** window consists of two main views that will be explained in the upcoming sections.

Universes / Profiles

In the **Universes / Profiles** view, we can select a Universe and insert new data or business profile to that Universe (the left-hand side panel). Then, we can assign this profile to users or groups (the right panel). After that, we can control security profile options from the panel at the bottom. The main focus of this window is to show the users and groups assigned to a specific security profile.

> This view should be used if your main focus is security profiles. Indeed, it is mainly used when the point of entrance is security rules because, as the first step, you will first define them and then they will be applied to the users or groups.

Users / Groups

This is the opposite view. We can use the **Users / Groups** view to display the list of security profiles assigned to a specific user or group. As the first step, we will select a user or a group from the left-hand side panel, then the list of security profiles assigned will be displayed. You can manage (add or remove) security profiles in this view as in the previous one.

In order to do this, we need to perform the following steps (flagged in the next screenshot):

1. Select a user or group.
2. Select a Universe.
3. The list of security profiles (data as well as business) assigned to the selected user or group that is related to the selected Universe will be displayed in both the bottom panels.

> This view should be used if your main focus is users. This means that we have a list of users and we want to manage security profiles for those users.

We can see the **Security Editor** window for the **Users/Groups** view in the following screenshot:

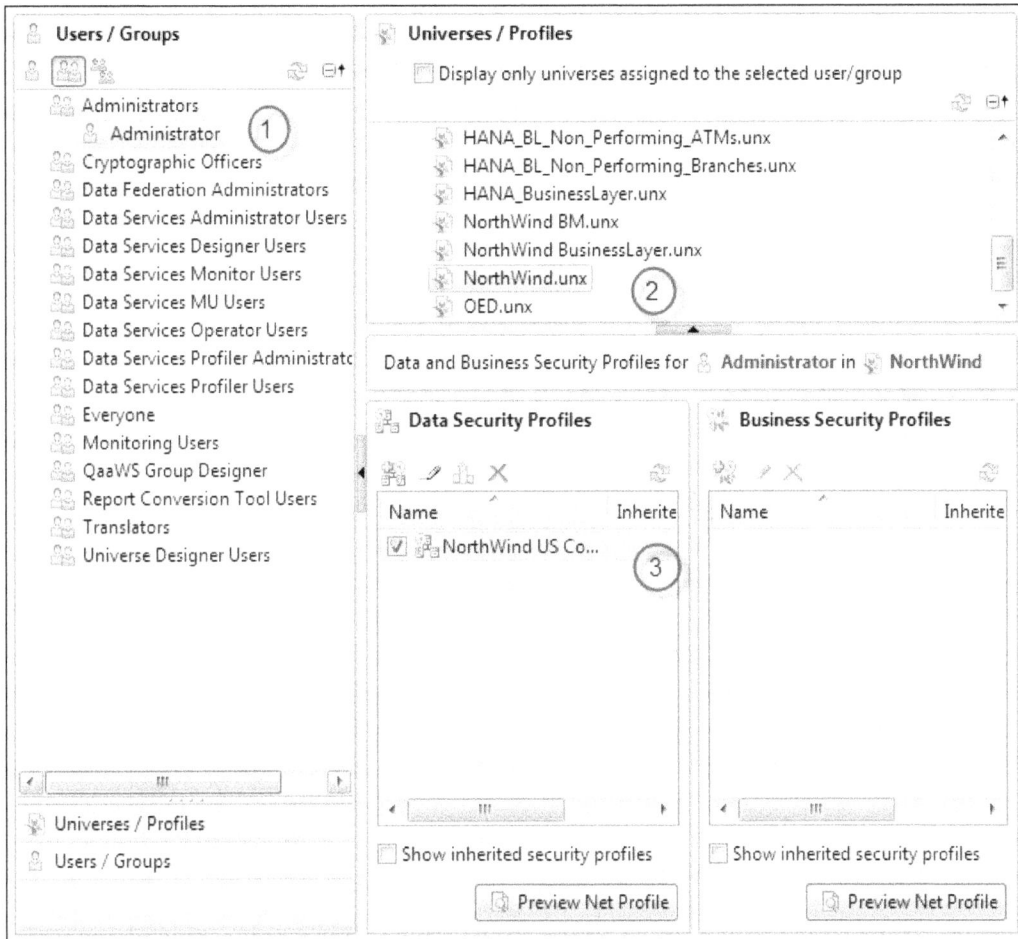

In the upcoming sections, we will learn how to create Data and Business Security Profiles.

> In the IDT, there are two types of security profiles (data and business) that can be managed from the Security Editor; in the UDT, there is only one type of security profile (known as **security restriction**) and it is managed by navigating to **Tools | Manage Security**.

Understanding Data Security Profiles

Data Security Profiles are a set of rules and restrictions related to data. Usually, they will target the Data Foundation resource.

Let's try to create a Data Security Profile together with the following steps:

1. Click on the Security Editor icon from the main IDT toolbar.
2. Make sure that you are in the **Universes/Profiles** view.
3. Click on the **Insert Data Security Profile** icon.

   The following window will open:

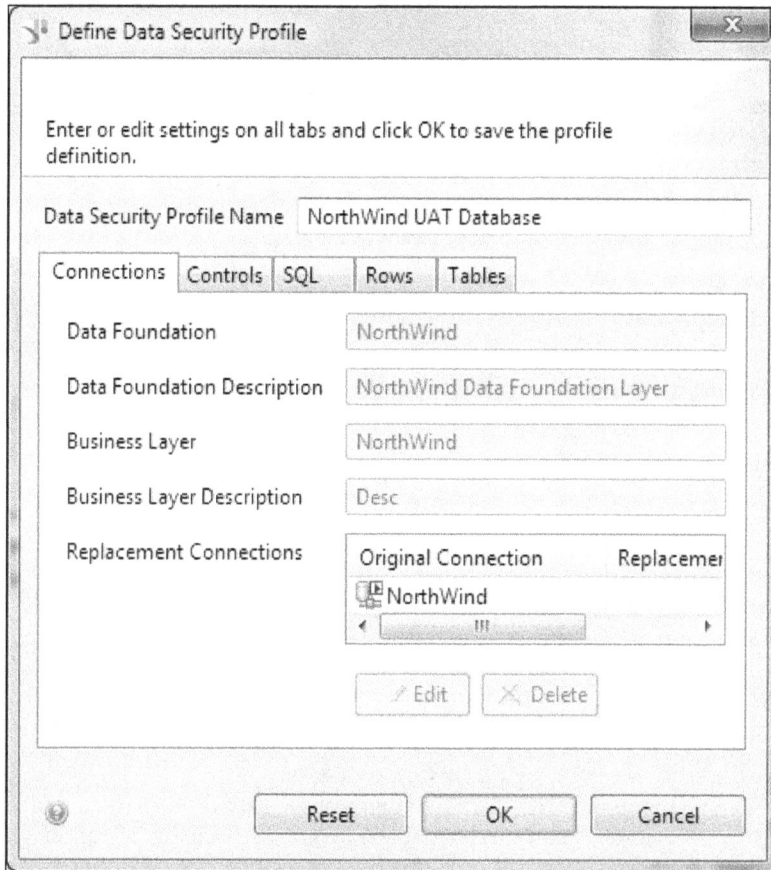

As we can see, there are five main categories for data restriction rules; these are explained in the upcoming sections.

Connections

In the **Connections** view, we can override the default connection used by the assigned user to connect to the Universe. For example, let's assume that we have two database connections (Production and Testing) and we want Universe testers to see only the testing environment while the business users should see the Production database.

In this case, we will create a security profile and assign it to the Universe tester user to restrict his/her access to the UAT database with the following steps:

1. Type NorthWind UAT Database as the Data Security Profile's name.
2. Then, in **Replacement Connections**, select the NorthWind.cnx connection and click on **Edit**. The **Define Replacement Connection** window will open.
3. Select **Northwind UAT** from the list and click on **OK**. The NorthWind UAT Database Data Security Profile is created successfully.

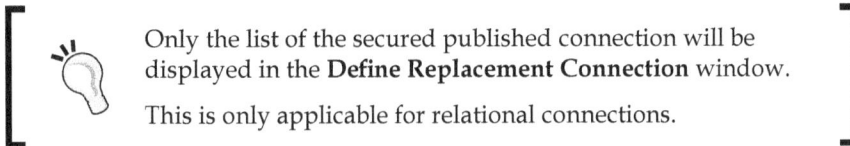

> Only the list of the secured published connection will be displayed in the **Define Replacement Connection** window.
>
> This is only applicable for relational connections.

We can see the definition of the NorthWind UAT Database Data Security Profile in the following screenshot:

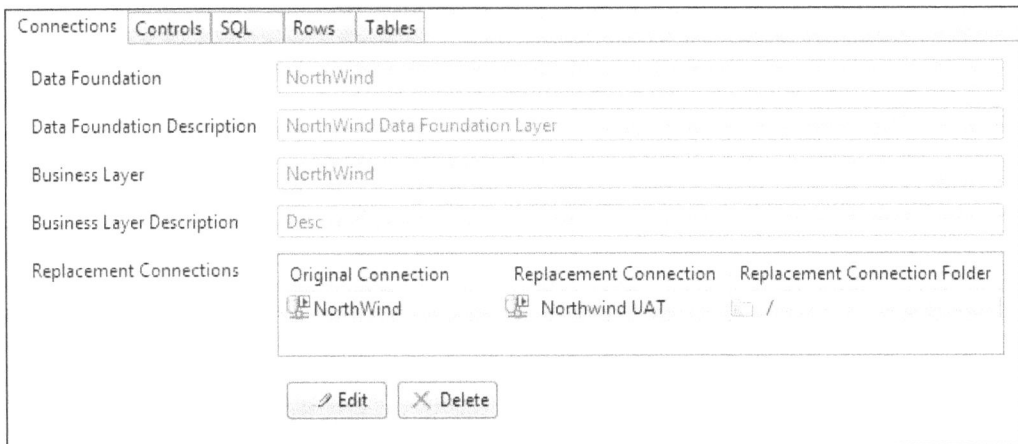

Then, we need to assign this profile to the **Administrator** user with the following steps:

1. Select the NorthWind UAT database security profile from the left panel.
2. Select the **Administrator** user from the right panel.

3. Click on the left arrow to assign this security profile for this user.

> We assigned this Data Security Profile to **Administrator** as we don't have any tester user. This is just for an example.
>
> You can define a replacement connection for each connection specified in a multisource Universe.

We can see in the following screenshot that the `NorthWind UAT Database` security profile is created under `NorthWind` Universes:

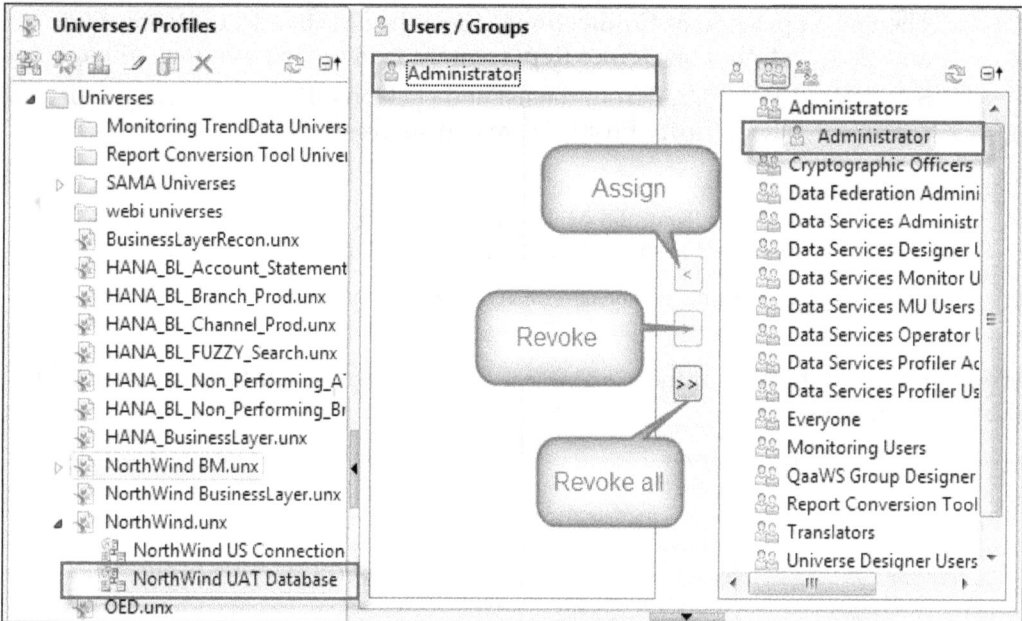

Controls

Let's assume that we have a specific user group and they have access to many detailed operational reports that are built on top of our `NorthWind` Universe. We want to give a priority to BI and analytics reports and we want to limit the operational data inquiries to a maximum of 10,000 rows or 15 minutes of execution time. We can use a Data Security Profile using the **Controls** tab to apply this restriction using the following steps:

1. Create a new Data Security Profile.

2. Type `Limited operational reports` in the profile name.

3. Navigate to the **Controls** tab.

4. Set the following:

   ○ **Limit size of result set to**: **10000 rows**

   ○ **Limit execution time to**: **10 minutes**

   ○ **Warn if cost estimate exceeds**: **5 minutes**

Note that this will override the default controls defined within the Universe. The override control will be displayed as bold. In our case, we only overdid the **Limit size of result set to** default value and so it will be displayed in bold as we can see in the following screenshot:

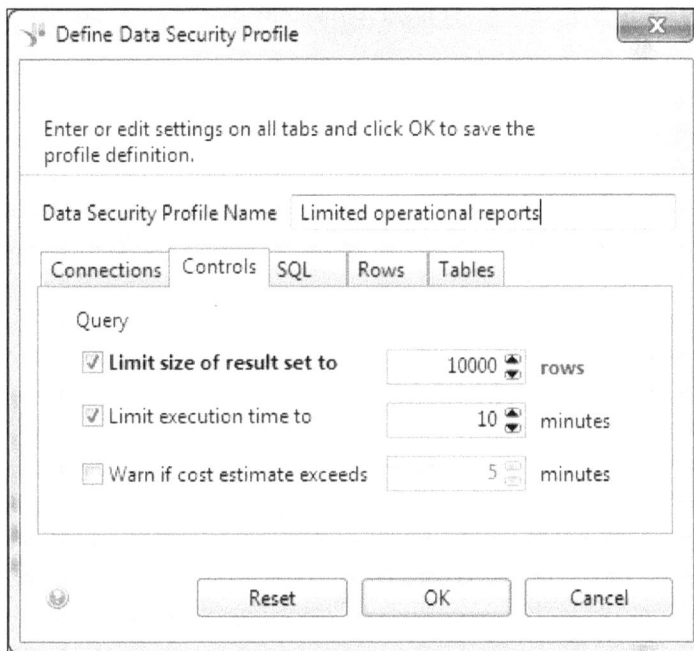

SQL

We can use the **SQL** tab to allow (or disallow) the end user to use some SQL features such as:

- **Allow use of subqueries**
- **Allow use of union, intersect, and minus operators**
- **Allow complex operands in Query Panel**

The SQL features are divided into three main categories:

- **Query**: In this area, we can control query options such as subqueries, set operations (union, intersect, and minus), and apply complex operands

- **Multiple Paths**: In this area, we can control multiple path options to overcome design traps as discussed in *Chapter 7, The Data Foundation Layer – Advanced Topics*

- **Cartesian Products**: In this area, we can allow or disallow Cartesian products

> The select rules here will also override the default SQL options defined in the Universe for the assigned user only.

We can see the **SQL** tab of the **Define Data Security Profile** window in the following screenshot:

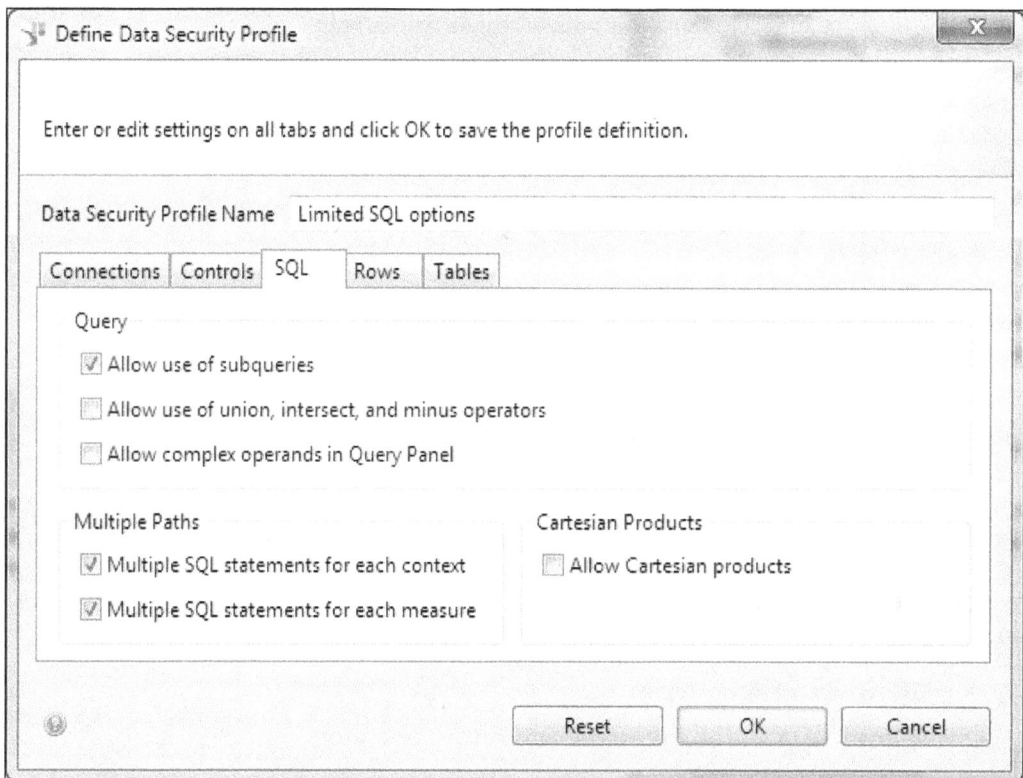

Rows

We can use the **Rows** tab to restrict the data retrieved for the assigned user. Let's assume we want to restrict the Chicago office manager to seeing only orders shipped to Chicago. To do this, let's perform the following steps:

1. Create a new Data Security Profile.

2. Type `Shipped to Chicago` in the **Data Security Profile Name** field.

3. Navigate to the **Rows** tab as shown in the following screenshot:

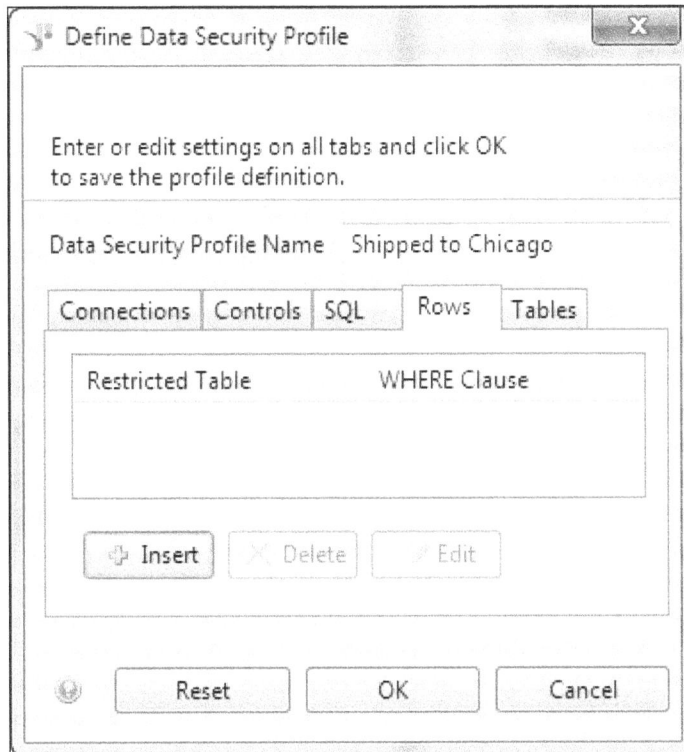

4. Then we need to click on the **Insert** button.

5. Select the `Orders` table.

6. Type the following query in the **WHERE Clause** field:

```
Orders."Ship City"='Chicago'
```

We can see the preceding query in the following screenshot:

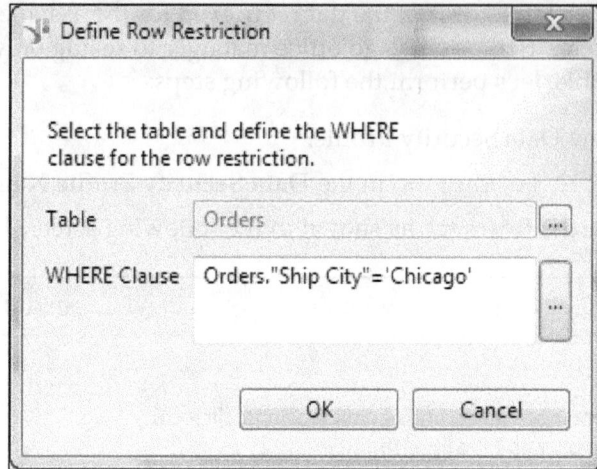

This profile will add the defined **WHERE Clause** field to any query generated by the assigned user if, and only if, it selects from the `Orders` table.

> We can define multiple row restrictions in the same profile.
>
> The **WHERE Clause** restrictions will be used only when the corresponding tables will be queried by the assigned users.
>
> Don't allow end users to use the customized SQL query in the report as they can edit the generated query and remove the line defined in this restriction.
>
> You need to build a security matrix first as explained in the final section of this chapter to avoid assigning two contradicting profiles to the same user/group. For example, you can build two profiles, one to the filter on `"Ship City"` = `'Chicago'` and the other one on `"Ship City"` = `'New York'`. If you applied both of them to the same user/group, then you would not get any records.

We can see the **Rows** tab in the **Define Data Security Profile** window in the following screenshot:

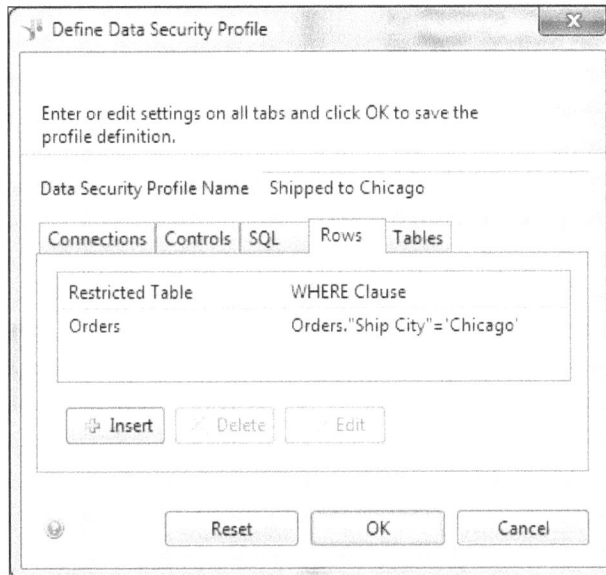

Tables

We can use the **Tables** tab to replace one table or view at runtime with another one. We can select a table from one of the connections defined with the Universe or with another table from the Data Foundation resource.

Let's assume that we have two finance tables. The first one contains the published figures, while the second one contains the actual confidential figures. We want all the users to see only the published figures, while we want any user in the executives user group to see the confidential information.

In this case, we will use the finance published figures table in our Universe and we will create a data profile to switch this table at runtime if any user from the executives group tries to access this table.

Now, let's try to create a Data Security Profile that will replace the table at runtime based on the logged in user using the following steps:

1. Create a new data profile under the `NorthWind` Universe.
2. Type `Replace Table` in the profile name.

3. Navigate to the **Tables** tab as shown in the following screenshot:

4. Now, let's click on the **Insert** button and define the original table and the replacement for this table, as shown in the following screenshot:

This concludes the Data Security Profiles section and we will discuss Business Security Profiles in the upcoming section.

Understanding Business Security Profiles

Business Security Profiles are a set of rules and restrictions related to the Business layer in our Universe. The main focus of these types of profiles is to restrict or grant access to folders and objects inside the Business layer to the right users. There are three main categories of security rules inside this security profile type:

- **Create Query**
- **Display Data**
- **Filters**

Let's learn about each of these types one by one in the upcoming sections.

Create Query

In the **Create Query** view, we can restrict the objects that end users can use in the query editor while building the report query. We can grant or deny access to:

- Business layer views
- Folders and business objects in the Business layer

The end user will be able to see and use only the granted objects and Business layer views, while he/she will not be able to see or access the denied ones.

Let's create a Business Security Profile to assign the following permissions to the assigned users:

- Grant access on the **Orders** business view
- Deny access to `Customer Information | Contact Info.`

To use this view, perform the following steps:

1. Create a new Business Security Profile and navigate to the **Create Query** tab, as shown in the following screenshot:

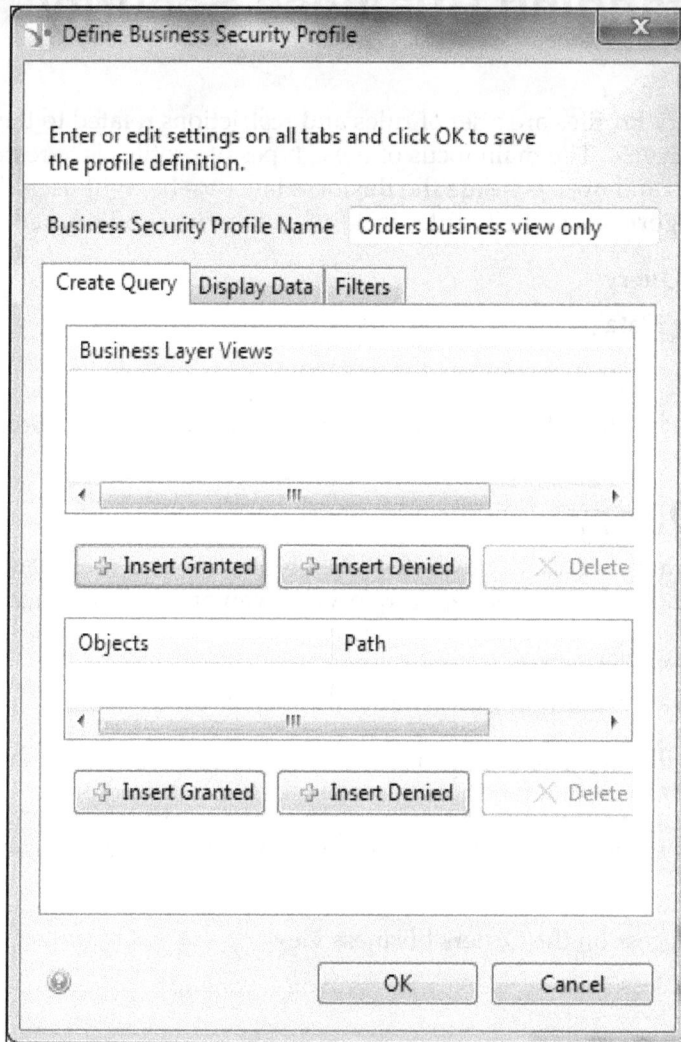

2. In the **Business Layer Views** area, click on the **Insert Granted** button.

3. Then select the **Orders** business view from the list, as shown in the following screenshot:

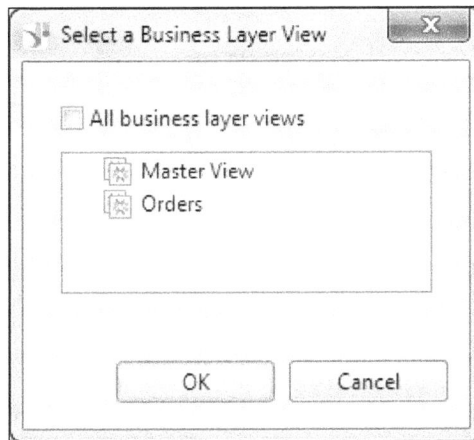

Now, let's add a restriction to deny access to the assigned user on the `Contact Info.` folder using the following steps:

1. Click on the **Insert Denied** icon on the **Objects** area.

2. Navigate to `Customer Information | Contact Info.` and click on **OK**, as shown in the following screenshot:

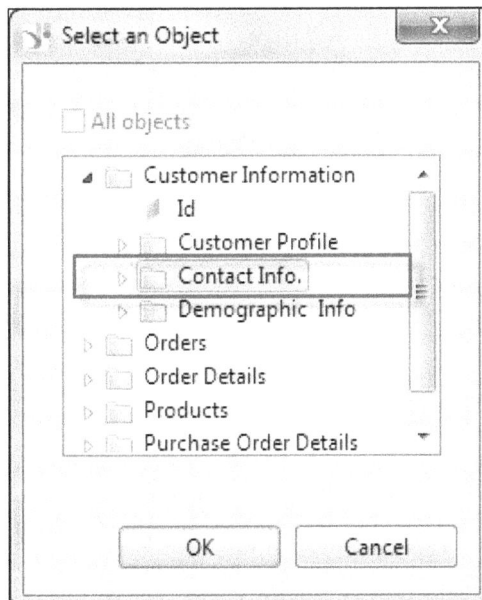

The Business Security Profile should look like the following screenshot:

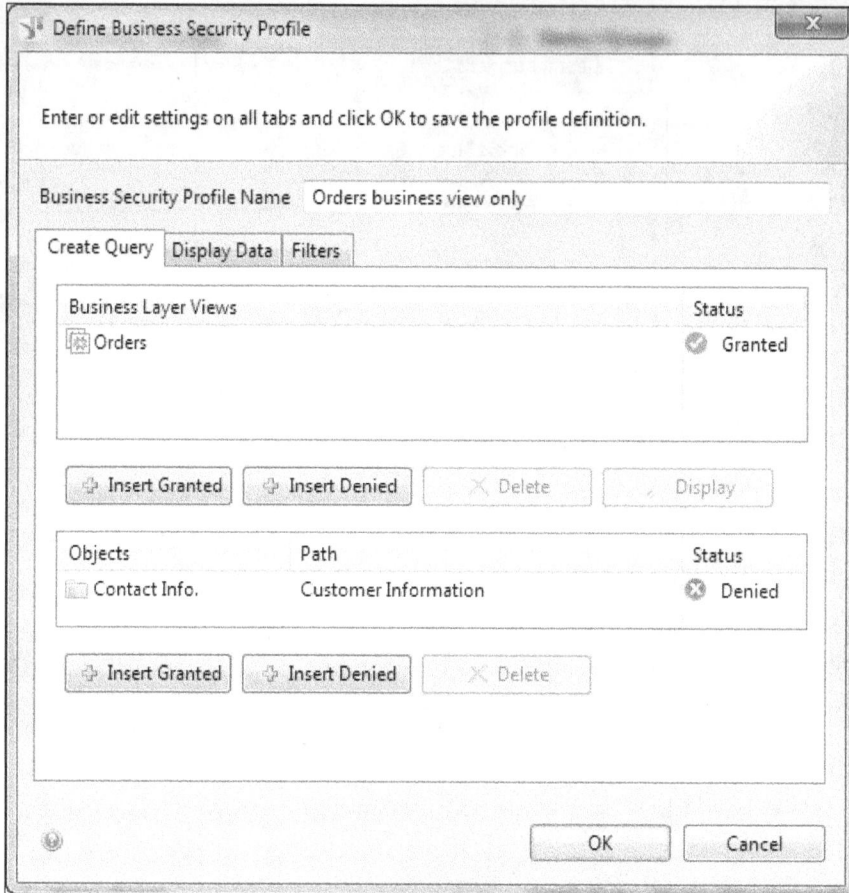

After applying this profile to a business user, he/she will be able to see objects under the **Orders** view only when it is the granted view; at the same time, he will not be able to see any object under the Contact Info. folder, because access to this folder is explicitly denied in this profile even if it is a part of the granted **Orders** view.

Display Data restriction

The **Display Data** restriction is the same as the **Create Query** restriction feature. The only difference is that **Create Query** will be used to manage assigned user permissions on the objects that will be used in the query editor, while **Display Data** will manage the data that can be displayed by the end user. You can follow the same steps used to create a **Create Query** Business Security Profile but in the **Display Data** tab, shown in the following screenshot:

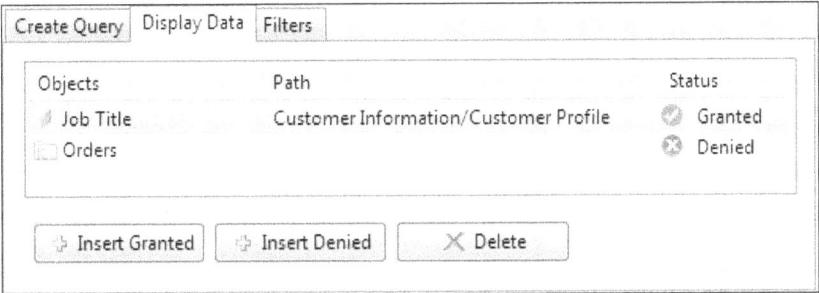

Create Query	Display Data	Filters		
Objects		Path		Status
Job Title		Customer Information/Customer Profile		Granted
Orders				Denied

Insert Granted	Insert Denied	Delete

Filters

Filters are similar to the row level security that we used in the Data Security Profiles. The only difference is that the **Rows** restriction is used only when the affected table is referred in the assigned user query. In the **Filters** restriction category, in Business Security Profiles, it will force and apply this condition on the assigned user (no matter what the selected objects and the referenced tables are). The **Filters** tab is shown in the following screenshot:

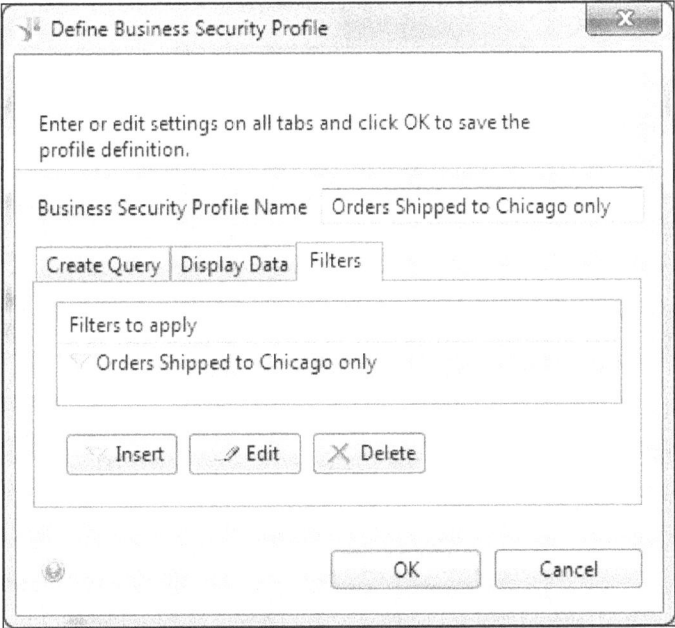

Define Business Security Profile

Enter or edit settings on all tabs and click OK to save the profile definition.

Business Security Profile Name   Orders Shipped to Chicago only

Create Query	Display Data	Filters

Filters to apply

   Orders Shipped to Chicago only

Insert	Edit	Delete

OK	Cancel

In the upcoming section, we will learn how to create a security matrix to map security profiles to the associated users and groups.

The security matrix

A security matrix is a mapping between users and profiles. We use a security matrix as the first step to defining what kind of restriction rule will be created and to whom it should be assigned. This is one of the best practices because it will give a single place to document and manage the security profiles.

We can have only one security matrix mapping that shows the relationship between users and profiles or we can even make it more detailed by breaking this relationship into two matrices. The first one will show the mapping between profiles and restriction rules, while the other one will show the relation between the users and profiles.

The following is a sample security matrix:

User/Profile	Profile # 1	Profile # 2	Profile # 3
User # 1	X		
Group # 1		X	X
User # 2			X

In the following table, we can see the security setting assigned to each profile:

Security setting/Profile	Profile # 1	Profile # 2	Profile # 3
Replace table TABLE1		TABLE2	
Set the maximum retrieved rows	1000		500
Allow the use of the inner join		Yes	Yes
Business layer view	**Master View**	Orders	

Summary

In this chapter, we talked about the security model applied inside the SAP BO IDT and we learned that by default any user will be able to access all objects, folders, and data that can be retrieved from the assigned Universe. We also received an introduction about the importance of managing our Universe security.

After that, we learned how to use the Security Editor to create Data and Business Security Profiles and how to configure restriction rules inside each security profile type.

Finally, we discussed the importance of a security matrix and how this can help us to build the right security profiles and assign it to the right people.

In the next chapter, we will learn how to share Universe resources among Universe designers by utilizing the multiuser development environment.

10
A Multiuser Development Environment

In this chapter, we will talk about how to manage work in a multiuser development environment. Usually, more than one developer will work together to develop the same Universe. Each developer will be responsible for developing a specific area but, in the end, the Universe will be merged with all the resources developed, in order to deliver a single point of truth.

One aspect that we will discuss in this chapter is how to make the resources of all Universes available to all users. We will be able to achieve this by sharing our project on the BO server (repository) instead of saving it on our local filesystem.

Another aspect is how to promote a Universe from one environment to another, for example, from the development or testing environment to production. This is different from upgrading a Universe that will transform an old Universe version to a new one. For example, for upgrading a Universe from XI 3.1 to BO R 4.x, Universe promotion and upgrade topics are more related to the BO server administration, which is out of the scope our book, but it is very important to have an idea about the main promotion and upgrade process. This chapter will help us have a high-level view on these topics; we will focus on how this will help us in our main target, that is, how to create a Universe.

[
For more information on *Promotion Management in SAP Business Objects BI Platform 4.0*, you can refer to
http://scn.sap.com/docs/DOC-50451.
]

In this chapter, we will cover the following topics:

- The difference between local and shared projects
- Using project synchronization to synchronize your local and shared projects
- The difference between Universe promotion and upgrade
- Using life cycle management to promote a Universe
- Using the upgrade wizard to upgrade a Universe

Working with projects

We already created a local project in *Chapter 3, Creating Our First Universe*, and we know that a project is a folder that will contain all Universe resources, such as data connection, Data Foundation, and Business layer. In this section, we will talk about other project types that we can create using the IDT. Then, we will talk about how to manage and synchronize our local and shared projects.

There are two types of projects that we can create:

- Local projects
- Shared projects

Let's take a look at both of them.

Local projects

A local project is a folder that will be stored locally on your machine is accessible any time from the IDT **Local Projects** window or by using the **Open Project** option from the **File** menu. The resources inside this project will be available only for the local machine users, and no one else will be able to access them. Let's take a look at the various operations that we can perform on local projects.

Creating a local project

We already created a local project in *Chapter 3, Creating Our First Universe,* to hold all the resources related to the NorthWind Universe.

Opening a local project

Now, assume that we already have some local projects on our local machine and we want to open them. This can be done using the following steps:

1. Go to the **File** menu and click on **Open Project**.

2. Select or browse to your root directory, or select an archived file if you want to open a project from an archived file.

3. Select the project that you want to open from **Projects**.

> You can check **Copy projects into workspace** if you just want to create a copy instead of opening the original project's files in the IDT.

We can see the **Import Existing Projects** window in the following screenshot:

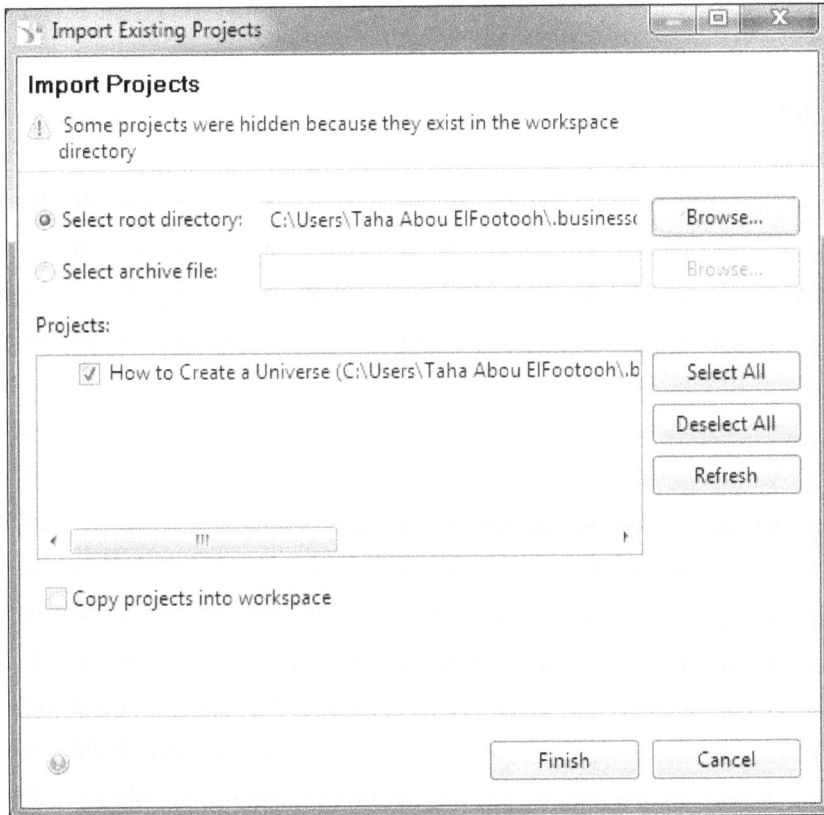

Next, we will learn how to delete a local project.

> Your local projects will be stored in the Workspace folder by default.
>
> Projects are a new concept introduced in the IDT, and there is no equivalent for them in the UDT.

Deleting a local project

To delete a local project, you have two options: to remove it from the IDT's **Local Projects** window only or to permanently remove it from your file management system (disk). The first option will only remove your project from the **Local Projects** window; it can be retrieved later on from the project folder on your machine, while the other option can't be undone. To delete a project, perform the following steps:

1. Right-click on your project and select **Delete**. Alternatively, just select your project and press the *Delete* key.

2. If you want to remove it only from the **Local Projects** window, just click on **Yes**.

3. If you want to remove it permanently from you file management system, then click on **Delete project contents on Disk (can't be undone)** and then on **Yes**, as shown in the following screenshot:

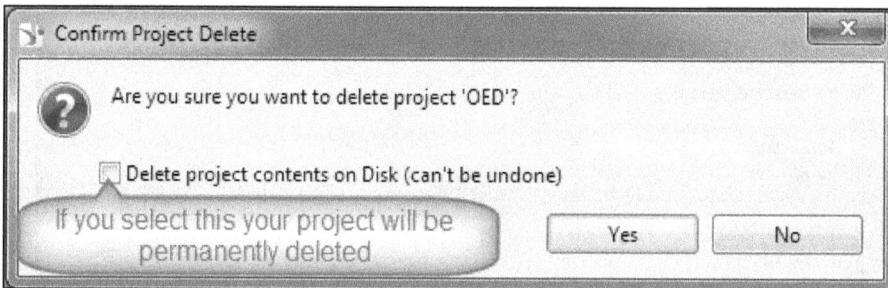

Shared projects

A shared project is a folder that will be stored on the server repository and will be available for other users and developers. The authorized users will be able to import this project and synchronize it with their local projects or just import and use it. The shared project is used to facilitate the multiuser development environment because, normally, in projects that involve several business areas, you will have many developers working on the same Universe. The shared project is a place where we can store and share all project-related resources. We can also manage our shared project and synchronize it with our local projects. This should take place as soon as we complete the development for one part, test it, and make it available to be used by the others. Let's take a look at the operations that we can perform on shared projects.

Creating a shared project

To create a shared project, we should have a local project created first. This local project contains all the resources needed by your Universe, such as data connection, Data Foundation, and Business layer. To share your project, we need to perform the following steps:

1. Right-click on the NorthWind Universe.
2. Select **New Shared Project...** from the menu displayed.
3. Select your system or session, and enter your username and password.
4. A new empty shared project with the same name will be created on the server repository.

We can see the **New Shared Project...** option in the following screenshot:

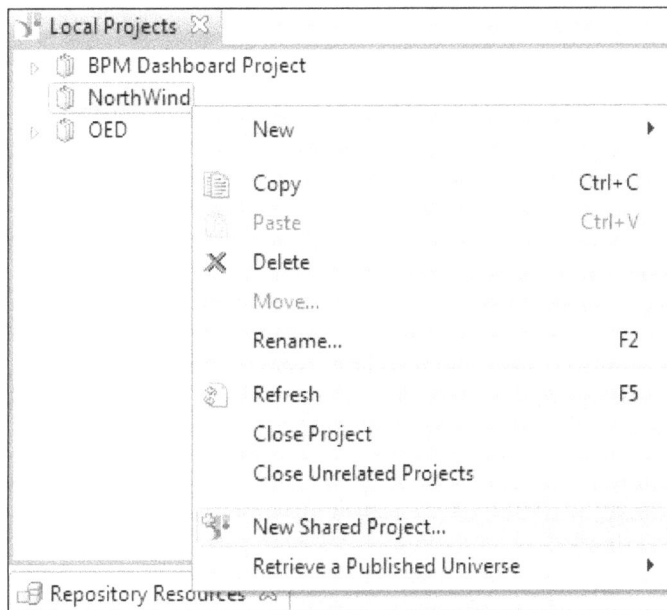

Renaming and deleting a shared project

To rename or delete your shared project, we need to perform the following steps:

1. Open your **Project Synchronization** window.
2. Log in to your CMS system.
3. Select a shared project from the **Shared Project** list.
4. Click on **Rename** and enter the new name in the pop-up window. Alternatively, click on **Delete** to delete the selected shared project.

> The local project resources will no longer be synchronized with your renamed shared project.
>
> The local project will not be affected if you delete the shared folder.

We can see the **Project Synchronization** window in the following screenshot:

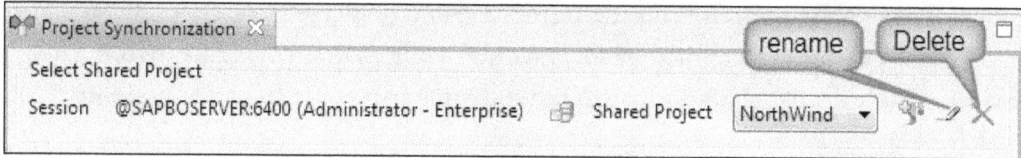

Synchronizing projects

We can use the **Project Synchronization** window to synchronize our local projects with our shared projects and vice versa.

> There is still a possibility that one designer can overwrite the Universe's shared resources.

Before we go further and see what we can do using the **Project Synchronization** window, let's take a look at main panels:

- **The top panel**: This is used to select a session and then select a shared project from the **Shared Project** list. We can also create, rename, and delete shared projects from this area, as discussed earlier.

- **The left panel**: This will display your local project's resources along with its synchronization status. In the following table, we will list and describe all the possible statuses:

Status	Description
Synchronized	The resource is up to date, and the local version exactly matches with the shared repository version.
Changed Locally	The local resource version is not matching with the shared repository resource version. You may save your local version to the server and overlook the shared one, or you may retrieve the shared resource version and update your local one.
Added Locally	The local resource file is not part of the shared project, which is stored on the server. You may add it to the shared project by selecting the **Save to server** icon.

- **The right panel**: Here, you can see your shared project resources along with each resource version. You can also lock and unlock project resources from this panel.

We can see the **Project Synchronization** window and the main panels in the following screenshot:

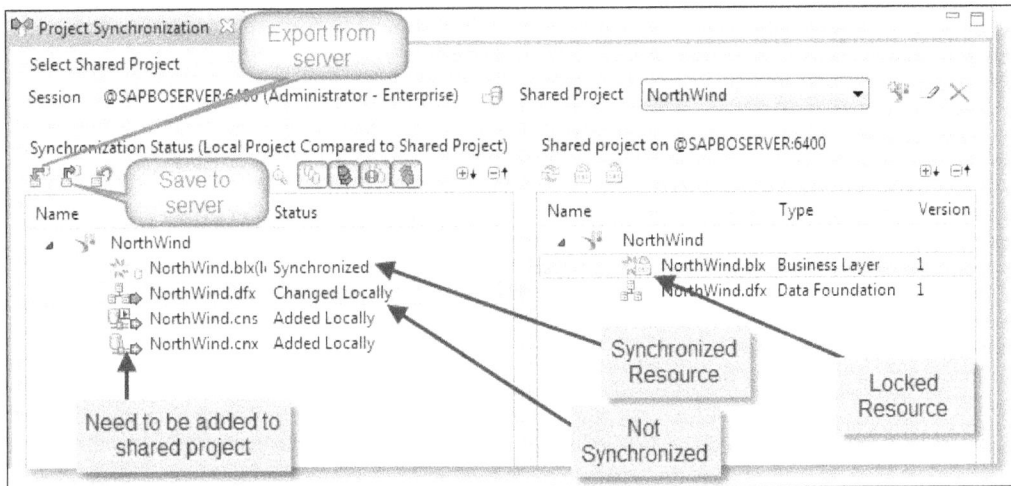

You can perform the following actions in the **Project Synchronization** window:

- **Save to server**: This is done when you want to update and overwrite the shared project resource with the version that you have locally. Normally, this happens when the local resource is the most current one.

- **Get from server**: This is done when you want to retrieve the shared project resource to overwrite the local one. Normally, this happens when the shared resource version is the most current one. This functionality is the complement of the previous option (**Save to server**).

- **Lock shared resource**: When you retrieve a shared resource from the BO server to start working on it, you should lock this resource on the server. This is just to let other developers know that someone is currently updating this resource. Note that authorized users with the right privilege can remove the lock later on.

- **Unlock shared resource**: After you complete your updates on the resource and save it to the server, you have to unlock it to let everyone know that you completed your work and they can do their modification.

The lock and unlock shared resource are very useful, and they act like development protocols.

Promotion and the life cycle management console

In real life, we will need at least two environments to have a healthy development life cycle. Normally, we will need a development server to develop our new Universes and make any required modifications. We will also need a production server that will have the live version of our Universe. Sometimes, we might implement a testing environment as well, to test our developed Universes before moving it to production.

The main purpose of the **life cycle management** (LCM) console is to help us promote objects such as reports, users, and Universes, among BO environments. Our focus here will be on Universes, but the same concept described here applies on the other objects as well. If you used to work with BO's previous releases such as BO XI 3.X, then you should consider the **Import Wizard** functionality. Promotion here is a new term for migrations that we previously used with Import Wizard. You will notice that many terminologies have been changed and renamed in BO release 4. However, don't worry; it it's just a matter of time before you memorize and master them.

We need to define some terms related to the life cycle management console before we start creating a promotion job together.

> The life cycle management console is not a new tool, as it was used to manage Universe version control in BO XI 3.X. This functionality was supposed to be installed in the complement of the BO server installation before the BO 4 version; now, however, it is fully integrated in the installation process.

Promoting a Universe from one environment to another

We can promote a Universe from one environment to another using one of the two methods, described as follows:

- **The BIAR file**: In this method, we will promote a Universe by exporting it to a LCMBIAR file, which is a normal BIAR file. We can use this file later on and import it to another environment.

> We can use BIAR files to take backups as well.
>
> The BIAR file can also contain other objects such as reports, users, and LOVs. In this chapter, we will focus on the Universe object as it is our main topic.

- **Live to Live**: This means that we will promote a Universe on the fly, from one environment to another. Both environments should be up, and this will be done through an LCM job.

Now, let's try to promote our `NorthWind` Universe.

> The best practice is to promote from the development environment to the testing environment and from the development environment to the production environment. It is not recommended that you promote from testing to production.
>
> You might need to adjust the Universe connection after promotion if you have, for example, a specific development connection and another one for production.

Promoting NorthWind using the LCMBIAR file

In this method, we will create a LCMBIAR file that will contain objects that we want to promote (migrate) from one environment to another, as shown in the following diagram:

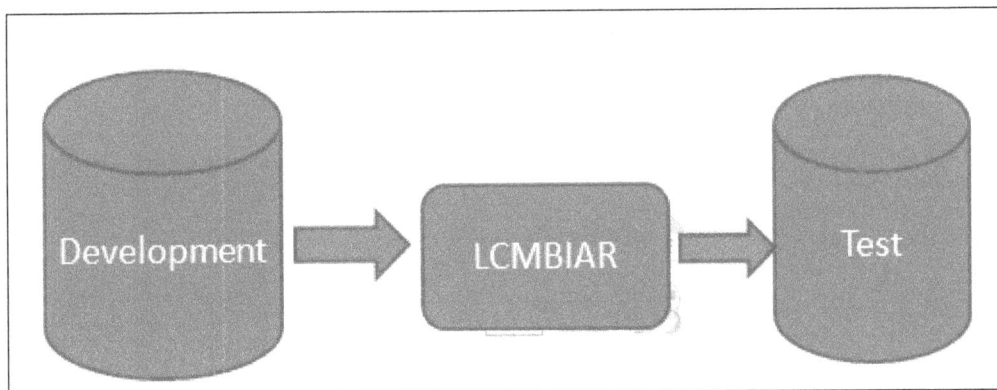

Perform the following steps to migrate from one environment to another:

1. Open the **Central Management Console (CMC)** by entering
   `http://<BO_Serevr_Name>:<Port>/BOE/CMC` in your browser window.

2. Then, log in to your system using your username and password.

3. Navigate to the **Manage** area and select **Promotion Management**, as shown in the following screenshot:

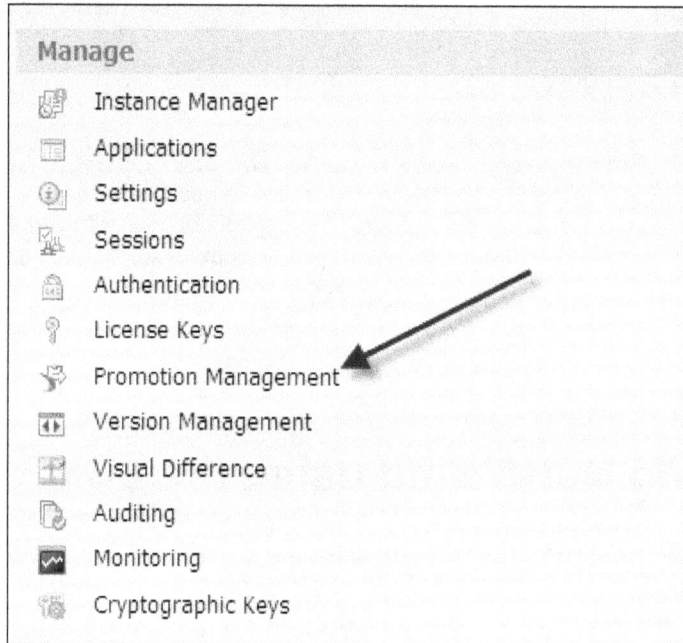

4. Select a new job from the **Promotion Jobs** window, as shown in the following screenshot:

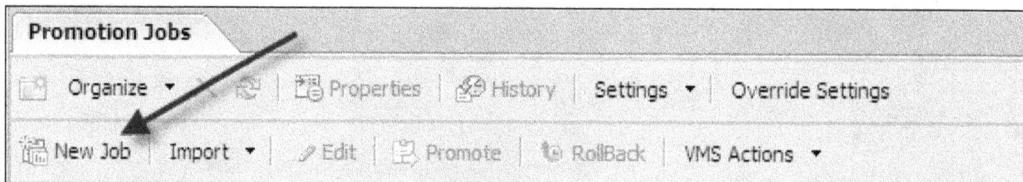

5. Enter NorthWind in the job's **Name** field.

6. Enter the description and location in which you want to save this promotion job, as shown in the following screenshot:

Fields marked with an asterisk (*) are mandatory fields

Name*:   NorthWind

Description:

Keywords:

Save Job in*:   Promotion Jobs

📁 Copy an Existing Job

📁 Browse

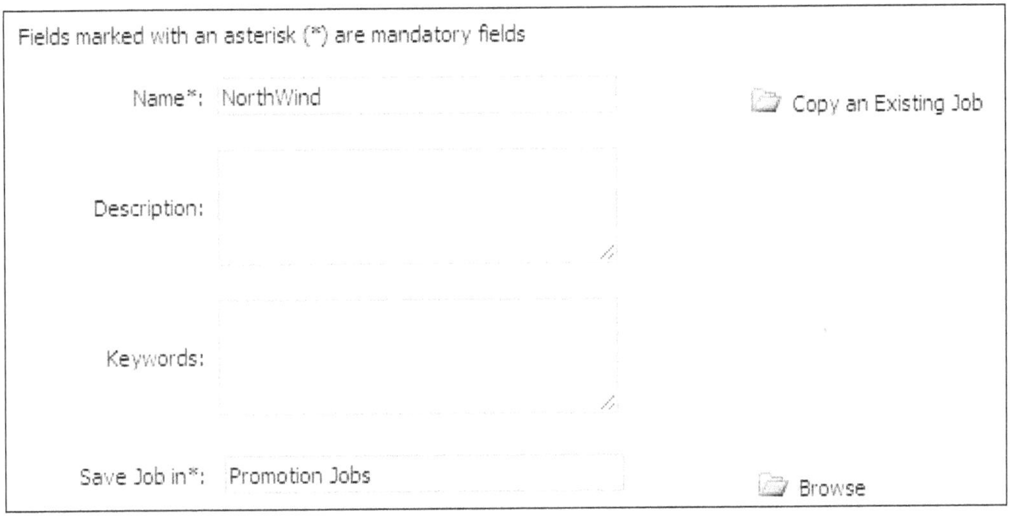

7. After that, select **Login to a New CMS** from the **Source** drop-down menu and enter your BO server information, as shown in the following screenshot:

Source *:   Login to a New CMS

Destination :

Create   Cancel

Login To System   ? □ ×

System :   SAPBOSERVER:6400   ▼

User Name :   Administrator

Password :   ••••••••

Authentication :   Enterprise   ▼

Login   Cancel

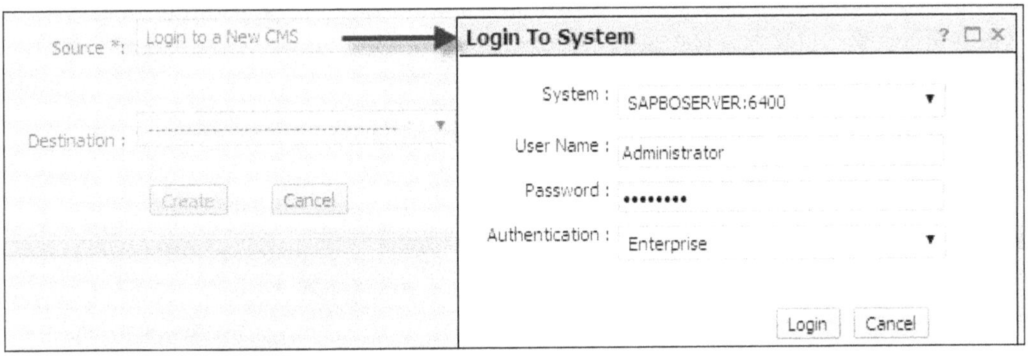

8. Finally, select **Output to LCMBIAR File** from the **Destination** drop-down menu and then click on **Create**, as shown in the following screenshot:

Destination :   ------------------------------------   ▼

Output to LCMBIAR File

SAPBOSERVER:6400

Login to a New CMS

9. Now, the **Add Objects - from System** window will open, and we should start selecting the objects that we want to include in this promotion job. For now, we just have our NorthWind Universe, and we don't have any reports or users to promote. Select the Universe with the following steps:

   1. Navigate to Universes on the left panel.
   2. Select the NorthWind Universe and click on the **Add & Close** button.

Congratulations! We finally created our first promotion job. You can click on the **Promote** button to generate the LCMBIAR file that we can use to migrate our NorthWind Universe to another BO environment.

> After creating a promotion job, we can still add objects to this job and also schedule it to run at a specific time.

Promoting NorthWind using the Live to Live method

The Live to Live method is exactly similar to the previous one (the LCMBIAR file method) but, instead of setting our destination with the LCMBIAR file, we will set our destination with the target BO environment directly. The promotion job will migrate the selected objects from the source system to the destination system directly, without creating any temporary BIAR files.

In the following diagram, we can see that we can promote a Universe from the **Development** environment to the **Test** environment. We can also promote a Universe from **Test** to **Production** or from **Development** to **Production** directly.

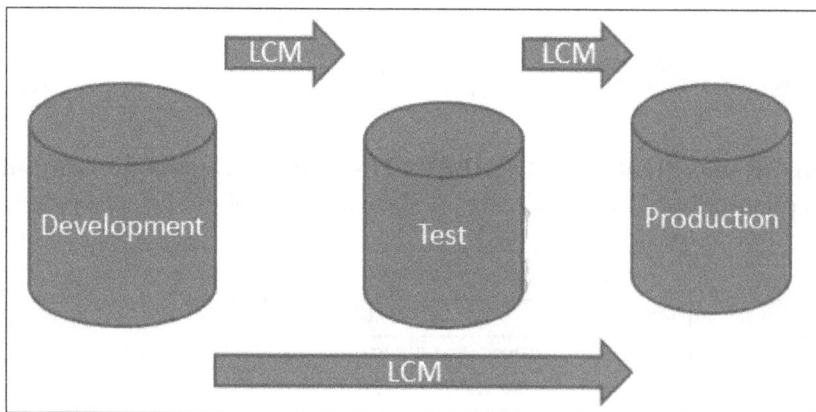

To create a Live to Live promotion job, follow exactly the same steps that we used to create the promotion job using the LCMBIAR file, but enter the target BO environment in the **Destination** field.

The Upgrade Management Tool

The Upgrade Management Tool is used to migrate BO objects from the XIR3.x and XIR2SP2 environments to the newer version. We might just need this tool once during the upgrade process. The Upgrade Management Tool works in the same way as the LCM. You can upgrade your objects using a BIAR file or the Live to Live method. This topic is mainly related to the BO administration but you should know, at least, what we can use this tool for.

> The Upgrade Management Tool in SAP BO 4.x is equivalent to **Import Wizard** in the previous releases.
>
> You can refer to the SAP Community Network (http://scn.sap.com/welcome) for more information about the Upgrade Management Tool. To upgrade to BI4.X, refer to http://wiki.scn.sap.com/wiki/display/BOBJ/How+to+Upgrade+to+BI4.0.

Converting UNV to the new Universe UNX extension

The Universes created by Universe designer will be saved with the .unv extension; on the other hand, the Universes created by the IDT will be saved as .unx. We can still use the Universe designer to create .unv Universes but then we will not be able to make use of the new features provided by the IDT. We will also not be able to call this Universe from the new SAP tools such as SAP Lumira and SAP Explorer.

To convert a .unv Universe, let's perform the following steps:

1. Open the IDT and create a new empty local project.

2. Click on **Convert .unv Universe…**, as shown in the following screenshot:

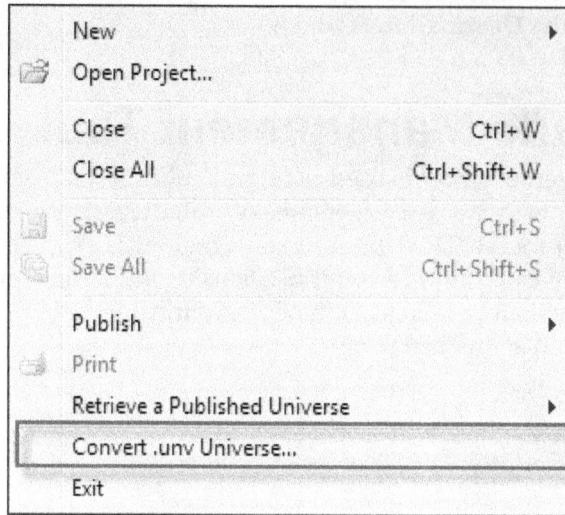

	New	▶
📂	Open Project…	
	Close	Ctrl+W
	Close All	Ctrl+Shift+W
	Save	Ctrl+S
	Save All	Ctrl+Shift+S
	Publish	▶
	Print	
	Retrieve a Published Universe	▶
	Convert .unv Universe…	
	Exit	

3. Then, select the .unv Universe to convert it. We can browse and select a Universe from the local filesystem or initiate a session and retrieve a .unv Universe from a repository.

4. Then, select the destination for the converted version, as shown in the following screenshot:

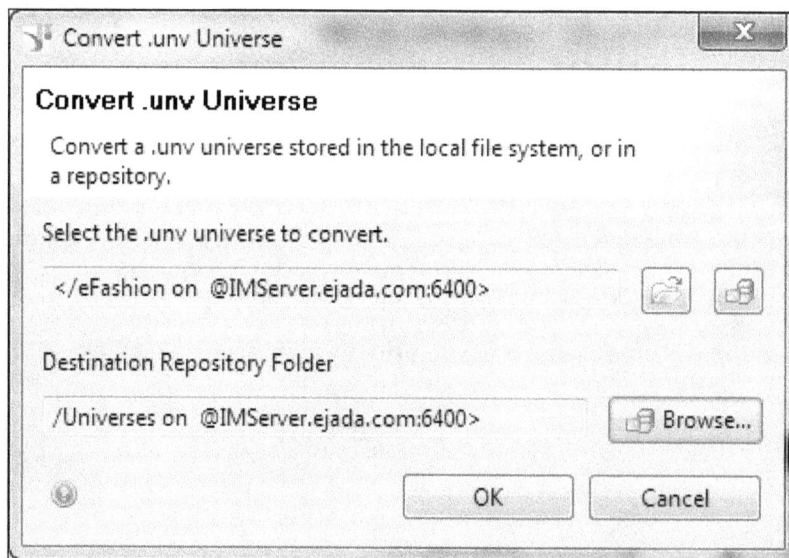

Convert .unv Universe

Convert a .unv universe stored in the local file system, or in a repository.

Select the .unv universe to convert.

</eFashion on @IMServer.ejada.com:6400>

Destination Repository Folder

/Universes on @IMServer.ejada.com:6400>   Browse…

OK   Cancel

You will get an error message that describes the reason behind the error if anything went wrong during the conversion process. Otherwise, you will see the converted .unx version in the selected destination folder.

> We need to convert our old migrated .unv Universes if we want to migrate them from a former SAP BO release such as SAP BO XI 3.x. This is very important in order to be able to use the new features.
>
> We can convert only one Universe at a time.

Summary

We have arrived at the end of the chapter. In this chapter, we learned how to share our project on the BO repository to make it available for other developers as well. Then, we learned how to use LCM to promote a BO object using the LCMBIAR file or the Live to Live method. Finally, we got to know the difference between the Upgrade Management Tool and LCM.

Index

Symbols

@Aggregate_Aware() function **236**
@DerivedTable() function **236, 237**
@Prompt() function
  about 237, 238
  using, in derived table 68
@Select() function **238**
@Variable() function **238**
@Where() function **238**

A

Access Level option, Advanced tab **129**
Access Modules Processors (AMPs) **72**
Add to View function **93**
adoption level, BI Maturity Model **25**
advanced analytics level, BI Maturity
    Model **25**
advanced Business layer properties
  about 241
  accessing 241
  Change Data Foundation... button 243, 244
  Description field 242
  Parameters window 244
  Summary... button 243
advanced Data Foundation layer properties
  about 172, 173
  description 173
  parameters 175
  SQL options 174
  summary 174
advanced design techniques,
    Data Foundation
  about 170
  alias table 170
  context 170

Data Foundation layer properties 172
  shortcut join 171
Advanced tab
  about 128, 129
  Access Level option 129
  Database Format section 131
  Display option 132
  list of values (LOV) 132
  Objects can be used in section 131
aggregate awareness
  about 225
  aggregated objects, defining 228-230
  aggregated tables, inserting 226-228
  aggregation navigation, detecting 230-234
alias table
  about 63, 170
  creating 63, 64
  used, for fixing loop 203, 204
  used, for solving chasm trap 195
attributes, business objects types
  about 140
  creating 141

B

basic BI level, BI Maturity Model **25**
BI
  about 7, 8
  concepts 8
  data warehouse (DWH) 11
  foresight 11
  hindsight 11
  insight 11
  knowledge pyramid 9
  reporting tools architecture 14
BIAR file **274**

[PACKT] enterprise

PUBLISHING — professional expertise distilled

Thank you for buying
Creating Universes with
SAP BusinessObjects

About Packt Publishing

Packt, pronounced 'packed', published its first book "Mastering phpMyAdmin for Effective MySQL Management" in April 2004 and subsequently continued to specialize in publishing highly focused books on specific technologies and solutions.

Our books and publications share the experiences of your fellow IT professionals in adapting and customizing today's systems, applications, and frameworks. Our solution based books give you the knowledge and power to customize the software and technologies you're using to get the job done. Packt books are more specific and less general than the IT books you have seen in the past. Our unique business model allows us to bring you more focused information, giving you more of what you need to know, and less of what you don't.

Packt is a modern, yet unique publishing company, which focuses on producing quality, cutting-edge books for communities of developers, administrators, and newbies alike. For more information, please visit our website: www.packtpub.com.

About Packt Enterprise

In 2010, Packt launched two new brands, Packt Enterprise and Packt Open Source, in order to continue its focus on specialization. This book is part of the Packt Enterprise brand, home to books published on enterprise software – software created by major vendors, including (but not limited to) IBM, Microsoft and Oracle, often for use in other corporations. Its titles will offer information relevant to a range of users of this software, including administrators, developers, architects, and end users.

Writing for Packt

We welcome all inquiries from people who are interested in authoring. Book proposals should be sent to author@packtpub.com. If your book idea is still at an early stage and you would like to discuss it first before writing a formal book proposal, contact us; one of our commissioning editors will get in touch with you.

We're not just looking for published authors; if you have strong technical skills but no writing experience, our experienced editors can help you develop a writing career, or simply get some additional reward for your expertise.

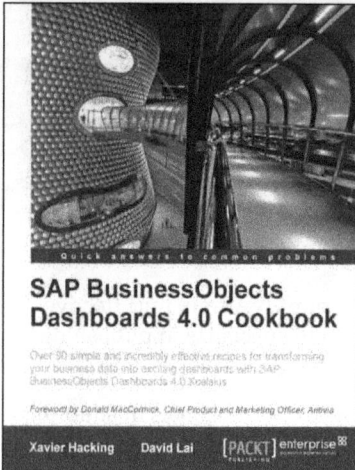

SAP BusinessObjects Dashboards 4.0 Cookbook

ISBN: 978-1-84968-178-0   Paperback: 352 pages

Over 90 simple and incredibly effective recipes for transforming your business data into exciting dashboards with SAP BusinessObjects Dashboards 4.0 Xcelsius

1. Learn valuable Dashboard Design best practices and tips through easy-to-follow recipes.

2. Become skilled in using and configuring all Dashboard Design components.

3. Learn how to apply Dynamic Visibility to enhance your dashboards.

4. Get introduced to the most important add-ons available for Dashboard Design with the most up-to-date information for Dashboards 4.0.

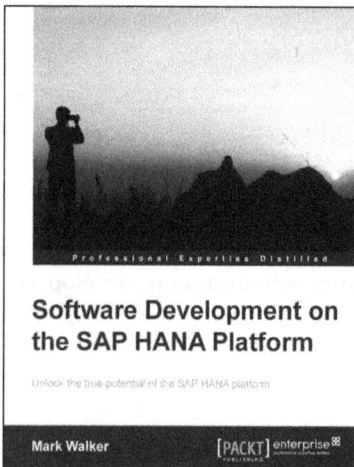

Software Development on the SAP HANA Platform

ISBN: 978-1-84968-940-3   Paperback: 328 pages

Unlock the true potential of the SAP HANA platform

1. Learn SAP HANA from an expert.

2. Go from installation and setup to running your own processes in a matter of hours.

3. Cover all the advanced implementations of SAP HANA to truly become a HANA master.

Please check **www.PacktPub.com** for information on our titles

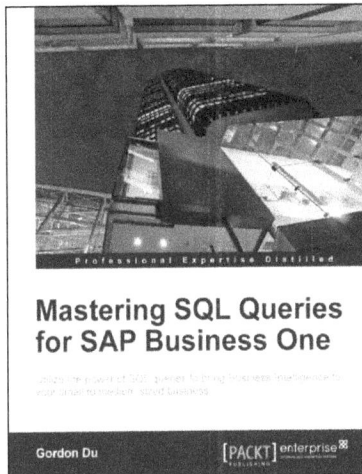

Mastering SQL Queries for SAP Business One

ISBN: 978-1-84968-236-7   Paperback: 352 pages

Utilize the power of SQL queries to bring Business Intelligence to your small to medium-sized business

1. Practical SAP query examples from a SAP Business One expert.

2. Detailed steps to create and troubleshoot SQL queries for alerts, approvals, Formatted Searches, and Crystal Reports.

3. Understand the importance and benefit of keeping SQL queries simple and easy to understand.

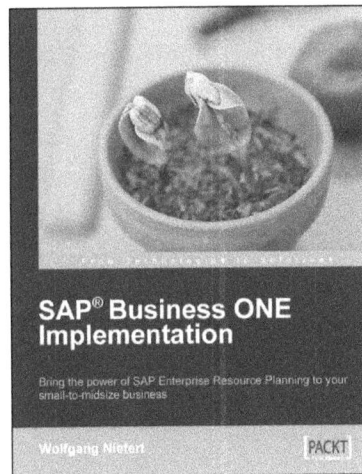

SAP® Business ONE Implementation

ISBN: 978-1-84719-638-5   Paperback: 320 pages

Bring the power of SAP Enterprise Resource Planning to your small-to-midsize business

1. Get SAP B1 up and running quickly and optimize your business, inventory, and manage your warehouse.

2. Understand how to run reports and take advantage of real-time information.

3. Complete an express implementation from start to finish.

4. Real-world examples with step-by-step explanations.

www.ingramcontent.com/pod-product-compliance
Lightning Source LLC
Chambersburg PA
CBHW080936220326
41598CB00034B/5794